The Viennese Waltz

The Viennese Waltz

Decadence and the Decline of Austria's Unconscious

Danielle Hood

LEXINGTON BOOKS
Lanham • Boulder • New York • London

Published by Lexington Books
An imprint of The Rowman & Littlefield Publishing Group, Inc.
4501 Forbes Boulevard, Suite 200, Lanham, Maryland 20706
www.rowman.com

86-90 Paul Street, London EC2A 4NE

Copyright © 2022 by The Rowman & Littlefield Publishing Group, Inc.

All rights reserved. No part of this book may be reproduced in any form or by any electronic or mechanical means, including information storage and retrieval systems, without written permission from the publisher, except by a reviewer who may quote passages in a review.

British Library Cataloguing in Publication Information Available

Library of Congress Cataloging-in-Publication Data

Names: Hood, Danielle, author.
Title: The viennese waltz : decadence and the decline of Austria's unconscious / Danielle Hood.
Description: Lanham : Lexington Books, 2022. | Includes bibliographical references and index.
Identifiers: LCCN 2022015417 (print) | LCCN 2022015418 (ebook) | ISBN 9781793653925 (cloth) | ISBN 9781793653949 (paperback) | ISBN 9781793653932 (ebook)
Subjects: LCSH: Music—Austria—19th century—History and criticism. | Music—Austria—20th century—History and criticism. | Anxiety in music. | Uncanny, The (Psychoanalysis) | Music—Social aspects—Austia—History—20th century. | Music—Social aspects—Austria—History—19th century. | Waltzes—19th century—History and criticism. | Waltzes—20th century—History and criticism. | Mahler, Gustav, 1860-1911.—Criticism and interpretation.
Classification: LCC ML246.5 .H66 2022 (print) | LCC ML246.5 (ebook) | DDC 780.9436—dc23/eng/20220414
LC record available at https://lccn.loc.gov/2022015417
LC ebook record available at https://lccn.loc.gov/2022015418

For Ian and Clive,
for pushing me into this and supporting me through it.

Contents

Introduction	1
1 Topics in *Fin-de-Siècle* Vienna	7
2 Evolution of Viennese Cultural-Historical Topics: Romance, Freud and Authenticity	27
3 The Waltz and the 'Other'	45
4 Narrative and Deception	67
5 The Development of the Uncanny Narrative	83
6 Part 1. The Waltz and the Uncanny in Mahler's Seventh Symphony	115
6 Part 2. Mahler's Scherzos and the Uncanny Waltz	139
7 The Waltz as Pivot Point in Webern's Symphony Op. 21	155
Conclusion	177
Bibliography	183
Index	195
About the Author	203

Introduction

'The Viennese traditionally lived in two countries. One is on the map. The other is the imaginary region where wine flows, love triumphs and everything is silk-lined. This is the land of the waltz'.[1] So begins Hans Fantel's book *Johann Strauss* and lyrical as the language is it captures the consistently dualistic nature of being 'Viennese' in the nineteenth and twentieth centuries perfectly. For the last 100 years of the Habsburg dynasty, the gap between what was real and how the Viennese upper- and middle-classes lived grew exponentially. Encouraged by the Metternichian repression of outside influences and suppression of revolutionary ideas from the 1820s onward, the reality of Austria's loss of territory and standing in the European climate was at best ignored, at worst denied by the aristocracy and the bourgeoisie to whom the political quietness gave a sense of relief that instigated the Biedermeier era. Painters produced bucolic scenes of pastoral serenity and the waltz became the mainstay of the hedonistic, carefree upper-class society. As Fantel writes: 'if melody could be translated, a Viennese waltz would add up to a hundred ways of saying that, all considered, and with due allowance for everything, simply being alive is a cause for celebration'.[2]

However, the 'two countries' Fantel described were very much in opposition to each other, giving Vienna a dualistic nature both in the philosophical and psychological sense. Two disconnected worlds acted separately without interchange: those of the physical and the spiritual. The physical reality was that Austria suffered terrible losses of land and population during the various wars (against Napoleon, France and Prussia). The abolition of serfdom in 1780 and the advent of the industrial revolution caused the peasantry to flock to the city leading to overcrowding and poverty. Out of Metternich's oppression of outside influences and censorship, 'civil societies' grew – a form of surrogate politics practiced in cultural and business associations – and nationalism came to the fore. With the influx of peasants from other countries into the city, nationalism mixed with class conflicts creating an ethos of 'Otherness' between the Austro-Germans and the Exotic Other: the Czech's, Hungarians and Polish. The Dual Monarchy, created in 1867, went someway to relieving this conflict, although, in line with the inherent dualism of the Austrian society this only solved tensions on the surface. The Hungarians were not afforded equality in the government and the Compromise only served to marginalise the other nation states further to the extreme that the Czechs left the Reichsrat after being denied their national rights a year later.

Nevertheless, in the years 1866–1918 Vienna became, according to Steven Beller 'famous as a major centre of modern culture and thought that "invented the twentieth century"'.[3] There were greater transformations in economic, technological, social, political, cultural and intellectual spheres than at any other time. Strauss II's *The Blue Danube* premiered in 1867 at the World Exhibition in Paris and in 1874 the premiere of *Die Fledermaus* provided a welcome distraction from the stock market crash of 1873. The *Ringstraße*, a prestige project of neo-absolutism, was constructed during this period; its first street was opened in 1865, by Emperor Franz Joseph, while the entire project was only completed in 1916 the year of his death. By 1900, three major trends emerged: aestheticism and impressionism, progressive modernism and critical modernism.[4] The first emphasises the surface experience: the aesthetic form and the irrational psyche. With roots in French *decadence*, positivism and cultured irrationalism, the major contributors were artists and philosophers such as Richard Wagner and Friedrich Nietzsche. The progressive modernists were critical of political and religious institutions; they challenged authority and conservative bourgeois values in the name of freedom and equality. Finally, the critical modernists, such as Schoenberg, Adolf Loos and Karl Kraus rejected convention and ornamentation seeking to restore an ethical imperative to modern art 'so that the work became an essay in realising the artists "thought"'.[5] Freud's theories of the 'double' and the unconscious mind occupied by repressed primal urges because of self-imposed restrictions derive from the contemporary society's traditions and conventions; as such, he falls into the second category: progressive modernism.

It is not surprising that Freud developed his psychoanalytical methods and hypotheses at this time, based, as a lot of them are, on a dualistic approach; in particular the concept of the Uncanny: 'that class of the frightening which leads back to what is known of old and long familiar'.[6] To put it another way, something familiar that becomes unfamiliar (and often therefore frightening) like an empty child's swing rocking without any apparent propulsion; a music box sounding in an empty, creaking house; a winding path through a forest that is beautiful when sunlight beams through the leaves but terrifying in the night's shadow. The Uncanny takes in two major ideas by Freud.

The *doppelganger* or double – the notion of opposites collapsing into one another – is explained by Freud through Hoffman's story, the Sandman, in which Nathaniel falls in love with Olympia an automaton. Her maker/father, Coppelius and Nathaniel's father are what Freud termed the father-imago split. Here one father (Coppelius) tries to blind Nathaniel, and the other lovingly intercedes. The double is also demonstrated in the doll Olympia. As she is Coppelius's daughter, he made her, and Coppelius is, as part of the father-imago, Nathaniel's father, Freud hypothesises that Olympia is Nathaniel's 'disassociated complex', or the unconscious part of his split personality. This brings us to the other of Freud's hypotheses: the 'hypnoid state' or 'second state' where the analysand is paralysed in fear by something they are unconsciously repressing, for example in the case of Anna O., the case in which Schoenberg's *Erwartung* (1909) is supposedly based, she lost the ability to speak her native German and became almost completely paralysed. In music, this translates into the employment of devices that arrest the temporal development of the music, for example ostinatos and Michael Cherlin's 'time shards'.

The temporal narrative of the music is significant, particularly when combined with an analytical narrative utilising Topic Theory. This deconstructive style of analysis explores the placement of familiar sections of music (dances, marches etc.) that are still recognisable out of context on a syntagmatic axis. The emplotment of oppositional/juxtapositional relationships informs the narrative creating a commentary on the contemporaneous society and culture. The oppositional quality of the analytical method makes it a perfect tool for this dualistic era defining upper versus lower class, nature versus man, light versus dark, charm versus grotesque, conscious versus unconscious. Not only can topic theory help illuminate the subplots created in texted music, for example the verismo versus artificial subplot of Lehár's *The Merry Widow* (1905), or the upper versus lower class conflict in Strauss's *Die Fledermaus* (1874), but once these plots have been identified, the same arrangement of topics in un-texted music can be understood in a similar manner. This creates an historical precedent for understanding the work of musicians composing in the same cultural milieu, regardless of whether they compose what is considered 'light' or 'art' music. The work of composers of 'light' music, such as Strauss I and II, Lehár and Kálmán is just as significant as that of 'art' composers – Mahler, Schoenberg and Webern – as they often provide a satirical illustration of what life at the time was like politically, socially and culturally. The use of the same topics with the same satirical observations in Mahler's work as Strauss II's suggests that identical issues were encountered and endured by both composers. By analysing their music written over the last fifty years of the Habsburg Monarchy it is also possible to trace the decline of the Empire. From vicarious fear of external forces portrayed by the *ombra* and *tempesta* topics to a more personal psychological fear portrayed by the Uncanny narrative, a narrative evolved from the *ombra* and *tempesta* as the audience were presented less with natural or supernatural terrors and more with the anxieties of death and the unconscious mind.

The waltz and *Ländler* topics encapsulate all that has been discussed so far. Superficially, the dance evokes the quintessential Viennese idea of love, laughter, wine and women. However, in the hands of the Viennese composers mentioned above the waltz takes on multivalent significations. In *Die Fledermaus* its opposition to lower class dances and location in the narrative – whenever a deception plays out on stage – lends it a scornful signification of upper-class artifice. Its opposition to the *Ländler* in Mahler's Scherzos confirms the high/low-class conflict, while its identification as the Viennese national dance opposes it to the eastern mazurka, polka and *Csárdás* creating a nationalistic Western/Eastern dialectic. The waltz's signification as the Viennese dance and as the aristocratic society's dance means that its placement in the centre of the uncanny narrative's evolution by Mahler, Schoenberg and Webern produces a disparaging multivalent interpretation of society in general, of the Empire and the Habsburg monarchy, and of the Viennese in particular.

Chapter 1 introduces topic theory as the methodology used throughout this monograph. With the recent publication of books outlining and employing this methodology, such as Clive McClelland's *Ombra* (2013) and *Tempesta* (2019), Danuta Mirka's *Oxford Handbook of Topic Theory* (2014) and Joan Grimalt's *Mapping Musical Signification* (2021) a widened interest in the theory of topics has spawned. In this chapter, I have defined both the basics of the theory and a selection of the topics extant at the turn of the nineteenth century. Although there is a widening interest in this analytical method this is one of the few analyses which deal with post–twentieth-century compositions such as Webern's Symphony Op. 21.

Chapter 2 outlines the cultural-historical framework surrounding the evolution of the waltz and its varied signification. Once the issues, customs and noteworthy people of the time are identified and understood, it is possible to reveal associations between the significant themes and the topics employed. It also helps to explain the transformation of the topics prevalent in the contemporaneous works and the emergence of new topics such as the rational and psychological topics, nationalism and Romance.

The definition of the waltz and other national dances are introduced in chapter 3, such as the polka, and the *Style Hongrois* which incorporates both specific Hungarian dances and the more general 'Exotic Other' expounded by Jonathan Bellman and Derek Scott. This chapter explains how the waltz becomes charged with such varied signifieds, such a major identifier of the

Viennese society and aristocracy that even after the Empire decays it is still recognisable, and its impactful connotations understood.

Chapter 4 explains how topics can be read using narratology, the act of emplotting the topics into a musical narrative which lays out the 'story' of the work. There then follows three analyses of *Die Fledermaus*, Oscar Strauss's *Walzertraum* (1907) and *The Merry Widow* in order to create the historical trace needed to analyse the un-texted works of Mahler, Schoenberg and Webern. These analyses cement the signification of deception as Viennese identity (whether consciously or unconsciously) and the Freudian narrative of the double in 'light' music demonstrating that it was a concept that affected even those in the popular music spheres.

The Uncanny narrative is introduced and defined properly in chapter 5 with an explication of Freud's theories and an excellent example of the uncanny in Schoenberg's opp. 15 and 16, *Ewartung* and *Fünf Orchesterstücke* (both 1909). This chapter also explains why I refer to an Uncanny as a *narrative* rather than a topic as it is defined by Lawrence Kramer (1990) and Michael Klein (2005).

Chapter 6 has been split into two parts as they deal with two different ideas that nonetheless are inextricably linked. The first part describes the part the waltz plays in the Seventh Symphony, focussing on the Scherzo, but in the context of the symphony as a whole. It shows a recognisable parallel with the preceding analysis of Schoenberg's op. 16, although it was written four to five years earlier. The Uncanny is unmistakable in the narrative that plots the descent into the unconscious over the first three movements and the rise to happiness as the character of the symphony turns joyous and triumphant in the finale. The second part of chapter 6 demonstrates the transformative arc of the external fear of the *ombra* topic to the Uncanny narrative through an exploration of the Scherzo's from his Symphonies Three to Nine (excluding Eight). Over the course of time (1896–1909), the Scherzos encapsulate the evolution of fashion in dance form from the aristocratic minuet to the *Ländler* and waltz's class conflicts and finally the nationalistic conflicts illustrated by the initial *style hongrois* inflections, which became recognisable *volk* dances. The waltz and *Ländler* in these Scherzo's also become entangled with the Uncanny narrative, such that the waltz in each acts as the pivot point at the innermost depth of the unconscious hypnoid state before rising back into the conscious world, suggesting the dance is connected in some way to the primal trauma at the heart of Freud's premise.

Finally, chapter 7 proposes that despite the fact the Habsburg Monarchy dissolved in 1918, the effects felt by their decadence and subsequent decline were still felt by composers further away in time and distance. Mahler's Ninth Symphony was written in America and yet still displayed the disparaging Viennese narratives. In a similar fashion, Webern's Symphony Op. 21

was written ten years after the dissolution of the Monarchy and nevertheless described the same internal anxieties as the earlier works by his teacher Schoenberg and idol Mahler.

Overall, through analysis of the three domains of culture, topical narrative and Freudian methodologies I establish that the music of *fin-de-siècle* Vienna expresses the common issues and cultural events of Vienna 1900. Musical narratives parallel the ideas of the critical modernists through satirical observations constructed in the subplots caused by oppositions to and inflections by other topics. Progressive modernism is reflected in the humour and occasional scorn poured on the aristocratic classes, the industrial city and societal conventions by the oppositions of simplistic or heavenly pastoral and natural scenes with upper-class contrivances, such as the learned topic subclasses. And finally, but most significantly, is the manifestation of the anxieties inherent in a population torn apart by war, deprivation and a stagnant, constrictive government that retained power through distraction and artifice and the consequences of the loss of both the power and the veneer of revelry they hid behind.

NOTES

1. Hans Fantel, *Johann Strauss: Father and Son and their Era* (Newton Abbott: David and Charles, 1971), 9.
2. Ibid.
3. Beller, *A Concise History of Austria*, (Cambridge: Cambridge University Press, 2006), 142.
4. Ibid., 172.
5. Ibid.
6. Sigmund Freud, "The Uncanny", *The Standard Edition of the Complete Psychological Works of Sigmund Freud*, ed. and trans. James Strachey (London: Hogarth, 1964), 220.

Chapter 1
Topics in *Fin-de-Siècle* Vienna

Leonard Ratner, in his 1980 book *Classic Music*, formulated an analytical methodology to explore the plurality of different styles within the music of the eighteenth century. Drawing attention to the referential and mimetic qualities of the music, he posited that 'music developed a thesaurus of characteristic figures' typically derived from cultural contexts such as dance, worship, ceremony, the hunt and the military, as well as from the life of the lower classes.[1] Since then topic theory has become an intricately explored method with treatises exploring specific topics, like Clive McClelland's monographs on the *ombra* and *tempesta* topics and the exploration of dance topics by Eric Mckee, as well as explorations of the methodology itself, such as Kofi Agawu's *Playing With Signs* and Raymond Monelle's *The Sense of Music*[2]. It is with the method of extant topical categorisation, particularly between high and low classes, which is this chapter's focus. To be able to trace the topics used in post-1900 Vienna it is important to be able to trace the historical significations of topics present in not only nineteenth-century Vienna, but in all of Europe and to understand how they were perceived by contemporary composers. A specific description of dance topics is included as, as Mahler once remarked, 'all music stems from dance'.[3]

Ratner divided *topoi* into two categories: "types", fully worked-out pieces; and "styles", figures and progressions within a piece. He immediately qualifies this categorisation, however, with the statement that 'the distinction between types and styles is flexible; minuets and marches represent complete types of composition, but they also furnish styles for other pieces'.[4] These recognisable figures are then lifted out of context, thus enabling a string quartet to evoke a military fanfare, or an orchestra to play an aria, which leads to Danuta Mirka paraphrasing Ratner's definition of topics as *'musical styles and genres taken out of their proper context and used in another one'*.[5]

Although Ratner qualified his categorisation as "flexible", the distinction between "style" and "type" blurs almost to incomprehensibility. In his description of the different dance types there are numerous references to specific dance styles, for example the polonaise, which Ratner describes as a 'rather serious and deliberate style', and, just prior to this, the 'Swabian allemande style'.[6] In her introduction to the *Oxford Handbook of Topic Theory*, Mirka attempts to define Ratner's original presentation. She argues that '[i]f styles encompass broad affective zones, genres composed in these styles are related to specific affects'.[7] Mirka continues:

> This concerns, in particular, the instrumental genres that Mattheson calls 'small *Pièces*' [in which] each genre receives its typical affect. For example, the affect of the allemande is one of a 'contented or satisfied sprit', of the bourrée 'contentment and pleasantness', of the courante 'sweet hopefulness', of sarabande 'ambition', of the rigaudon 'trifling jocularity', of the passapied 'frivolity' [...] Affective characters of larger pieces are less specific. In symphonies, which form introductions to operas or church or chamber music, 'the expression of affects [...] would have to conform to those passions which predominate the work itself'.[8]

Mirka, therefore, equates these 'small compositions of determined character' with Ratner's "types". 'By contrast', she writes, 'larger compositions "of undetermined character", that is, such "which can acquire every character", are the genres that create opportunities for topics to mix together'.[9] It appears, then, that the difference between "style" and "type" is merely one of size. If a small piece is of one "determined" character, the topic involved is a type; if it is a larger "mixed" piece, it is a style.

Ratner further outlines two other levels of signification: the high, middle and low styles; and the chamber, church and theatrical styles, with which some of his topics are consequently associated. Ratner ascribes the proposition of the classification into the high, middle and low styles to Johann Adolphe Scheibe, although Mirka adds that others, including Johann Mattheson, also made the observation.[10] Ratner paraphrases Scheibe's description of each style:

> The *high style* must be stately and emphatic; the harmony must be full, the ideas fully carried through, the melody rich in invention, fresh, lively, and elevated. It should be used only for heroes, kings, and other great men and noble spirits; magnanimity, majesty, love of power, magnificence, pride, astonishment, anger, fear, madness, revenge, doubt, and other similar qualities and passions can only be expressed in the high style.
>
> The *middle style* is ingenious, pleasant, and flowing; it must please the listener rather than excite him or lead him to reflection. The melody must be clear,

lively, flowing, and well turned; harmony must serve only to make the melody clearer and must never dominate. [. . .] Joy, delight, love devotion, modesty, and patience are best imitated in this style.

The *low style* avoids all clever elaborations. [. . .] It represents nature in its simplest form, and is used for low-born persons and for objects and situations associated with them. Its characteristic embodiment is the shepherd; some others are beggars, slaves, poor prisoners, and farmers.[11]

The significance of this quotation is that it demonstrates that these styles are not based solely on society's class system, but that the emotional character of the music denotes its placement within these categories. Robert Hatten notes, therefore, that it is the 'degree of dignity' that is the determining factor.[12] As such, he provides a table which represents his interpretation of the hierarchy of Ratner's original presentation.[13] His construal offers four levels: I. Codes of feelings and passions, linked to pace, intervals and motives; II. Styles based on locale/occasion/situation (e.g. ecclesiastical or theatrical) and degree of dignity (high/middle/low styles); III. Topics: either types or styles; IV. Pictorialism, word painting and imitation of sounds of nature.

Hatten's table emphasises the aforementioned issue with the terminology associated with topic theory. The other two classifications posited by Ratner (via Mattheson, Scheibe and Meinrad Speiss) and adopted by Hatten, Mirka, Monelle *et al.*, are also termed "style", consequently creating an additional ambiguity in the classification hierarchy. A further complication is that this table is presented by Hatten under the subheading "Understanding Expressive Genres in Music", and introduced as a summary of the 'historical classifications of musical topics' supplied by Ratner.[14] This not only adds a new, undefined, term – genre – but also places the third sub-category "topics" as an historical classification of itself. While Hatten does acknowledge the 'overlapping use of terms' and the 'inevitably messy categories', he does not attempt to resolve the problem.[15]

In his 2008 book *Music as Discourse*, Kofi Agawu attempts to solve the terminological problem by labelling the high, middle and low styles as topics in their own right, and placing them in his topical universe alongside extant topics, such as the learned style, the march and the polonaise. He avoids the distinction between "type" and "style" altogether, and discusses the location/ occasion categorisation only in terms of eighteenth-century "public realms" of topics and nineteenth-century "private realms", a division originally suggested by Johann Georg Sulzer, who groups the church and theatrical styles as "public" and the chamber style as "private".[16] This distinction begins to explain why the uncanny could gain such a presence in nineteenth- to twentieth-century music. The retreat into "private realms" describes not only the transfer of music into the bourgeois and aristocratic salon, but the transference of the audiences encounter of musical action from outside of their own experiential sphere, that of kings and gods more authentic experience of their own private emotions. This will be discussed in more detail later.

Nevertheless, the characters that Scheibe connects with each of the high, middle and low styles are still class conventions; the high style is for 'heroes, kings, [. . .] great men and noble spirits', while the low style embodies shepherds, 'beggars, slaves, poor prisoners, and farmers'. The emotional characteristics which follow – 'power, magnificence, pride', or 'joy, delight, [and] love' – are stereotypical character traits associated with the classes, attributed to them by educated members of the upper class. Hence, these are idealised versions of the different classes, just as some topics are romanticised versions of an ideal rather than significations of the brutal truth.[17] It is therefore important when analysing a work topically to understand the period of time from which the piece comes, since, as Monelle points out, 'both signifier and signified have their roots in the social, cultural, and technological world. In the case of indexical topics, the signifier—the sign, embodied in a musical event—will naturally tend to be contemporary'.[18] He presents as an example the hunt topic:

> It is a little surprising to find that the heroic, manly, noble hunt evoked by music, portrayed in operas and described in hunting books, was not very much practiced in the lands of its chief currency, the Austro-German territories of eighteenth-century Europe. Hunting was cowardly and ignoble, and the fanciful mythology of the noble hunt was cultivated partly to redeem this. The musical topic was significative of an older, more sporting hunt, but it was also significative of the falseness of contemporary heroism [. . .].[19]

The 'historical trace' of each topic, as Monelle terms it, will then enable the analyst to form a coherent plotline from the topical narrative. A discourse then evolves through this notion, merging topics from contrasting classes, or subtly altering the topics to mock the class with which they are associated. In Micznik's article, "Mahler and the Power of Genre", the author suggests that Mahler's music has 'slipped into a parody version of a waltz with grotesque overtones'.[20] By transferring the waltz into a low register – orchestrating the theme with trombones, bass clarinet, bass tuba and double bass – and inserting large leaps into the melody, Mahler has altered the initial association of the dance with the ballroom and 'hurled it into the street'.[21]

Even here, however, the difference between a style associated with topic, or one associated with function, location or degree of dignity is not clearly defined. The following diagram therefore attempts to refine this division. First, however, one more level of classification must be acknowledged. Monelle describes three musical topics, the pastoral, hunt and military, as 'great topical worlds that constitute musical and cultural genres'.[22] These topics include multifarious signifiers, which, Monelle suggests, make the signifieds 'complex and elusive'.[23] As such, included within the stages of classification are also multi-level topical associations, here named as large topical classes (also sometimes called super-topics, or 'dialects').[24] These are collections of musical gestures and topics which, when used in conjunction with each other, define a larger topical class.

The aspiration is therefore to identify the conventional topical universe as understood by, in this case, Viennese composers and listeners at the end of the nineteenth century. Hence, the topics provide evidence of how composers and listeners understood their own era and the goal is therefore to provide a source of insight into how the music may have been heard contemporaneously. In tandem with the cultural themes examined in the next chapter, those inherent specifically in the Viennese *fin-de-siècle*, the "story" level of the hermeneutic reading will be based less on the interpretant's subjective construal than an attempt at an historically objective appraisal.[25] This is achieved by constructing a new hierarchy listing the order in which the work will be analysed, from the identification of the progressions, motives, intervals, pace or tempo and so on, which signify the topic – or subtopic of a larger topical class – to the categorisation of that topic into its respective associations of determination, class and finally social purpose. Not all topics will signify both social class and purpose, just as not all topics are part of a larger class. Table 1.1 is a structural diagram that sets out the associations of each topic within the Viennese nineteenth to twentieth century system. It shows that the associations are not always straightforward; for example the pastoral topical class can signify all three social classes, depending on the signifiers present within the music, but the four dance pastoral sub-topics are all low class. Similarly, the brilliant topic does not belong to a larger topical class, nor is it associated with a social class; instead, based as it is on virtuosic concertos, it is classed as chamber music. The dotted lines appear when the topic is not connected to the first line it crosses, for example the sensibility topic is not a dance, but is connected to the middle class and chamber music. The break in the overarching line above the lament and *pianto* indicates that, while the two topics are associated with both the theatre and the church, there is no association between the two categories "Church" and "Theatre".

This diagram explicates not only the topoi present in the middle of the nineteenth century when most scholars believe topic theory is most useful, but also includes *topoi* which will emerge through the analyses and discussions in this manuscript and are specific to Vienna and the discernment of the Viennese contemporary composers. The latter *topoi* will be presented in later chapters, however it is important first to outline and understand the extant

Table 1.1 Table of Topics Present c. 1900, Their Topical Classes and Associative Classes.*Topics in bold are large topical classes, Rational is underlined as it encompasses the Learned Style Topical Class.

	High	Middle	Low	Non-affiliated
Theatre	Lament *Pianto* *Ombra* Sensibility *Tempesta* *Opera Seria* **Rational** • Authentic		*Opera Buffa* *Alla Turc* *Alla Zoppa*	
Church	Lament *Pianto* <u>**Rational***</u> **Learned Style*** • Strict style • *Alla Breve* • Bound Style **Pastoral**			
Chamber		Romantic Sensibility Singing Style **Pastoral**		Fantasia Brilliant Cadenza
Psychological	*Ombra* *Tempesta*	Romantic Sensibility		
Dance	Gavotte Sarabande Bourée Waltz	Minuet Waltz	Contradanse **National** • Mazurka • *Style Hongrois* • *Ländler* • Waltz • Polka **Pastoral** • Gigue • Siciliene • *Ländler*	
Military	Cavalry Horse Fanfare March		March Marching Band **National** • Janissary music	
Hunt	Horn Fifths Noble Horse **Pastoral**			

Classical topological lexicography in order to be able to perform a hermeneutic reading of them in juxtaposition to the contemporary topoi.

HIGH CLASS TOPICS

As shown above, the *topoi* considered high class include the large topical classes of the learned style, the rational style, the military, the hunt, the pastoral as well as a majority of the dances. The inclusion of the learned style here has to do with a combination of Hatten's 'degree of dignity' and Elaine Sisman's explanation that

> [c]onnecting learned style with rhetoric are several separate but related complexes of ideas: the idea of an older, antiquated style dependent upon strict rules; the idea of a musical *topos* or topic; the idea of an elevated style; and the idea of difficulty inherent in learnedness, and thus the propriety of taxing the understanding of the audience.[26]

Keith Chapin, in his detailed appraisal of the learned style agrees with Sisman's assessment adding that it is the elaborate, or wrought style, which moves the learned style style 'toward the ethos of the high [class] in general'.[27]

With "elaborate" or "wrought style" (*gearbeitete Schreibart*) one moves both to the broadest conception of the learned style and also to the heart of its logic, to the issues that held together the panoply of styles in a loose stylistic and conceptual field. The term can refer to the strict discipline required for dissonance control, to the figural elaboration of simple counterpoint, to the imitative treatment of a theme, or to polyphonic textures. It can also point to highly developed textures in general, including those characteristic of the fantasia and the symphony, or to what was later described as 'motivic-thematic working'.[28]

The military, hunt and pastoral topical classes have been admirably elucidated by Raymond Monelle in his 2006 manuscript however a few notes should be made concerning the class denotations of each. The hunt is the simplest of the three to categorise in this way as culturally the hunt is often portrayed as a favourite pastime of the nobility, and this learned convention is how Ratner justifies the high-class association of this topic. Monelle, however, acquaints the reader with the idea that 'much hunting was ignoble, squalid and cruel during this period'.[29] It is, then, 'the cultural hunt—the *chasse écrite*—[that] remained heroic and glorious'.[30] It is the idea of the hunt, rather than the bloody reality of it, that is symbolised by this topic, making the signification arbitrary in a way similar to the military topic outlined above. The hunt topic eventually became synonymous with the forest, an association which continued through the Romantic period, and thus with the myths and fairy stories that emerged from the forest – nymphs, dryads and so on – adding romantic and supernatural facets to the topic, as will be explained in more detail in chapter 6.2. Generic hunt signifiers include '6/8 meter, triadic melodies outlining primarily tonic and dominant chords, horn-call *bicinia*, and regular periodicity'; however, in addition, two common subtopics of the hunt topical class are the horse topic and horn fifths.[31]

The military style is more indefinite in its allegiance to a particular class. In the eighteenth century, the march had both dance and ceremonial associations. It served to remind the audience of the 'cavalier and manly virtues ascribed to him', evoking overtones of the noble houses and their court guards, as well as suggestions of medieval valour and idealistic heroism.[32] Like the minuet, the march is easily adapted to different situations, and therefore has various recognisable varieties, for instance, rustic, civic, church, military and funeral.[33] Monelle also outlines 'equestrian marches' which are in compound time, 12/8 or 6/8, as the dotted rhythms and triplet signifiers are easily adapted to this metre. The distinction between the two can be heard in the 'galloping' rhythm of the equestrian march accentuated by the compound time signature, bringing to mind the cavalry charges rather than infantry marches, and is connected to the noble horse of the hunt topic. The military topic is also linked to the hunt topical class through similarities in their brass calls. The fanfare and the horn fifths (sometimes also termed horn calls) are similar due to their rhythmic properties, the difference being that horn calls are usually harmonically based on a tonic–dominant–tonic progression, whereas the fanfare is arpeggio based. The connotations of the topics are both aristocratic, but with an urban outlook for the military topic and a rural aspect to the hunt. This rurality also associates it with the low-style pastoral topic, as it connotes the countryside, with forests and open fields through which the hunt chases; yet rather than being associated with the rural peasant class, as the pastoral topic tends to be, it instead signifies the rural aristocracy. Through the hunt style's link with the military *and* the pastoral topic, it can be used as a pivotal topic within the dialectic of the work so that a piece can begin with the military topic and end with the pastoral topic without the use of any major transformative devices.

Where most topics can be codified as *either* high, middle *or* low class, the pastoral topic encompasses all three. This topic is a large topical class which encompasses a hierarchy of topics and signifiers that, singly or combined, imply the pastoral topic. At the lowest level are signifiers that cannot be used individually, and therefore cannot be called topics, for example the timbre of the flute and oboe, or bagpipe drones which mimic the shepherd with his pipe, a classic pastoral image. These become significant only when combined with subtopics that are recognisable when functioning alone; in this case, the musette, siciliano, gigue and the pastorale itself. These are subtopics rather than fully fledged topics because even when they do function independently of the others they still imply the pastoral world, signified by pedal points and ostinati, promoting temporal and harmonic stasis, and 'the quality of simplicity from which a cultivated person could learn'.[34] This quality is achieved by limiting the vocal range and minimising leaps, while keeping the rhythm repetitive and dance-like.

Monelle quotes Hermann Jung when suggesting that the signifieds of the pastoral topic are two conflicting views of country life: the 'heavenly paradise' on one hand and the 'evocation of brute peasantry' on the other.[35] These polarised associations became more significant in light of the dream of escapism that became common in the early 1900s, when industrialisation drew labourers into the towns and cities. The town dwellers longed to "get back to nature", or at least their idealised, simplified version of this idyllic paradise; this topic then highlighted the town dwellers' attitude of superiority over the peasant population.

Within the theatrical umbrella class, we find, first and foremost, *opera seria*. *Opera seria* took shape in response to French criticism of 'undisciplined, irrational and often licentious' Italian librettos of the early eighteenth century and became one of the favourite pastimes European aristocracy alongside courtly dances.[36] Librettos were instead based on Aristotelian dramatic principles to become 'worthy of the civilised state now enjoyed'.[37] Although the librettos were often based on past events or mythological subjects, tragic endings were discouraged in order to teach a moral lesson; the writers were encouraged to portray what should have happened if a moral system was followed, rather than what actually did happen. As McClymonds and Heartz state 'poets were admonished to strive for simplicity, naturalness, verisimilitude and dignity, and to instruct as well as to entertain. The end result should be of high enough literary quality to be enjoyed as literature'.[38]

Initially, at the beginning of the eighteenth century, the action progressed through *secco recitative* (accompanied by basso-continuo) interrupted sporadically by da capo arias accompanied by orchestral instrumentation. However, at intense dramatic moments an *accompagnato recitative* (accompanied by the whole orchestra) is used.[39] Occasionally, no more than one or two scenes, a speech would be set in *recitativo obbligato* 'where strings provide expressive ritornellos and obbligato motivic commentary in vocal caesuras'.[40] The arias were mostly placed at the end of the scene and known as "exit arias" so the singer could leave the stage to the applause. At the close of some of the Acts, duos are employed; typically love songs between the star attractions. The distribution of arias between the cast was based on rank, with the prima uomo, or *divo*, and the prima donna, or *diva,* taking the most. The tenor (usually playing a patriarch or King) would rank second behind the primo's. Advisors and confidants would only be awarded one or two each.[41] Because of the da capo A-B-A structure of the arias they were enclosed pieces, usually giving voice to a sentiment and used by the singers when A is reprised to show of the *primo*'s virtuosic vocal acrobatics. Because it is an enclosed unit, and there was often only a loose connection between the aria and the preceding scene, singers would substitute a favoured aria from a different opera so long as it conveyed the appropriate emotion, affections which much alternates between successive arias.[42]

One of the greatest *opera seria* librettist was Pietro Metastasio (1698–1782) whose librettos dominated the Italian repertory during the 1750s.[43] His operas focused principally on love, but also the Enlightenment ideals as characters 'overcame selfish human desires in order to achieve greatness in though and deed in a world where monarch and subject alike must adhere to the highest moral principles'.[44] Thereafter, a mounting interest in *opera buffa* eroded his monopoly.[45] Among these, Alessandro Scarlatti, Johann A. Hasse, Niccolò Jommelli and C. G. Gluck, whose celebrated *Orfeo ed Euridice* premiered in Vienna in 1762. This opera is the first of Gluck's "reform" operas in which he introduced simplicity in both the music and drama, attempting to 'erase the harsh lines of demarcation between action (recitative) and reflection (aria) and to create a musical and dramatic unity from diverse components of chorus, air, ballet and ensemble'.[46] The da capo arias with their coloratura and the alternation between these and the 'regular and restrictive' *recitative secco* have disappeared.[47] Instead, a chorus assumes a greater role, the recitative is orchestrated throughout (providing passion and colour not available in a *secco recitative*) and the arias are placed at powerful dramatic points.[48] Grimalt suggests that the reform, attributed to Gluck but simultaneously adapted by other composers, consisted mostly of assimilating some *opera buffa* elements and involved increased relevance of orchestral colours, particularly adopting *accompagnato recitative* at the expense of the old *secco*, inclusion of bass voices in serious works, inclusion of chorus and soloist ensembles and the development of musically coherent constructions, especially at the close of an act.[49] Despite the inclusion of these *buffa* elements, however, Grimalt notes that the fundamental difference between the serious and comic is the representation of the "marvellous", many of which were representations of the supernatural. 'The appearance of gods and magic', Grimalt tells us, 'offers great many opportunities to display awesome machineries, a fundamental asset of both *tragédie lyrique* and *opera seria* that allowed the representation of miraculous events with mechanical devices'.[50]

Representations of awe-inspiring supernatural and natural "marvels" in opera are signified by the *ombra* and *tempesta* topics. Both these topics use similar signifiers: mainly minor keys; shifting modulations; "surprise" progressions; bold, chromatic harmony; disjunct, fragmented melodies with wide leaps; repeated notes, pedals and ostinatos in the bass; restless, syncopated rhythms and sudden dynamic contrasts. In this way, McClelland offers 'they can therefore be viewed as representing different sides of the same coin'.[51] The main difference between the two topics involve tempo and this is tied in with what each topic signifies. 'In general', McClelland tells us, 'it can be said that *ombra* is reserved for darkly ceremonial or ominous references, while *tempesta* applies to cataclysmic events or emotional outbursts'.[52] The *ombra* topic is described in greater detail later as it plays a major part in the emergence of the uncanny narrative and will therefore not be too closely illustrated here. The *ombra's* denotation of the supernatural in opera and sacred music dates from the Renaissance onwards, however in seventeenth- and eighteenth-century opera *ombra* represented oracles, demons, gods and witches as well as ritualistic ceremonies that were designed to inspire awe and horror among the audience. It is this link with religion and the church, malevolent or otherwise, and the slow, heartbeat-like recitatives that categorise the *ombra* as a high-class topic, while the *tempesta* is not class affiliated as it signifies natural storms – 'whether supernaturally instigated or not,' McClelland adds –, metaphorical signs of turbulent emotions and to accompany scenes of pursuit or flight.[53] The emotional representation of the *tempesta* links it with one other high-class topic, the sensibility style or *Empfindsamkeit*. In Matthew Head's definition of sensibility, he states that it refers

> to human disposition, not to musical materials. It identified a capacity to respond with pleasure or pain, with feeling, and with self-awareness to the impressions made on the body and mind by the senses. Consciousness, subjectivity, and reflexivity are key terms in conceptualising sensibility, which referred not simply to a capacity to be moved but also to an awareness of that capacity and its moral obligations'.[54]

It served as an early defense of sense (in this instance referring to the senses and emotions) over reason and rationalism, and was also therefore a reaction to the 'strict' or 'learned' style.[55] Ratner posits this topic as a parallel to *Sturm und Drang*, using the dramatic fluidity that shifts quickly from one emotion to another to support this theory. The *Sturm und Drang* topic, however, has come under intense criticism in the last decade with Monelle commenting in 2010 that 'it is probably no longer OK to speak of a "Sturm und Drang" topic'.[56] McClelland concurs stating that 'The use of *Sturm und Drang* in relation to music is certainly problematic, and it must now be recognised that it is no longer fit for purpose in the discipline of topic theory. In order to establish specific topical references more clearly, the *Sturm* really needs to be separated from the *Drang*. The *Sturm* characteristics are relatively easy to identify, deriving as they do from essentially pictorial representations of storms, whereas *Drang* is rather more difficult to pin down'.[57] McClelland instead proposes the use of the term *tempesta* for all references that are storm-related, although he also adduces that the musical style also reflects pursuit or metaphorically depicts rage and madness. As such, the intimate quality of C.P.E. Bach's keyboard sonatas (as the main proponent of this style) helps to distinguish the refined *Empfindsamkeit* topic from the more declamatory *tempesta* style.[58] In similar fashion to the *tempesta* topic, this topic has also been defined as a 'pre-Romantic' Classical topic.[59]

According to Ratner this style is signified by 'rapid changes in mood, broken figures, interrupted continuity, elaborate ornamentation, pregnant pauses, shifting, uncertain, often dissonant harmony'.[60] Monelle, however, states that the 'style of *Empfindsamkeit* is largely founded on the affective appoggiatura, a component of the "*pianto*" topic'.[61] While still associating it with the keyboard fantasias, it is the appoggiatura that Monelle claims gives the music its emotional disposition:

> Here the formula always resolves a dissonance and is always stressed; that is, it is an appoggiatura. An example is given from a fantasia in the *Musikalisches Vielerley* of 1770. It shows a series of *pianti*, each dissonant, ending with the recitative formula of a falling fourth. In this very chromatic passage, all figures are minor seconds. Elsewhere, major seconds alternate freely with minor, often keeping the figure within the mode. This is the true style of *Empfindsamkeit* [. . .] And, indeed, the figure may rise as well as fall.[62]

LOW CLASS TOPICS

In some of the high-class topics mentioned above, it is suggested that their associations are perceived, rather than authentic representations, for example the hunt as noble rather than the 'ignoble, squalid and cruel' reality. As is so often the case in historical discourses, because the low-class topoi are more the upper class's notion of the lower class, rather than a real representation, these topics tend toward the comic or grotesque. For example, the *opera buffa* style and *alla turca* were often used to inject some comedy into a scene, or piece of music.[63] In Mozart's opera *Die Entführung aus dem Serail* (1782), he used Turkish inferences as a comic counterpoint to Osmin's rage, invoking the 'play' on topics that is so easily executed when utilising the class system that is being outlined. Although for many topics the meaningfulness of the class signification can change through time, the signification of nationalistic topics has remained the same into the nineteenth century as they are linked to the *Volk*, folk or commoner. Jonathan Bellman posits that the signifiers of the *alla turca style* suggest a 'lack of musical sophistication' through a 'mechanical approach to music-making', which lends an air of contempt to the music, highlighting its use as a source of comic value.⁶⁴ *Opera buffa* reflected a perception of everyday life with both comic and serious characters. This was achieved using local settings and dialects, cementing the association of the topic with the lower classes, and an often witty observation of the human condition within a contemporary context.⁶⁵ The topic as recognisable in instrumental music is, Mary Hunter writes, ambiguous. Ratner describes 'comic-rhetoric', rather than *opera buffa* specifically, as 'quick juxtapositions of contrasting ideas, short lively figures, active interplay of dialogue, light textures, marked articulation, [and] unexpected turns'.⁶⁶ The main signifier for this topic, Allanbrook suggests, is 'an all-inclusive image of a peopled topological space, [. . .] without the precise story-bound meanings that a text provides'.⁶⁷ Therefore, a variety of contrasting topics, particularly contrasting in class, will inevitably bring into play ideas of dialogism and theatricality, at which point, Hunter explains, opera will be invoked.⁶⁸

Dances

Different dances represent different times and social classes; for example, the sarabande, minuet, gavotte and bourrée are considered upper-class, while a depiction of the low-class dances – the musette, gigue, pastorale and siciliano – are seen as such owing to their association with the pastoral topical class to which they also belong. The nationalist dances, that is the polka, *stile hongrois,* the polka, and of course the waltz and *Ländler* will be discussed in the next chapters as their class depiction is rooted in the Viennese perception of them, rather than emerging directly into the eighteenth- and nineteenth-century courts. As most upper class dances can be traced back to aristocratic courts and ballrooms, they are not, per se, associated with church, chamber or theatre music. However, as these types of composition were often written or transcribed for the piano for use in the salon in the nineteenth century, they can be associated to a higher degree with chamber music. Leonard Ratner observed that 'there is hardly a major work in this [Classical] era that does not borrow heavily from the dance'.⁶⁹ This, Eric McKee suggests, is 'not surprising given that social dancing, whether in the ballroom, in the beer hall, or in the home, was by far the most popular social activity of the time'.⁷⁰ Moreover, McKee writes that

> the choreographies of each dance (and the manner in which one performed them) were associated with particular feelings or motions of the soul (*Gemüthsbewegungen*), ethical states, and indications of one's social class.

And, according to eighteenth-century writers, the vocabulary of dance gestures encompassed the entire gamut of the human condition from grave to gay, from noble to vulgar.[71]

The sarabande's central features are its slow tempo, prompting it to be described by Ratner as a slow minuet; triple time, with an emphasis on the second beat; and 'heavily dotted rhythms and lavish ornamentation'.[72] The dance is often in a minor key, which, along with its serious character represents the high class in much the same way as the learned style's 'elevated' intellectualism does.[73] The gavotte, a French court dance in duple time, often had a pastoral affect such as a drone and was frequently employed in the Baroque suite, often appearing after the more serious movements like the sarabande. The dance itself consists of repeated four or eight bar phrases and is uncomplicated rhythmically and harmonically. It is notable for its 'caesura' after the second crotchet of the bar and the half-bar anacrusis (usually two crotchets), a rhythm which Ratner claims 'accommodated a melody of elegance, poise, and self-containment'.[74] To provide a strong rhythmic bassline to this melody, Alberti basses are often used as their 'tick-tock' rhythms 'help to accentuate the separate strokes of the three strong beats'.[75] In the nineteenth century, many lightweight drawing-room pieces were written in the gavotte style, therefore transferring its associations from the aristocratic ballroom to the gallant chamber style.[76]

The minuet style uses a triple time signature (either 3/4 or 3/8), a moderate tempo, and generally begins on the downbeat. Melanie Lowe describes it as 'typically homophonic, with a simple and normally unembellished melodic style; in its hierarchical and symmetrical phrase structure, the minuet epitomizes Classic structural balance and contrast. Moreover, the minuet is the archetype of Classic form: two-reprise form usually presented in the I–V, X–I key-area plan (or I–III, X–I for those few dances in the minor mode)'[77] – hence Ratner's suggestion that it was 'associated with the elegant world of court and salon'.[78] 'Indeed', Lowe notes, '"noble" was the first word of choice among 18th-century critics to describe the Classic minuet's affect'.[79] Sulzer, for example, characterises the minuet as having 'a noble and charming deportment, but combined with simplicity'.[80] This simplicity, however, does not contradict the nobility inherent in this topic; rather it indicates the Enlightenment's aesthetic concept of *noble simplicité*, which Lowe observes 'imparts further sincerity'.[81] Scheibe places this in opposition to the high-class connotations of the learned style, as he 'consider[s] "the natural" and "the clear" to be true signs of the good style, two values clearly opposed to the "artificial" and "indistinct" style of fugal writing and counterpoint'.[82] The fundamental style of this dance, however, is such that it is capable of great ranges of expression, as Ratner illustrates by providing examples of the dance with an 'elegant vein', a 'rustic flavour', and a 'deeply pathetic mood'.[83] It is, therefore, a valuable integration topic, one which can 'tolerate the overlay of another style or topical reference' such as the military, hunt or pastoral (outlined more fully below).[84] Since this dance is able to integrate with lower class topics, for example in the rustic manner suggested by Ratner, it is possible it could itself be seen as having interchangeable associations. However, it is more likely that its use instead highlights the differing classes of the topics, creating juxtaposition between the dance and the topic with which it is integrated.

The bourrée and the contredanse are similar enough to be discussed together, indeed Ratner says of the contredanse: 'if we quicken the pace of the bourrée, the music will be in the style of the contradanse'.[85] In 'Ballroom Dances of the Late Eighteenth Century', McKee provides an account of the 'prototypical features' of the contredanse, identifying three types: the *contredanse anglaise*, the *contredanse française* and the *contredanse allemande*, however, he notes that the Viennese favoured the *contredanse anglaise* hence that is the dance referred to from here. The salient difference between them is in fact their class associations. The bourée 'was rather lively in manner, calling for lightness in performance'; this '*di mezzo carattere* ("of the middle rank")' style was frequently used in Classical music, although not as the structure for an entire movement.[86] The musical markers of the contredanse give it a 'spirited, playful and gay character: [. . .] lively tempo, major mode, clear and uncomplicated melodic organization, and simple rhythms with a swinging gait (triplet figures are common), [and] are set in duple meter, either simple (2/4) or compound (6/8)'.[87] Simplicity, McKee claims, citing the lexicons of Jean-Jacques Rousseau, Charles Compan and Koch, is at the core of the contredanse.[88] It is not the noble simplicity of the minuet, however, but the rustic simplicity of its origins in the English village, which therefore associate it principally with the lower class. Allanbrook explains that contredanses 'portray customs, amusements, and love intrigues of the common people. Movements and leaps are a little less abandoned, but still lively, rather mischievous, and very striking. They must always be amusing and merry. The main thing in them is agility, a quick, artful movement, and a mischievous affect'.[89] Grimalt explains that the main feature of the contredanse 'is the way it is danced: by practically walking', however, he also identifies distinctive musical characteristics.[90] The dance is usually in duple meter with an *oompah-pah-pah* rhythm (quaver rest then three quavers) and it is diatonic or pentatonic with a small range and basic harmony suggesting folk songs and instrumentation.[91] It is often used as a closing function, appearing at the conclusion to a work, particularly in many of the Viennese Classical composers' (Beethoven, Mozart Haydn) symphonies and sonatas. Grimalt suggests this is because it 'represent[s. . .] the longed-for new, egalitarian times' and that more exclusive dances such as the minuet are 'displaced and overcome by the dance that anyone can take part in'.[92] He terms this the changeover narrative: a musical narrative that begins in minor keys and in high-class topical signification but transforms to the major mode and to lower topical classes like the contredanse, the *Ländler* and the Gigue.[93]

Specific dances considered low class are not as easy to identify, however there are certain identifiers that are common to all. Julia Sutton writes that 'drums and double-reed instruments [. . .] were considered to be grotesque or peasant types and were excluded from [...] high society'.[94] The musette is an excellent example of this as it is a dance whose 'pastoral style is suggestive of the sound of a musette or bagpipe' which, while of aristocratic design, was used to play rustic dances.[95] There is typically a drone in the bass on the tonic and the melodies are in conjunct motion and often in quick note values.[96] The 'Gavotte ou la musette' in J. S. Bach's Third English Suite (BWV808) demonstrates how the musette drone could be integrated into other topics to indicate the pastoral and therefore change the signification of the topic. As Hutton explains, 'Theatrical conventions governed the choice of dance types within a flexible, evolving framework that composers both within and outside the theatre could draw upon; the pastoral realm, for example, could be evoked by the sounds of a passepied, *musette* or gavotte'.[97]

It would appear then that there are a number of different ways to distinguish between high and low topics. Whether it is through the introduction of pastoral effects, such as drums, drones and double-reed instruments – although as shown, not all pastoral references are of the low style –, through connotations of national dances or the chatter of the ordinary *volk* in the *opera buffa style* it is not a plain depiction of the lower class that is signified. Instead, it is a contemptuous, satirical perception of the lower classes as awkward and clumsy in opposition to the noble elegance of the dances that 'carried the weight of tradition and remained a vehicle for demonstrating proper deportment and the disciplined use of the body that was seen as essential for anyone aspiring to social standing'.[98] While this chapter has concentrated on the Classical period, the customary period in which topoi are considered useful, this perception seems to be as virulent in *fin-de-siècle* Vienna as it was in the eighteenth-century European centres. However, what does change is the political and court-orientated realm in which topic theory traditionally operates.

NOTES

1. Leonard G. Ratner, *Classic Music: Expression, Form, and Style* (London: Collier Macmillan, 1980), 9.

2. Clive McClelland, *Ombra: Supernatural Music in the Eighteenth Century* (Plymouth: Lexington, 2012) and *Tempesta: Stormy Music in the Eighteenth Century* (London: Lexington, 2017); Eric McKee, *Decorum of the Minuet, Delirium of*

the Waltz: A Study of Dance Music Relations in 3/4 Time (Bloomington: Indiana University Press, 2012).

3. Natalie Bauer-Lechtner, *Recollections of Gustav Mahler,* trans. Dika Newlin, ed. Peter Franklin (Cambridge: Cambridge University Press, 1980), 239–240.

4. Ratner, *Classic Music,* 9.

5. Danuta Mirka, ed., introduction to *Oxford Handbook of Topic Theory* (Oxford: Oxford University Press, 2014), 2; italics in original.

6. Ratner, *Classic Music,* 9.

7. Ernest C. Harris, *Johann Matthesson's* Der Volkommene Capellmeister*: A Revised Translation with Critical Commentary* (Ann Arbor, MI: UMI Research, 1981), 467, quoted in Mirka, *Oxford Handbook of Topic Theory* "Introduction", 7.

8. Harris, *Johann Matthesson's* Der Volkommene Capellmeister, 467, quoted in Mirka, "Introduction", 7.

9. Mirka, "Introduction", 21.

10. Mirka, "Introduction", 4.

11. Johann Adolph Scheibe, *Critische Musikus* (Leipzig: Breitkopf, 1745), 126ff.

12. Robert Hatten, *Musical Meaning in Beethoven: Markedness, Meaning and Interpretation* (Bloomington: Indiana University Press, 1994), 77.

13. Hatten, *Musical Meaning in Beethoven,* 74.

14. Hatten, *Musical Meaning in Beethoven.*

15. Hatten, *Musical Meaning in Beethoven,* 75.

16. Kofi Agawu, *Music as Discourse: Semiotic Adventures in Romantic Music* (New York: Oxford University Press, 2008), 42–44; Johann Georg Sulzer, *Allgemeine Theorie der schönen Künste*, 2nd ed., vol. 1 (Hildesheim: Georg Olms, 1994), 441.

17. For example the hunt, which is associated with nobility and the thrill of the chase, rather than a vicious blood sport, or the medieval valour and heroism of the military style, ideals far removed from the horrors of war.

18. Raymond Monelle, *The Musical Topic: Hunt, Military and Pastoral* (Bloomington, IN: Indiana University Press, 2006), 29–30.

19. Monelle, *The Musical Topic: Hunt, Military and Pastoral*, 30.

20. Vera Micznik, "On Mahler and the Power of Genre" *The Journal of Musicology* 12, no. 2 (Spring 1994), 137.

21. Micznik, "On Mahler and the Power of Genre".

22. Monelle, *The Musical Topic: Hunt, Military and Pastoral*, 5.

23. Monelle, *The Musical Topic: Hunt, Military and Pastoral.*

24. The term 'dialects' is taken from Janice Dickensheet, "Nineteenth-Century Topical Analysis: A Lexicon of Romantic *Topoi"*, *Pendragon Review* 2, no. 2 (2003), 27.

25. The "story" level referred to here is a term used in narrative methodology and is explained fully in chapter 4.

26. Elaine Sisman, *Mozart: The Jupiter Symphony* (Cambridge: Cambridge University Press, 1993), 68.

27. Keith Chapin, "Learned Style and Learned Styles", *Oxford Handbook of Topic Theory*, 310.

28. Johann Christian Lobe, *"Motivische-thematische Arbeit"*, *Compositions-Lehre: Oder umfassende Theorie der thematischen Arbeit und den modernen*

Instrumentalformen (Weimar: Voigt, 1844), quoted in Keith Chapin, "Learned Style", *Oxford Handbook of Topic Theory,* 310.

29. Monelle, *The Sense of Music* (Princeton and Oxford: Princeton University Press, 2000), 26.

30. Monelle, *The Sense of Music,* 26.

31. Melanie Lowe, "Amateur Topical Competencies", *Oxford Handbook of Topic Theory,* 619.

32. Ratner, *Classic Music,* 16.

33. Monelle, *The Sense of Music,* 26.

34. Monelle, *The Musical Topic: Hunt, Military and Pastoral,* 220.

35. Hermann Jung, *Die Pastorale: Studien zur Geschichte eines musikalischen Topos* (Bern: Francke, 1980), 144–51, quoted in Monelle, *The Sense of Music,* 191.

36. Opera seria (It: 'serious opera') Marita P. McClymonds and Daniel Heartz. https://doi-org.nls.idm.oclc.org/10.1093/gmo/9781561592630.article.20385 (accessed 3/1/2022).

37. Opera seria (It: 'serious opera') Marita P. McClymonds and Daniel Heartz. https://doi-org.nls.idm.oclc.org/10.1093/gmo/9781561592630.article.20385, (accessed 3/1/2022).

38. Opera seria (It: 'serious opera') Marita P. McClymonds and Daniel Heartz. https://doi-org.nls.idm.oclc.org/10.1093/gmo/9781561592630.article.20385, (accessed on 3/1/2022).

39. Joan Grimalt, *Mapping Musical Signification* (Switzerland: Springer, 2020), 307.

40. Opera seria (It: 'serious opera') Marita P. McClymonds and Daniel Heartz. https://doi-org.nls.idm.oclc.org/10.1093/gmo/9781561592630.article.20385 (accessed on 3/1/2022).

41. Opera seria (It: 'serious opera') Marita P. McClymonds and Daniel Heartz. https://doi-org.nls.idm.oclc.org/10.1093/gmo/9781561592630.article.20385 (accessed on 3/1/2022) and Joan Grimalt, *Mapping Musical Signification,* 307.

42. Opera seria (It: 'serious opera') Marita P. McClymonds and Daniel Heartz. https://doi-org.nls.idm.oclc.org/10.1093/gmo/9781561592630.article.20385 (accessed on 3/1/2022).

43. Joan Grimalt, *Mapping Musical Signification,* 307.

44. Opera seria (It: 'serious opera') Marita P. McClymonds and Daniel Heartz. https://doi-org.nls.idm.oclc.org/10.1093/gmo/9781561592630.article.20385 (accessed on 3/1/2022).

45. Opera seria (It: 'serious opera') Marita P. McClymonds and Daniel Heartz. https://doi-org.nls.idm.oclc.org/10.1093/gmo/9781561592630.article.20385 (accessed on 3/1/2022).

46. Hayes, Jeremy (2002). "Orfeo ed Euridice". Grove Music Online (8th ed.). Oxford University Press. doi:10.1093/gmo/9781561592630.article.O008226 (accessed 3/1/2022); quote from Opera seria (It: 'serious opera') Marita P. McClymonds and Daniel Heartz. https://doi-org.nls.idm.oclc.org/10.1093/gmo/9781561592630.article.20385 (accessed on 3/1/2022).

47. Hayes, Jeremy (2002). "Orfeo ed Euridice". Grove Music Online (8th ed.). Oxford University Press. doi:10.1093/gmo/9781561592630.article.O008226 (accessed 3/1/2022).

48. Hayes, Jeremy (2002). "Orfeo ed Euridice". Grove Music Online (8th ed.). Oxford University Press. doi:10.1093/gmo/9781561592630.article.O008226 (accessed 3/1/2022).

49. Joan Grimalt, *Mapping Musical Signification*, 309.

50. Grimalt, *Mapping Musical Signification*, 308.

51. Clive McClelland, "*Ombra* and *Tempesta*" *Oxford Handbook of Topic Theory,* 285.

52. McClelland, "*Ombra* and *Tempesta*" *Oxford Handbook of Topic Theory*.

53. McClelland, "*Ombra* and *Tempesta*" *Oxford Handbook of Topic Theory,* 286.

54. Matthew Head, "Fantasia and Sensibility", *Oxford Handbook of Topic Theory* 264.

55. Daniel Heartz and Bruce Alan Brown, "Empfindsamkeit", in *Grove Music Online. Oxford Music Online.* http://0-www.oxfordmusiconline.com.wam.leeds.ac.uk/subscriber/article/grove/music/08774 (accessed July 20, 2015).

56. Monelle, *The Sense of Music*, 110.

57. McClelland, "*Ombra* and *Tempesta*" *Oxford Handbook of Topic Theory,* 281.

58. Daniel Heartz and Bruce Alan Brown, "Empfindsamkeit".

59. Jim Samson, "Romanticism", in *Grove Music Online. Oxford Music Online.* http://0-www.oxfordmusiconline.com.wam.leeds.ac.uk/subscriber/article/grove/music/23751 (accessed May 5, 2011).

60. Samson, "Romanticism".

61. Monelle, *The Sense of Music*, 31.

62. Monelle, *The Sense of Music,* 70–71.

63. Ratner, *Classic Music*, 3.

64. Jonathan Bellman. "Toward a Lexicon for the *Style hongrois*" *The Journal of Musicology* 9, no. 2 (Spring 1991), 214–237, 218.

65. Piero Weiss and Julian Budden, "Opera buffa", in *Grove Music Online. Oxford Music Online.* http://0-www.oxfordmusiconline.com.wam.leeds.ac.uk/subscriber/article/grove/music/43721 (accessed July 20, 2015).

66. Ratner, *Classic Music*, 395.

67. Wye. J. Allanbrook, *The Secular Commedia: Comic mimesis in Eighteenth-Century Instrumental Music* (Berkeley: University of California Press, 2014); Mary Hunter, "Topics and Opera Buffa", *Oxford Handbook of Topic Theory*, 61.

68. Hunter, "Topics and Opera Buffa", 62.

69. Ratner, *Classic Music,* 18.

70. Eric McKee, "Ballroom Dances of the Late Eighteenth Century", *Oxford Handbook of Topic Theory* 164; also see Lawrence M. Zbikowski, "Music and Dance in the *Ancien Régime*", *Oxford Handbook of Topic Theory*, 143–163.

71. McKee, "Ballroom Dances", 164.

72. Ratner, *Classic Music*, 11; Wye J. Allanbrook, *Rhythmic Gesture in Mozart: Le Nozze Di Figaro and Don Giovanni* (London: University of Chicago Press, 1983), 37.

73. Ratner, *Classic Music*, 12.
74. Ratner, *Classic Music*, 14.
75. Allanbrook, *Rhythmic Gesture in Mozart*, 50.
76. Wendy Thompson and Jane Bellingham, "Gavotte", in *The Oxford Companion to Music*, ed. Alison Latham. *Oxford Music Online*. http://0-www.oxfordmusiconline.com.wam.leeds.ac.uk/subscriber/article/opr/t114/e2800 (accessed July 20, 2015).
77. Melanie Lowe, "Falling from Grace", 172–173.
78. Melanie Lowe, "Falling from Grace", 172–173; Ratner, *Classic Music*, 9; W. J. Allanbrook also links this dance with the *ancien régime*, an observation paralleled by Eric McKee, who noted that it was one of the only dances still performed in court in the eighteenth century. He states that it was 'artfully simple yet fiendishly difficult to master, the minuet not only was the choreographic ideal of natural(ized) grace and noble simplicity, but also represented the collective historical weight and power of the *ancien régime*. Thus the minuet was both a current dance and a historical dance' (Eric Mckee, "Ballroom Dances", *Oxford Handbook of Topic Theory*, 168).
79. Lowe, "Falling from Grace", 173.
80. Sulzer, *Allgemeine Theorie der schönen Künste*, 3, 388; Lowe, "Falling from Grace", 173–174.
81. Lowe, "Falling from Grace", 174.
82. Scheibe, *Critische Musikus*, 274, quoted in Lowe, "Falling from Grace", 175.
83. Ratner, *Classic Music*, 10.
84. Allanbrook, *Rhythmic Gesture in Mozart*, 35–36.
85. Allanbrook, *Rhythmic Gesture in Mozart*, 35–36.
86. Ratner, *Classic Music*, 13.
87. Eric McKee. "Ballroom Dances of the Late Eighteenth Century", *Oxford Handbook of Topic Theory*, 168–170.
88. Charles Compan, *Dictionnaire de Danse* (Paris: Cailleau, 1787), 101; Heinrich C. Koch, *Musikalische Lexicon* (Hildesheim: George Olms, 1964), 535; Jean-Jacques Rousseau, "Menuet", in *Encyclopédie*, ed. Denis Diterot and Jean d'Alembert, vol. 10 (Paris: Briasson, 1751–1772), 122.
89. Allanbrook, *Rhythmic Gesture in Mozart*, 63.
90. Grimalt, *Mapping Musical Signification*, 291.
91. Joan Grimalt, *Mapping Musical Signification*, 291.
92. Joan Grimalt, *Mapping Musical Signification*, 292.
93. Joan Grimalt, *Mapping Musical Signification*, 292.
94. Julia Sutton, "Dance" *Grove Music Online* https://doi-org.nls.idm.oclc.org/10.1093/gmo/9781561592630.article.45795 (accessed 04/03/21).
95. Anthony Baines, revised by Robert A Green and Meredith Ellis Little, "Musette" *Grove Music Online*. https://doi-org.nls.idm.oclc.org/10.1093/gmo/9781561592630.article.19398 (accessed 04/03/21).
96. Baines, revised by Robert A Green and Meredith Ellis Little, "Musette".
97. Sutton, "Dance" *Grove Music Online*.
98. Rebecca Harris-Warrick, "Dance" *Grove Music Online*. https://doi-org.nls.idm.oclc.org/10.1093/gmo/9781561592630.article.45795 (accessed 04/03/21).

Chapter 2

Evolution of Viennese Cultural-Historical Topics

Romance, Freud and Authenticity

If topics are historically situated, as Monelle claims, then to understand the significance of the topics used in the music of *fin-de-siècle* Vienna it is vital to achieve an understanding of the cultural-historical framework that surrounds the works. This helps not only to form a comprehensive narrative provided by known topics, but also explain how other topics and their associations have transformed. It also facilitates the identification of new topics that emerge from the critical historical moment in which the music was conceived. By isolating the main themes and issues occurring at the turn of the twentieth century in Vienna it is possible to reveal associations between the significant themes and the new topics.

The new styles that surfaced at this point in history appeared to be independent of the past, as if, in Carl E. Schorske's words, 'history had become useless to [them]'.[1] This is not completely so, however: history had not become "useless", but rather the young Viennese had become disheartened with where their past had brought them. It was not only in music that this aversion occurred; similar movements emerged in literature, architecture, philosophy and politics simultaneously. As Allan Janik and Stephen Toulmin point out, attempting to explain one of these movements without exploring the others would be to ignore the most significant point, 'namely that they *were* all going on in this same place at this same time'.[2] I can therefore conclude that not only did these movements have an effect on each other's development, but that the political and social development of Austria at the time had a part to play in their formation.

Schorske, in his authoritative work on *fin-de-siècle* Vienna, presents the thesis that the remarkable emergence of such progression within the arts, psychology and politics, was a result of the 'failure of liberalism'.[3] This theory proposes that the modernists "assaulted" the 'value system of classical liberalism-in-ascendancy within which they had been reared'.[4] Schorske sets out the different reasons why the failure of liberalism affected the leading figures of the time, focussing on a movement away from the previous generation's rational life into an instinctual one, and the use by the liberals of 'undemocratic devices' to retain power. He also looks at how the artists attempted to integrate with the aristocracy through art, and how the rise of nationalism and anti-Semitism affected Viennese life and politics.

LIBERALISM AND RATIONALISM

When in 1867 the Liberal party rose to power in Vienna, they came to be associated with rationalist intellectuals and the highly moralistic bourgeois class. The basic beliefs of the Liberals were their faith in reason and progress, their economic power, and their cultural elitism, characterised by their pro-German stance, resentment of the Catholic Church, and 'a profound distrust of anti-intellectual trends'.[5] In this way, the Liberal party connected less with the liberalism of the revolutionaries of 1848, and more with the capitalists and, therefore, the Jews.[6] Meyer explains that the rise of many Jews into 'financially comfortable circumstances' caused anxiety in the artisan and shop-keeping classes whose economic territory was threatened.[7] The Liberal's method of maintaining power was also questionable, as Janik glibly writes: 'the liberals were not very liberal and in their own illiberalism provoked an even more dangerous illiberalism that destroyed them politically'.[8] He refers to the act of restricting the franchise to men paying over 10 florins in tax. This excluded the working classes and the *Bürgertum* or "little men", alienating, in essence, approximately ninety-five percent of the population, but, crucially, not the "financially comfortable" Jews, prompting the famous quotation from Robert Musil's novel *The Man without Qualities*: 'before the law all citizens were equal, but not everyone, of course, was a citizen'.[9] The expansion of the franchise, which began in 1882, meant that the disgruntled artisans gained a vote, and in 1897, in an increasing atmosphere of anti-Semitism, the Liberals lost power to Karl Lueger and the Christian Social Party.

Schorske theorises that the remarkable emergence of such progression within the arts, psychology and politics was a result of the "failure of liberalism".[10] Meyer, summing up Schorske's argument, explains that 'the rapid rise and equally rapid decline of the fortunes of liberalism caused such bitter disappointment on the part of Vienna's bourgeoisie that it retreated from the political scene and sought refuge in the aesthetic sphere'.[11] The values of the old Viennese bourgeoisie centred upon rationalism and positivism – upon the ideal of a man with disciplined conformity and moralistic good taste – and it was against this that the young Viennese rebelled. They felt there was a side to life that could not be dealt with rationally, an emotional side their fathers were repressing, and to them 'human beings ignored emotions at their peril'.[12] Within the universities, the politics of Richard Wagner and Friedrich Nietzsche formed the new cultural rationale. Schorske explains that

> [c]ritical of the rational state and the scientific spirit, both thinkers exalted archaic Greek culture as models for the regeneration of German society. Wagner added to the glorification of the polis the special allure of Germanic myth, thus enriching his archaic communitarian vision with a national-populist appeal for the young German militants. Both thinkers affirmed instinct, vindicating its claims against 'bourgeois' reason and the analytic spirit.[13]

Schorske suggests that the generational rebellion against the fathers and their values could be the reason for the 'sharp break from a tie with the past', but only on the most obvious level.[14] It is interesting however that Schorske, unlike other scholars, considers both of the generation's values – the first moral and scientific, and the second aesthetic – as part of the liberal culture. Other scholars portray the new generation as moving away from the political altogether and, Beller suggests, into the 'cultural temple of the aesthetic and psychological, where the historical world held no sway'.[15] Beller continues that modernism therefore appears to be the 'introspective response of artists and thinkers who, in Schorske's phrase, were not so much alienated *from* their class as *with* it'.[16] Meyer attributes this wholesale alienation of the bourgeois class to a collective guilt due to their continued social and economic power despite Liberalism's political demise.[17] Their response, she claims, stems from their self-perception of being 'in contrast to a decadent, self serving, exploitative, and corrupt nobility whose continued political power was justified by nothing but the chance of birth right'.[18] Hence, moral clarity became the maxim of the bourgeois class. The 1873 stock exchange crash, caused predominantly by Liberal economic policies, left the bourgeoisie partially responsible for misery faced primarily by the lower classes.[19] As such, Meyer argues that the authors of the time, represented in her article by Hugo von Hofmannsthal, Arthur Schnitzler and Leopold von Andrian, characterised their protagonists as 'victims [. . .] under siege', and as Other to both the aristocrats and the working class, effectively marginalising themselves as 'outsiders'.[20] Meyer explains that

> [t]orn as Vienna 1900's writers are, between a flight from politics into culture and an inclusion of politics in culture, they try to straddle both positions by

inscribing into their texts the figure of the split bourgeois subject who is alternately blamed for his own position and vindicated as a victim of forces greater than himself.[21]

In rebellion against the duplicitous nature of these moral values, Karl Kraus became the spokesperson of the modernists in an attempt to 'bite at the hypocrisy that passed in Old Vienna for morality, and at the twaddle that passed for art'.[22] His polemical articles in *Die Fackel*, the newspaper he wrote and produced, were aimed mostly at the lack of integrity displayed by his fellow Viennese. Janik and Toulmin provide a plausible explanation as to why these satirical attacks on others became so important to the development of modernism:

> This was a society in which all established media, or means of expression—from the language of politics across the board to the principal of architectural design—had seemingly lost touch with their intended 'messages', and had been robbed of all capacity to perform their proper functions. [...] Kraus's one-man debate had wider implications also. Very soon it woke echoes in other fields of intellectual and artistic activity, and broadened into the demand for a critique of the means of expression used in all fields – for example, for a stripping away of all that conventional and meaningless decoration with which sentimentality had encumbered the creative arts, so as to restore the expressive capacities they needed in order to fulfil their original and proper functions once again.[23]

Hermann Broch labelled this outdated and hypocritical sense of morality a "value vacuum" and it is here that Janik challenges Schorske's "failure of liberalism" thesis with what he has called the "critical modernism" paradigm. This idea turns on the notion that 'the most important contribution of *fin-de-siècle* Vienna to our culture is a particularly sceptical healthy reaction against the spellbinding power that modernity exerts upon us'.[24] Janik describes critical modernism as a "*scathing diagnosis*" of the great amount of power ascribed at the time to art to move us emotionally, and a "*strategy*" for contending with the narcissistic and theatrical "religion of art".[25] Among those he counts as critical modernists are Arnold Schoenberg, Hermann Broch, Georg Trakl and Ludwig Wittgenstein. To this list, I will add Johann Strauss II and Franz Lehár, as it is their satirical use of class-associated topics that gives us the critical populist view of the liberal bourgeois. This will begin to be demonstrated in chapter three, however, Janik's critical modernism becomes the basis for the narrative of the Second Vienna School and their direct predecessors, as well as the subject of some of the more popular contemporary operettas. A definition of the signifiers of the rational topical class can be found later in this chapter along with its dialectical opposite to the psychological topical class.

PSYCHE

Freud as the Central Psychoanalytical Personality

The central essay in Schorske's collection is based on the conceptual patricide at the heart of the psychological theme running throughout the rest of the work. The protagonist of this chapter is, ironically, the staunch liberalist Freud. Schorske posits that until the 1890s the political tension existed between the liberals and the conservatives. Closer to the turn of the century, however, the changed social strata caused conflict between the lower classes and the old elites. Freud, the author explains, 'belonged to the group most threatened: Viennese liberal Jewry'.[26] Schorske outlines how, through a series of analyses of his own dreams, Freud had to 'neutralise politics by reducing it to psychological categories'.[27] This, along with the death of his father in 1896, led to his basic analytic principle outlined in *The Interpretation of Dreams*: that a dream is the fulfilment of a wish, or in subsequent chapters that 'a dream is a (disguised) fulfilment of a (suppressed) wish', what Freud calls the principle of distortion.[28] The first dream, of Irma's Injection, represented his professional frustration and self-doubt.[29] The second dream of The Uncle with the Yellow Beard, expressed the 'unseemly moral consequences' stemming from the political hindrance within his professional career (namely, not making a professor because of his religious beliefs).[30] His wish signified within the dream is for the power to eradicate his professional frustration, by 'step[ping] into the minister's shoes'.[31] Therefore, his professional wish *disguised* his political one:

> It is only now that I begin to see that it translates me from being in the somber present to the hopeful days of the bourgeois Ministry, and completely fulfils what was then my youthful ambition. In treating my two estimable and learned colleagues, merely because they are Jews, so badly, [. . .] I am acting as though I were the Minister; I have put myself in his place. What a revenge I take upon his Excellency! He refuses to appoint me *Professor extraordinarius*, and so in my dream I put myself in his place.[32]

From the principle of distortion, Freud wove analogies to explain the essential nature of consciousness. Schorske explains that '[t]he dream thought confronts the same problem in the psyche of the dreamer as "the political writer who has disagreeable truths to tell those in authority"'.[33] If there is a strong censor, the writer must disguise his assertions; the two social powers, ruler and people, are then comparable to the two psychic forces, superego and id. Freud argues that '[o]ne of these forces constructs the wish which is expressed by the dream, while the other exercises censorship upon this dream-wish and by the use of censorship, forcibly brings about distortion in the expression of the wish'.[34] This is the basis of the unconscious, the two psychic forces acting upon the ego (or I) to balance one another. The unconscious is formed, Freud suggests, as a repression of the Oedipus complex, the desire to have sexual relations with the parent of the opposite sex in rivalry with the same-sex parent. As Freud's theories at first centred on male children, the father is the child's rival, against whose rules and restrictions the child rebels.

Freud's Oedipal Complex: the Father/Son Conflict of the Failure of Liberalism

In *The Interpretation of Dreams*, Freud analyses several of his own dreams in order to discuss his various theories. The Revolutionary Dream describes the Oedipus complex, while also acting as an analogy to Schorske's failure of liberalism thesis. In this dream, Freud experiences an outburst of anger at the aristocratic Count Thun and flees through the halls of the university, 'that is, through academia', Schorske notes.[35] The final scene is set on a railway station platform in the company of his dying father, who, because of his blindness, needs Freud to hold a urinal for him. Schorske terms this dream his 'last explosive hail-and-farewell to politics', but also observes that in his own analysis Freud focussed not on the political rejection but on the final scene. He recalled how in reality his father had reprimanded him for urinating in his parent's bedroom, that he had 'disregarded the rules which modesty lays down'.[36] His Father responded that the 'boy will come to nothing', hence, by helping the old man to urinate it is as if he says, '[y]ou see I *have* come to something', taking vengeance of an intellectual kind, not on Count Thun, as he wished to do in his waking life just before he had the dream, but on the father.[37]

The Oedipus complex is not, therefore, just a conflict between a boy and his father, but an individual and society, as Freud explains:

> A Prince is known as father of his country; the father is the oldest, first, and for children the only authority, and from his autocratic power the other social authorities have developed in the history of human civilisation.[38]

As such, it is a metaphor for Schorske's thesis; the central principle of Freud's political theory being that politics is reducible to the conflict between father and son, and that the conclusion, drawn from the Revolutionary

Dream, is conquest of the father through flight into academia. Michael Roth explains that 'for all, generational and political conflict are represented in private terms or are imagined as inevitable Oedipal combat'.[39] Schorske simplifies this as 'patricide replaces regicide; psychoanalysis overcomes history. Politics is neutralised by a counterpolitical psychology'.[40]

Psychology in Literature

The theme that runs throughout Schorske's essays is the "psychological man" who emerged out of the political frustration of the time.[41] 'Anxiety, impotence, [and] a heightened awareness of the brutality of social existence' were the central features of the Viennese people.[42] Therefore, he argues, there was a rebellion against the liberal credo of morality and reason above all else – a rebellion against the contemporary authority which led to a turn inwards toward the psyche and the instinctual life – to a flight into academia and art. To illustrate this, Schorske begins by discussing the psyche within the literary works of Hofmannsthal and Schnitzler, the latter of which, Roth notes, diagnosed the tension between politics and the psyche "with extraordinary acumen".[43] However, Roth continues, while admirably 'unmask[ing] the pretensions of society's values' Schnitzler was 'unable to generate any values of his own'.[44]

Hofmannsthal, on the other hand, Roth writes, attempted to 'imagine an art that would offer a communal possibility beyond these crises rather than only describe them'.[45] Schorske comments that

> [e]ngagement in life, Hofmannsthal felt, demands the capacity to resolve, to will. This capacity implies commitment to the irrational, in which alone resolution and will are grounded. Thus affirmation of the instinctual reopened for the aesthete the door to the life of action and society.[46]

It is, then the "capacity to will", to desire, or as Freud puts it to "wish" that leads one towards the psychological, or instinctual. Schorske then examines Hofmannsthal's *The Tower* (*Der Turm*), written in 1927, his assessment of which symbolises the political crisis of the time:

> The father justifies political repression, as the Austrian liberals had done, by the rationale of order based on law. His subjects, his imprisoned son among them, are excluded from participation in the ceremony of the whole; hence they turn to aggression. Where law ignores instinct, instinct rebels and subverts order. [...] The poet prince, however, masters his aggressions and seeks to redeem the society with a new dynamic form of social order, a form inspired by the unifying, non-repressive paradigm of art.[47]

Hence, Hofmannsthal campaigns for a fusion between the instinctual and the rational, for a need to comprehend human feelings as well as rational, restrictive and often corrupt morality.[48]

THE RATIONAL AND PSYCHOLOGICAL AS TOPICS

The transformation that developed from rationalism shows society moving from the previous generations' positivist, disciplined conformity through the next generation's rebellion into the psychological, before finally resulting in Kraus's authentic ideal. I intend to show here how this relates to the music of *fin-de-siècle* Vienna. When identifying the 'rational' as a topic, allied with the first mode of the transformation, it becomes clear that it is a topical class. It is signified by the structures of the Classical period, for example, sonata form, rondo form and so on, as well as the use of diatonic harmony and traditional orchestration. The topics that also signify this topical class are the learned style, chorale topic and the aria topic; topics mostly associated with the high style and the (Catholic) church. The alliance of these subtopics with the sociological concept of rationalism can be clarified both in the foundation of tonality and in its opposition to the emotional and the representation of the psyche. As John H. Mueller describes: 'Either we have language, meaning, discourse, and reality (the orderly, the rational, the cerebral), [. . .] or we have the unstructured world of ruptured, ecstatic, *jouissance*, replete with luscious, Dionysion, hedonistic pleasures'.[49] Regarding the former, Martin writes that 'the development of the music [i.e. Western polyvocal music] necessitated a system of notation, but that system itself stimulated further development in the direction of rationalisation – imposing standard practices permitting greater complexity, facilitating compositional work by specialists and the development of musical theory'.[50] The learned topic embodies the rationalisation of music, it is the "orderly", "rational" and "cerebral" side of Mueller's coin, the second side of which, the second phase of the transformation, is outlined below. This topic possesses links with the overt Classical architecture of the Ringstraße, the monumental construction of which, Schorske asserts, became a 'symbolic focus of [the modernist] critique [...] "*Ringstraßenstil*" became a quite general term of opprobrium by which a generation of doubting, critical, and aesthetically sensitive sons rejected their self-confident, parvenu fathers'.[51]

The second phase of the transformation witnesses the arrival of what I have termed psychological topics. Some of these topics are "pre-Romantic" topics, for example sensibility style (*Empfindsamkeit*), *ombra* and *tempesta*, whose emotional significance make them more suited to the music of the time. For instance, although *tempesta* is traditionally associated with Classicism, it is a perfect topic to present emotion within a work, and is therefore classed here as a Romantic topic. The term "Romantic" has been generally applied to the post-Beethoven period, from roughly 1830 to the beginning of the twentieth century. Initially, it grew as an opposition to the formal aspects of Classicality, with Karl August Kahlert, a nineteenth-century musicologist, explaining the difference as 'classical composers being more interested in the formal structure of music, romantic composers in free, untrammelled expression'.[52] This development of expression was shared in the political and intellectual worlds, growing through the discovery of the individual as a prevailing force. As the practice of patronage began to disappear, the focus on the individual gave Romantic music an inner quality. This gave composers the opportunity to 'make their own statement'; and, according to the influence of Kant's philosophical position, 'the romantic artist, privileged by his genius, would reveal the world was grounded in self', hence, the growing exploitation of expression as the basis of aesthetic value over formal considerations.[53] For their newfound expressive desires, German composers began to look to other arts for inspiration, especially poetry, and particularly that of Goethe and Schiller. This propensity led to the rise of the *Lied*, a genre Jim Samson suggests 'might sustain a claim to be the quintessential romantic genre', a statement he qualifies succinctly:

> In its intimate, confessional character it epitomised the autobiographical character of romantic art. In its narrative, descriptive aspects it reflected the programmatic, referentialist tendencies of the music of the period. In its evocation of folksong it echoed a wider nineteenth-century idealisation of *Volksgeist*. And above all in its response to the new lyric poetry of the early nineteenth-century it provided a model of the Romantic impulse towards a fusion of the arts.[54]

Formal differences between Romantic and Classical works also began to be explored. Works became monadic, considered as single units containing their own meaning and not referencing other genres or eras, but instead utilising an "ideology of organicism".[55] Through a preoccupation with unity, whole pieces were conceived and built around a basic shape or idea: a *Grundgestalt*. Structural weight was then given to the development of this motive, weakening the Classical foundation of a tonal structure. Where tonal structure was still employed, it shifted away from strict diatonic harmony towards more chromatic elements, affecting an increasingly dissonant quality to works. This notion of non-referential art, of which "absolute" music became the epitome, demonstrates the concept of Romanticism as defined by its opposition to Classicality and its "Apollonian" features, and gives rise to the next step of the transformation towards "authenticity".

AUTHENTICITY

While Schorske exposes the revolutionary new utilitarian trend that marked the "critical modernists" through looking at the work of Otto Wagner, it is Timms who introduces the reasons for this sudden cultural change: that the difference between the façade of Austrian life and the economic and social reality were like 'the costumes of a public masquerade'.[56] The resplendent military uniforms were 'designed to divert away attention from the fact that military pay was appallingly low' and 'the colourful artifice in civilian dress as well concealed an underlying instability'. This aesthetic smokescreen, based on the pre-industrial eras, resonated on a far larger scale to take in the architecture itself. This type of aesthetic nostalgia added to the "myth" of a secure city at ease.[57]

The architect Otto Wagner's overruling concept was to move away from the overtly ornamental Baroque and Renaissance styles, instead letting the functionality of the object, room or building he was designing be the point of departure for the design itself. In 1895, Wagner suggested that 'all modern forms must correspond to new materials and the new requirements of our time, if they are to fit modern mankind. [...] What is impractical can never be beautiful'.[58]

This radical departure from the conservative Viennese habit of copying ornate styles of the past reverberated throughout the culture of the time, exemplified by such modernists as Loos, another architect, Kraus and his polemic, as seen above, and Schoenberg and his pupils, such as Max Deutsch. In Smith's exposition of Schoenberg and his circle, the author conducted an interview with Deutsch, in which he explained what Loos and Schoenberg were doing: '[f]irst, in general manner, necessity [...] and the second term is intensity. That is the criterion that you can find in the works of these four men [Kraus, Loos, Schoenberg and Kokoschka]. And that is, too, Schoenberg's way to teach for the students – what is absolutely necessary. Write down what is necessary! And don't write down what you are really not very [...] [clear about]'.[59] It is Webern's work that provides, perhaps, the clearest example of this aspiration to reveal the structure of a piece rather than veil it with complicated expression and ornamentation, thereby producing a sparse, simple, but ultimately striking work. And so it is Webern's work which will ultimately bring together the strands of the waltz, the uncanny and Vienna *Schmäh* in chapter nine.[60]

ROMANCE

With the emergence of emotion within the works of *fin-de-siècle* composers, a Romance topic was destined to appear. This topic can be found in abundance among the songs of operettas, where, as always, love is a popular central theme. This topic is signified first by a moderate tempo and the presence of either an Alberti bass, or an ascending pizzicato bass. The melody is rhythmically regular, usually extending to crotchets and quavers only, no quicker, and often takes the shape of an arch. The instrumentation is string-based with a range that extends over the octave, sixth or seventh. These signifiers stem from the romances (and romanzas) of the eighteenth-century *opéra comique*, including François-André Danican Philidor's *Le sorcier* (1764), Pierre-Alexandre Monsigny's *Le roi et le fermier* (1762) and André Grétry's *L'amitié à l'épreuve* (1770). Heartz describes the operatic romance as being in the rhythm of the slow gavotte, or *gavotte tendre*, employing an overall major-minor-major structure, and in *alla breve* time.[61] It is also often accompanied by plucked strings to simulate the guitar (e.g. Pedrillo's romance "In Mohrenland gefangen war" in Mozart's *Die Entführung aus dem Serail* (1782)).[62] Jack Sage adds that 'the genre's strophic form, unadorned melody, subordinate accompaniment and simple expression' gave the music its 'qualities of naturalness, simplicity and naivety'.[63]

Examples of this topic can be found in 'Deinen süßen Rosenmund' from Lehár's *Paganini* and 'Dein ist mein ganzes Herz' from *Das Land des Lächelns* (figure 2.1), one of the most famous love songs written for the tenor Richard Tauber (affectionately labelled *Tauberlied* by Franz Lehár himself). The rising pizzicato bass and octave doubling in the strings is clear, as is the moderate tempo marking.

Johann Strauss II uses this topic as a method of accentuating the duplicity of this emotion in *Die Fledermaus*. In No. 4 'So muß allein ich bleiben', the topic appears at the beginning of the song when Rosalinde mourns the jailing of her husband for eight whole days. However, as is clear by this point,

Figure 2.1 *Lehár,* Das Land des Lächelns, *"Dein ist mein ganzes Herz", bb. 4–6.* (Wien: Josef Weinberger, 1931).

none of the three protagonists intends to stay alone and all are planning secretly to go to Prince Orlofsky's ball. As the song becomes more ironic the romance topic disappears. In No. 5 'Trinklied', the romance topic appears briefly from bars 13–20, when Alfred speaks of the misleading nature of love, juxtaposing the topic against the text to accentuate the satirical nature of the song.

NATIONALISM

In his article assessing Schorske's "powerful work", Scott Spector counters the "failure of liberalism" thesis, suggesting that 'such a conclusion would assume that the cultural sphere was at least imagined to be separate from the sphere of political conflict, when in fact, especially in Weltsch's Prague, just the opposite was supposed'.[64] In response to the argument of 'modern culture as political surrogate for a marginalized liberal bourgeoisie', Spector suggests instead that politics inhabited the modern cultural sphere, and that culture was used to marginalise the other nations within the Empire.[65] Consequently, the *fin-de-siècle* culture, based on Germanic ideals, evolved 'as a combative site of identity construction and defence, and as an instrument of power over those outside of the privileged national/cultural circle'.[66] Spector explains:

> [t]he 'liberal' component of German liberalism, the commitment to liberal politics, had undermined the 'German' component in late nineteenth-century Bohemia. If German hegemony was to be preserved in some form, the discourse which privileged the Germans as the unique Central European *Kulturnation* had to be recovered and reinforced. Further, there was a need to address the conflict between a German claim to power, legitimated by 'culture', and the competing Czech claim, legitimated by liberal 'politics'. The establishment of the primacy of culture, then, became more important than ever.[67]

Similarly to the Jews being seen as outsiders or "Others", the nations that made up the Dual Monarchy of Austria-Hungary were never felt to be fully part of the Empire.[68] This was not only a product of Austro-German racism, but also came about through attempts made by the smaller nations to retain their heritage and language, and to further their independence. Language became a major catalyst of nationalist protest. The liberal bureaucracy was attempting to germanise the imperial administration, to make it more streamlined, while at the same time the most prestigious gymnasia and universities were mainly German speaking. The Austrian tie with Germany, Austria having been the head of Prussia at one time, was strong and it was felt that the German culture was superior to that of the "Other" nations.

This push towards German nationalist sentiment by the administration led, seemingly inexorably, to Hungarian and Czech reactions. The Hungarians demanded hegemony over their army and for their soldiers to communicate in Hungarian, while the Czechs campaigned for a university that taught in their own language.

As discussed above, the liberals' "social base" was comprised mostly of those of German nationality. Schorske describes how the German liberals thought to use nationality to their own advantage, by functioning as "tutor and teacher" to the minority peoples, rather than 'keep them as ignorant bondsman' as the aristocracy had done. With this munificent gesture nationality itself would hold together the multinational state.[69] By joining with the masses against a common foe – the aristocracy – the liberals hoped to form a cohesive whole. However, every German nationalist sentiment articulated against the "enemy above" produced antagonistic action from the Slavic patriots below. When the Germanism was played down by the liberals it resulted in them being 'branded as traitors to nationalism by an anti-liberal German *petite bourgeoisie*'.[70]

At one point, the Austrian Empire had been the largest empire in Europe. However, in the 1700s and 1800s it gradually lost its territories, along with its military might. In 1858 Austria was defeated in the Franco-Austrian War and in 1866 by the Prussians at Königgrätz. This led to a new self-consciousness within the empire, resulting in a profound emphasis on Austrian cultural and musical prowess. The Austrians searched for a new identity, one that could be used to show the rest of Europe that they were still a powerful force in some way, and found one in Strauss's debut of his composition the 'Blue Danube Waltz' at the 1867 World Exhibition in Paris. Crittenden illustrates the way in which Strauss became 'a symbol of power and prestige equally as important in the popular imagination as territorial control or political alliances', and Traubner agrees, claiming he was 'as cherished as the venerable Emperor himself'.[71]

As the Austro-Hungarian Empire's military prowess was withering, its urban life was also changing. In 1781 serfdom was abolished, meaning that men who could not afford tenure on the land moved into the cities and towns. From the 1800s onwards, therefore, peasant reforms and industrialisation within the city of Vienna led to a large influx of labour into the capital. During the decade ending in 1890s the population almost doubled, and by 1910 it had risen from under 1,000,000 to over 2,000,000.[72] In this case, Edward Timms notes that

> the economic and social changes which in Britain had been spread over three centuries were in Austria crammed into a period of forty years. [...] The process of modernisation, far from strengthening the state (as in the German Reich), accelerated the tendency towards disintegration, as each national group asserted its own identity.[73]

Therefore, in direct proportion to the rise of this Viennese identity crisis, the nationalist sentiment in and towards the other nations of Austria also rose, precipitated by the industrialisation of the cities and towns. This creation of division within Vienna fed into the conception of nationalism as exotic "Other".

Nationalism as Exotic "Other"

Folk music in Vienna was used both to give the minorities a sense of independence and identity and to highlight the contrariness of their culture to the Austrian German culture and therefore the imbalance between the two nations. Judit Frigyesi writes that

> [i]n this context, nationalism appears to be a political force used in the discourse – or, better, struggle – between smaller and larger nations: it is a negative force when used to oppress the smaller nations and a positive one when used to liberate the oppressed ones.[74]

As such, nationalism is meaningfully undistinguished from incongruent nations other than as in opposition to "Viennese". Bartók similarly identifies the link between folk music and the peasant class, implying that the other nations were regarded as "uncultured" and therefore subordinate:

> Folk music is the music of the class of population least affected by city culture, a music of a more or less great temporal as well as spatial extent, which is or sometime was alive as a spontaneous manifestation of musical impulse. According to this definition the peasant class, being the least affected by city culture, should be the carrier and propagator of folk music.[75]

The disparate nationalities stirred to patriotism by the inequalities of the time used folk music as a source of rebellion against the Imperial rule. Bartók, although living in Budapest at the time, announced in a letter to his mother in 1903 that he intended to 'carry on the nationalist struggle against Habsburg domination by scrupulously avoiding the German language and speaking only Hungarian'.[76] Hence, as the Czech and Hungarian universities were campaigning to educate and learn in their own language, so were composers writing in theirs. However, they continued to use the same source material as the German Austrians: the march. Patriotic marches are found throughout Viennese light music; for example, Act One of *Die Lustige Witwe* begins with a march that proclaims the sadness of the Pontevedrian people at being away from home, but the best illustration is the finale of Act Two of *Die Zigeunerbaron*. At this point Barinkay, Zsupán and Ottokar are leaving to join the Hussars to fight in Spain. The finale contains a recruiting march (taken from No. 12 ½), and also a cavalry march in compound time, which among other Hungarian characteristics uses fanfares on the clarinet rather than trumpet, the clarinet being the second solo instrument in Gypsy music after the fiddle.

The theatre composers instigated the use of folk music as a way of introducing the exotic and a sense of Other into their operettas. Crittenden states that Viennese operetta often features 'overt and specific reference to regions of the Habsburg monarchy in general and to Vienna in particular. This subjectified Vienna is often established as in opposition to some Other', for example, Pontevedria in *Die Lustige Witwe*, or Hungary in *Die Fledermaus* and *Der Zigeunerbaron*.[77] Vienna itself is usually represented by a waltz or polka, both of which symbolise the ceremonial nature of the Empire and the aristocratic nature of the city. Songs alluding to the decadence of life, for example, 'The Champagne Song' from *Die Fledermaus*, or 'O Vaterland' from *Die Lustige Witwe*, also reference it.

Although the waltz falls under the nationalist banner when categorising it as a topic, its contextual signifieds are connected, whether in juxtaposition or opposition, to all the cultural themes outlined in this chapter. It is the epitome of the failure of liberalism: an emotionally dizzying dance charged with lascivious overtones and therefore in opposition to the rational topic. It is often in the romantic style, filled with lush strings and soaring melodies and, of course – along with the polka – is the dance that identifies Austrian nationality, cemented as such by Strauss's 'Blue Danube Waltz' premiered at the World Exhibition in 1874. It is, therefore, the Ordinary the exotic Other is set against. In the next chapter this opposition will be looked at in more detail as the waltz, its signifiers, signifieds and contextual historiography are explored.

NOTES

1. Carl E. Schorske, *Fin-de-Siècle Vienna: Politics and Culture* (New York: Vintage, 1981), xvii.

2. Allan Janik and Stephen Toulmin, *Wittgenstein's Vienna* (London: Weidenfeld and Nicolson, 1973), 18.

3. This term is taken from Allan Janik, "Vienna 1900 Revisited: Paradigms and Problems", *Rethinking Vienna 1900*, vol. 3 of *Austrian and Habsburg Studies*, ed. Steven Beller (Oxford: Berghahn, 2001), 32.

4. Schorske, *Fin-de-Siècle Vienna*, xxvi.

5. Margaret Notley, "Brahms as Liberal: Genre, Style, and Politics in Late Nineteenth Century Vienna", *19th-Century Music* 17, no. 2 (Fall 1993), 108.

6. Schorske, *Fin-de-Siècle Vienna*, 117–118.

7. Imke Meyer, "The Insider as Outsider: Representations of the Bourgeoisie in *Fin-de-Siècle* Vienna" *Pacific Coast Philology* 44, no. 1 (2009), 2.

8. Janik, "Vienna 1900 Revisited", 34.
9. Robert Musil, *The Man without Qualities*, vol. 1 (London: Secker & Warburg, 1953), 33.
10. This term is taken from Janik, "Vienna 1900 Revisited", 32.
11. Meyer, "The Insider as Outsider", 2.
12. Hannah Hickman, *Robert Musil & the Culture of Vienna* (Kent: Croom Helm, 1984), 45.
13. Carl E. Schorske, "Generational Tension and Cultural Change: Reflections on the case of Vienna", *Daedalus* 107, no. 4 (Fall, 1978), 112–113.
14. Schorske. *Fin-de-Siècle Vienna*, xvii.
15. Beller, introduction to *Rethinking Vienna 1900*, 2.
16. Beller, introduction to *Rethinking Vienna 1900*, 3.
17. Meyer, "The Insider as Outsider", 3
18. Meyer, "The Insider as Outsider", 4.
19. Meyer, "The Insider as Outsider".
20. Meyer, "The Insider as Outsider", 6.
21. Meyer, "The Insider as Outsider", 10.
22. Janik and Toulmin, *Wittgenstein's Vienna*, 69–70.
23. Janik and Toulmin, *Wittgenstein's Vienna*, 30.
24. Janik, "Vienna 1900 Revisited", 40.
25. Janik, "Vienna 1900 Revisited", 40–41.
26. Schorske, *Fin-de-Siècle Vienna*, 185.
27. Schorske, *Fin-de-Siècle Vienna*, 186.
28. Freud. "The Interpretation of Dreams", *The Standard Edition of the Complete Psychological Works of Sigmund Freud*, ed. and trans. James Strachey (London: Hogarth,1964), vol. IV, 119.
29. The dream consisted of his examination of his friend Irma in which he found an infection in her throat and chest, caused in his dream by his colleague, Dr. M, administering an injection of propionic acid with a dirty syringe.
30. Schorske, *Fin-de-Siècle Vienna*, 187. Freud describes a dream in which his friend 'R' is his uncle, for whom he feels great affection. In the dream, his friend's face is altered, elongated and 'surrounded' by a yellow beard.
31. Schorske, *Fin-de-Siècle Vienna*, 187.
32. Freud, "The Interpretation of Dreams", *The Standard Edition*, vol. IV, 136.
33. Schorske, *Fin-de-Siècle Vienna*, 187.
34. Freud, "The Interpretation of Dreams", *The Standard Edition*, vol. IV, 193, quoted in Schorske, *Fin-de-Siècle Vienna*, 187.
35. Schorske, *Fin-de-Siècle Vienna*, 195.
36. Freud, "The Interpretation of Dreams", *The Standard Edition,* vol. IV, 216.
37. Freud, "The Interpretation of Dreams", *The Standard Edition,* vol. IV, 193.
38. Freud, "The Interpretation of Dreams", *The Standard Edition,* vol. IV, 193.
39. Michael S. Roth, "Performing History: Modernist Contextualism in Carl Schorske's *Fin-de-Siècle* Vienna", *The American Historical Review* 99, no. 3 (June 1994), 733.
40. Schorske, *Fin-de-Siècle Vienna*, 197.

41. Schorske, *Fin-de-Siècle Vienna*, 5.
42. Schorske, *Fin-de-Siècle Vienna*, 5.
43. Roth, "Performing History", 730.
44. Roth, "Performing History", 730.
45. Schorske, *Fin-de-Siècle Vienna*, 19, quoted in Roth, "Performing History", 731.
46. Schorske, *Fin-de-Siècle Vienna*, 19.
47. Schorske, *Fin-de-Siècle Vienna*, 21.
48. For further links between Hofmannsthal, Schnitzler and Freud see Imke Meyer, "The Insider as Outsider:", 7.
49. John H. Mueller, "Musical Taste and How it is Formed", in *The Routledge Reader on the Sociology of Music*, ed. John Shepherd and Kyle Devine (New York: Routledge, 2015), 50. The term *jouissance* is particularly apt in its psychoanalytic sense as Lacan introduced it as a foundation of the pleasure/pain principle, which in excess becomes suffering (see Néstor A. Braunstein, "Desire and jouissance in the teachings of Lacan" *The Cambridge Companion to Lacan*, ed. Jean-Michel Rabaté (Cambridge: Cambridge University Press, 2003)).
50. Peter J. Martin, *Sounds and Society: Themes in the Sociology of Music* (Manchester: Manchester University Press, 1995), 224.
51. Schorske, *Fin-de-Siècle Vienna*, 25. For further investigation into architecture and Vienna 1900 see Tag Gronburg, *Vienna: City of Modernity, 1890–1914* (Bern: Peter Lang, 2007).
52. Jim Samson, "Romanticism".
53. Jim Samson, "Romanticism". For an informative article detailing the development of psychological morality from Kant to Freud see Martin Wank, "Oedipus in the Fin de Siècle: A Reinvention of Legitimacy", *New Political Science* 19, no. 3 (1997): 59–73.
54. Jim Samson, "Romanticism".
55. Jim Samson, "Romanticism".
56. Edward Timms, *Karl Kraus: Apocalyptic Satirist* (London: Yale University Press, 1986), 21.
57. Timms, *Karl Kraus: Apocalyptic Satirist*, 21.
58. Münz, Ludwig and Gustav Künstler, *Adolf Loos: Pioneer of Modern Architecture* (Santa Barbara: Praeger, 1966), 14, quoted in Joan Allen Smith, *Schoenberg and His Circle* (London: Collier Macmillan, 1986), 23. This contains an implicit reference to William Morris's statement: 'Have nothing in your houses that you do not know to be useful, or believe to be beautiful'. William Morris, *On Art and Socialism*, ed. Norman Kelvin (New York: Dover Publications, 1999), 53.
59. Smith. *Schoenberg and His Circle*, 38.
60. Smith. *Schoenberg and His Circle*, 25.
61. Daniel Heartz "The Beginnings of the Operatic Romance: Rousseau, Sedaine, and Monsigny" *Eighteenth-Century Studies* 15, no. 2 (Winter, 1981–1982), 149–178.
62. Heartz, "The Beginnings of the Operatic Romance", 178.
63. Jack Sage, *et al.*, "Romance." *Grove Music Online. Oxford Music Online.* Oxford University Press. http://0-www.oxfordmusiconline.com.wam.leeds.ac.uk/subscriber/article/grove/music/23725 (accessed January 2, 2016).

64. Scott Spector, "Beyond the Aesthetic Garden: Politics and Culture on the Margins of Fin-de-Siècle Vienna" *Journal of the History of Ideas* 59, no. 4 (Oct 1998), 697.

65. Spector, "Beyond the Aesthetic Garden", 691.

66. Spector, "Beyond the Aesthetic Garden", 697.

67. Spector, "Beyond the Aesthetic Garden", 697–698.

68. The "Dual Monarchy" is another name for the Austro-Hungarian Empire, named such because of Emperor Francis Joseph's standing as King of Hungary and King and Emperor throughout the rest of the Monarchy. This is a direct result of the Compromise, or *Ausgleich* of 1867, an agreement between the emperor and the Magyar leadership of the Hungarian diet intended to turn the Habsburg Monarchy into a German-Magyar condominium with the Magyars ruling Hungary and the Austrian Germans ruling the rest of the Empire. This act, unsurprisingly, caused a certain amount of negativity throughout the rest of 'the lands represented in the Reichsrat' (This is the official name of the Austrian aspect; 'Austria' was not its legal name until 1915) because they felt neglected by this apparent favouritism. Count Richard Belcredi, at the Ministerial Council meeting on 1 February 1867, asserted that 'the monarch should not rely on specific nationalities but be above them all' (Beller, *A Concise History of Austria*, 143).

69. Schorske, *Fin-de-siècle Vienna*, 117.

70. Schorske, *Fin-de-siècle Vienna*, 117.

71. Camille Crittenden, *Johann Strauss and Vienna: Operetta and the Politics of Popular Culture* (Cambridge: Cambridge University Press, 2000), 96; Richard Traubner, *Operetta: A Theatrical History* (London: Routledge, 2003), 128.

72. Ilsa Barea, *Vienna: Legend and Reality* (Secker and Warburg: Vienna, 1966), 332, quoted in Timms, *Karl Kraus: Apocalyptic Satirist,* 15.

73. Timms, *Karl Kraus: Apocalyptic Satirist,* 12.

74. Judit Frigyesi, "Bela Bartók and the Concept of Nation and Volk in Modern Hungary", *The Musical Quarterly* 78, no. 2 (Summer 1994), 255.

75. Béla Bartók, *Essays,* ed. Benjamin Suchoff (London: Faber and Faber, 1976), 316.

76. Kate Trumpener, "Comparative Ethnomusicology: Nationalism, Race Purity, and the Legacy of the Austro-Hungarian Empire", in *Music and the Racial Imagination,* ed. Ronald M. Radano and Philip V. Bohlman (Chicago: University of Chicago Press, 2000), 406.

77. Crittenden, *Johann Strauss*, 120. For extensive discussion of the exotic Other in Western music see Jonathan Bellman, *The Exotic in Western Music* (Boston: Northeastern University Press, 1998); Georgina Born and David Hesmondhalgh, *Western Music and Its Others* (Berkeley: University of California Press, 2000); Matthew Head, *Orientalism, Masquerade, and Mozart's Turkish Music* (London: Royal Musical Association, 2000); Ralph Locke, *Musical Exoticism: Images and Reflections* (Cambridge: Cambridge University Press, 2009); Catherine Mayes, "Cultural Associations of Turkish and Hungarian-Gypsy Styles in the Late Eighteenth Century and their Compositional Implications", *Oxford Handbook of Topic Theory*; Derek B. Scott, "Orientalism and Musical Style", *The Musical Quarterly* 82, no. 2 (Summer 1998), 309–335.

Chapter 3

The Waltz and the 'Other'

The waltz did not appear in eighteenth-century Vienna as the fully formed much loved version we associate with the gay city now. By exploring its roots in folk dances and transference from the beerhalls to the dance halls of the Habsburg court a correlation can be demonstrated between the whirling dance and the flight from reality the Viennese revelled in during the nineteenth century. Finally, through its dialectic narrative with the contemporary nationalist styles and dances, such as the *style hongrois*, the mazurka and the *csárdás*, an alteration occurs from a satiric depiction of *Wiener Schmäh* to a high brow depiction of morality opposed to the immoral "low brow" folk topics.

The waltz as it is known today originated from a few folk dances: The *Deutsche Tanz* or *Ländler*, the *Dreher* and the *Langhaus*. The *Dreher*, meaning to turn, was a popular German dance from the mid-sixteenth century which, just as its successor, was opposed by the ministers of religion and the authorities because of its improper turns. During the Reformation, Luther himself showed he was no enemy of dancing 'very modestly, decently and respectably', for, he realised, the "sins and vice" were to be attributed not to the dance but the 'disorderly appetites of the dancers'.[1] The whirling steps of this dance nevertheless disappeared from the French court in the middle of the seventeenth century as the minuet began to dominate civilised Europe. The German ballroom, however, eschewed the variety of the French court and stuck with the *dreher* or the *Deustche* as it became known. The French, on the other hand, raised dancing to the rank of self-directed art that could be professionalised and taught hence the courtly society dances gradually removed themselves from the primitive instinct for movement, the erotic impulses of which had characterised folk dance throughout its entire social development.[2] Eduard Reeser informs us that it was the rise of the bourgeoisie in Europe in the mid-eighteenth century that began to reintroduce the folk dances to the ballrooms:

> The new striving after simplicity and naturalness that ran parallel with the transition from the *opera seria* to the musical play, from the coloratura aria to the song 'in popular style', and which also brought with it an intense interest in the old folk-songs, aroused opposition to the complicated ceremonial into which the dance had stiffened and enabled the folk-dance to place its unimpaired vitality at the service of the altered needs of the society dance.[3]

Before the *dreher* regained its footing, the way was eased by the introduction of the *contredanse* ("country dance"). The uncomplicated steps to the *rounds* and *longways* of the *contredanse* instigated a strong reaction to the complicated artifice of the minuet, but even this rustic dance wasn't bright enough to counter the whirling dance as it re-emerged to take its place in society. The *dreher* paved the way for the *Langhaus* which was an energetic dance that lent the waltz its slide, where the Ländler hops, and could therefore be danced at a greater pace than the *Ländler*. The *Langhaus* was originally treated similarly to the *dreher* as in 1595 a Dresden ordinance banned 'voluptuous turning, jumping, or running hither and yon' and religious sermons condemned the maidens that "allowed" themselves to be 'kissed and mauled about'.[4] Despite the warnings, the dance craze spread aggravating heart conditions and breathing problems until the deaths in Vienna were so numerous the police banned the dance altogether.

The *Ländler,* the closest ancestor of the waltz, is a German folk dance in 3/4 time and was most common in Austria, Switzerland and Southern Germany. It was generally a slow dance, although it was often performed faster in the west (Switzerland and Tyrol). Its original character has been preserved somewhat in the "Yodel", a jump of a seventh, and the emphasis the dance places on the second beat of the bar, rather than the first (as in the waltz). Despite the rareness of rural dances in 3/4, its unsophisticated form helped it to gain popularity with the upper classes. This was due to the hopping and whirling dance steps that formed the dance, regularly accompanied by *Paschen* or rhythmic hand clapping and stamping.[5] Other than the hopping style, it differs from the waltz as the woman revolves under the man's arm as well as the dancers moving in opposite directions and around each other back to back.[6] This raucous dance was in pronounced opposition to the stately minuet that was performed by the nobility of the time, and was procured by the Austrian court for use during their feasts when dramatic representations of scenes from peasant life were acted out and the *Ländler* was used to entertain.[7] It is possibly in this way that the dance most associated with the rural peasantry also began to become associated with the Austrian court.

The dance is usually in a major key, diatonic, with a melodic tendency towards arpeggio figures which may have been influenced by Alpine songs. The instrumentation comprises two violins, double bass and a wind instrument, for example a clarinet, or in earlier times, a shawm or recorder. Romantic composers often used this dance to evoke peasant or rural settings, for example, the Waltz in Act One of Weber's *Die Freischutz* is more likely a *Ländler*, as is the Carinthian tune from Berg's Violin Concerto. Vera Micznik also looks at how Mahler uses the *Ländler*, although his own version of it, and mentions the "rawness" of the dance.[8] This coarseness inherent in the early dance is the main point in which the waltz diverges from its original state to become the smooth, decidedly upper-class version that became so entwined with the Austrian national identity. The waltz is danced as a *Schleifer*, the feet being dragged along the floor, as only the smoothness of this glide could be danced fast enough for the whirling revolutions to be completed in time. Berg uses this to highlight class separation in his opera *Wozzeck*; a *Ländler* plays for the apprentices, soldiers and servant girls, but when the Drum Major is dancing with Marie they dance a waltz. The *Ländler* used here, despite its atonality, is still recognisable through the presence of arpeggio figures in the wind instruments and the oom-pah accompaniment in strings. The inclusion of the horns in this section also adds to the pastoral feel that is characteristic of the *Ländler*.

THE WALTZ: THE DANCERS, THE LOVERS, THE DRINKERS, THE MEMORIES[9]

The waltzes most characteristic feature is its emphasis on the first beat of the bar although in the earliest versions of the dance the three beats in the bar were accented separately, as seen in *Der aud das neue begeisterte und belebte Bernardon*, one of the earliest examples of a waltz written by Josef Kurz in 1754. It was only as the music got faster that the first beat accent became so important and distinguished it so prominently from the other revolving dances. Allanbrook identifies the harmonic and temporal signifiers of the waltz, asserting that 'the beat tends to be perceived on the measure level, and supporting harmonies rarely change more than once a measure, producing the cliché of the "oom-pah-pah" accompaniment, a salient feature both of the Deutsche Tanz and of the modern waltz'.[10]

The signifier of the Viennese dance as opposed to waltzes from other cultures is the 'slight anticipation of the second beat of the bar known as the *Atempause* (literally "breathing-space" [sic])', which gives the music an enchanting lilt paralleling the drag of the foot in the choreography.[11] The early waltz consisted of two times eight bar sections, played twelve times.

There was no introduction of coda, and a minimum of musical invention. Josef Lanner was the first to 'Viennize' the waltz adding brief introductions and codas and inventing melodies that Hanslick claimed 'sound like an echo of Schubert'.[12] His warmth and melodiousness was more traditionally Viennese than Strauss Senior's stronger syncopations and larger orchestra however it is Strauss the son who united these characteristics to compose the Austrian anthem *'An der Schönnen Blauen Donau'* in 1866. He still used some of the same orchestration devices his father introduced: staccato and pizzicato articulation; alterations in the timbral colours during phrases; cellos doubling the violins two octaves below or moving in parallel tenths; short figures highlighted by other instruments (such as the piccolo); trumpets and percussion playing distinctive rhythms to provide emphasis or to embellish a climax.

The melodies were still in short sections, but Strauss II rarely repeated a melody in a waltz, although he often borrowed material from his other works, such that Gartenberg concludes that 'each waltz, aside from introduction and *coda*, consisted of an average of five sections, each sections of two parts. Each part of each section presented a new original melody, ten original melodies per waltz, fifteen hundred original melodies in Strauss' waltzes alone!'[13] A recurrent motivic feature is the upward-leaping sixth, written either as a Scotch snap or, as in the *Blue Danube*, an *acciaccatura*, possibly a reference to the Alpine yodel leftover from its rural contemporary the *Ländler*. Grace notes were also frequently used, a characteristic of Strauss I's waltzes, such as in the *TäuberlnWalzer* op. 1 (1827) which also highlights his use of syncopation.[14] Scott also shows a "striking and revolutionary use" of "free-floating" major sixths and major sevenths and, for example in the *Kaiser-Walzer*, op 437 (1889), Strauss begins to use seconds and ninths.[15]

By the nineteenth century and onward, the Viennese waltz is topically associated with the middle and upper classes, although the working class enjoyed the dance just as much. At this point, while Austria was losing territory, Vienna's population boomed to over 400,000 as industrialisation and the liberation of the serfs caused mass migration from rural areas into the city. This not only created a large group of workers but also a rich and increasingly powerful bourgeois class. The dance's elite correlation stems simply from the fact that accounts given of the sensational dance halls are almost all from the elite perspective, and as the aristocrats avoided sharing the same social space as the working class – and the middle class if they could be evaded – we are left with a rather one-sided, but entrenched understanding of it. Joonas Jussi Sakari Korhonen tells us that although all classes loved the dance hall, they were still socially very segregated: 'While the nobility danced in palaces and salons, the middle- and lower-class people went dancing to public dance halls in the suburbs'.[16] Korhonen argues that as between 1780 and 1810, the number of dance halls increased from 15 to 50 creating a commercialisation of the dance culture. The elite, rather than accepting the influx of bourgeoisie into their inner-city dance halls, moved to suburban halls. As the bourgeois followed, they moved to dancing only at court and in private ballrooms where the bourgeois were not invited to attend. During *Fasching* – the Viennese carnival epitomised by the dressing up as other classes and celebrating in the same venues, such as the Redoute Hall – the nobility and other members of the elite attended but only watched the lower classes dance, never participated. Egon Gartenburg, however, tells us that these rules were broken in a typically irreverent Viennese style.

> Inevitably both aristocrat and burgher sought and gained entrance into each other's realm, often through the backstairs and secret doors deviously opened. The duchess engaged as a valet the handsome young man she had espied while passing a dance hall in her carriage. The count travelled the Prater meadows or to a secluded Grinzing inn in his closed private *Fiaker* with his wife's chambermaid; or even more amusing, he would hie himself to one of the innumerable comfortable dance halls in the suburbs, insuring anonymity within the smoky intimacy of burgherdom's dancing waves. There they danced and whirled, aristocrat and burgher's daughter, in each other's arms without question or qualm. Gone was the fingertip touch of the minuet, 'the model of taste and decorum'. All abandoned themselves to the inescapable fever of the waltz; losing themselves in sensual desire evoked by speed, wine, embrace, they forgot – for an evening – war and want.[17]

'When Vienna gets gay, the situation is truly grave'

This quote, uttered by Emperor Joseph II, epitomises the signified of the Viennese waltz in the first half of the nineteenth century: the portrayal of *Wiener Schmäh*, which, in the historian Beller's words, 'is essentially the talent for telling lies in an attractive manner. It is the verbal form of the kind of baroque architecture where all marble was really exquisitely painted wood'.[18] The citizens of Vienna likely knew the artificiality of their decadence (indeed it is what Kraus, Loos and Schoenberg campaigned against throughout their careers) and, since the lower classes were not financially capable of this type of deceit, *Schmäh* became the contrivance of the upper and middle classes. As Gartenberg describes earlier, the Viennese lost themselves in the dance mania in order to forget the military defeats, the loss of land to the Prussians and the strict draconian laws Prince Metternich imposed to keep order in a time when other countries monarchies were becoming constitutionalised.[19] He achieved an almost completely insulated country, shut off from the outside world and in doing created a Vienna longingly remembered as the

'*Gemütlichkeit* of Biedermeier Vienna'.[20] This atmosphere of cosiness, complacency and contentment grew in direct proportion to the bleakness of the political climate. Karl Kraus, known for his polemical articles in *Die Fackel*, was thought to have said 'In Berlin, everything is serious but not hopeless; in Vienna they are hopeless but not serious'.[21]

Since Metternich's laws prohibited more than three people gathering in public the Viennese converged in the only places they could – the dance hall and the coffee house. With only censored reports from the outside world, they turned inward and immersed themselves in the pleasures of dancing and celebrating. Gartenberg even suggests that in 1797 the only pastime that rivalled dancing was sex:

> half of Vienna's children were born out of wedlock. The gaiety, the loosening of fear and restraint, the light wine, the closeness of clinging bodies in a dance which was only a thinly veiled symbol of love-making, brought to Vienna in ever increasing measure an undesirable but inevitable part of the scene. Vienna's narrow streets near the *Sperl, Mondschein,* and *Apollo* dance halls swarmed with the denizens of the oldest profession; prostitution was rampant in Vienna.'[22]

Contemporary fiction reflected this cultural escapism. In 1834 Grillparzer wrote *Der Traum ein Leben (A Dream is Life)*, a Faustian drama which ends happily as the peasant Rustan wakes from a dream. This flight from reality, this artificial illusion of life, was loved by the Viennese who strongly identified with it. His next book, *Weh dem, der lügt!* (Woe to Him Who Lies!), in 1838 was the author's only comedy and surprisingly a failure as the idea of the hero being liberated by the truth was anathema to the general public. Even through the revolution in 1848, Vienna danced. Police measures repressed the working class whose conditions worsened by the day; an undercurrent of nationalist tension rippled through the city as workers from other parts of the Empire flocked to Vienna despite inadequate employment so that a '"proletariat" of landless labourers existed but not yet the capitalists to employ them.'[23] The proletariat provided a ready-made revolutionary army led by immature students who were themselves budding bureaucrats. Fuelled by bourgeois liberalism and popular nationalism and triggered by troops firing into a crowd and killing five people, the revolution successfully caused Metternich's flight to England and the monarchy's flight to Innsbruck, despite the authorities crushing the revolution itself. Even Strauss II and his brother Josef manned the barricade in October and while some of his pro-revolution works were confiscated and destroyed, some (like the *Revolutions-Marsch* op. 54) had already been published and distributed and therefore survived. That he was saved after the revolution was crushed speaks volumes to the importance put on the king of waltz and the musical escapism he provided the Viennese.

The monarchy returned in the presence of a new Emperor, Franz Josef, who ruled until his death in 1916 just two years before the final dissolution of the monarchy. His favoured style of rule was to maintain the status quo. Hans Sassman compared the new emperor's handling of the formalities of running the empire 'like a captain who can quickly paint his sinking ship'.[24] Hermann Broch to both a 'gay apocalypse' and a museum.[25] 'Vienna', Broch writes, 'became an "un-world city", and, without thereby becoming a small town, it sought small town tranquillity, small-town narrowmindedness, small-town pleasures, the charm of "once upon a time"'.[26] The town itself, however, expanded in 1857 as Franz Josef ordered the demolition of the walls and the four gates to construct the *Ringstraße*. Controversial with the aristocracy as it destroyed the four historic gates of Vienna – and therefore the "once-upon-a-time" *Alt Wien* of pre-March Vienna – and highlighted the rise of the bourgeoisie who were now rich enough to afford to build a house on the *Ringstraße*, it nevertheless embraced the Viennese culture of artificiality. The conception of art and architecture prevalent at the time meant it was considered gauche if a building revealed its purpose by its architecture. The prominent architect Gottfried Semper claimed that a house '"like a guest at a ball must be externally covered by a domino so that it cannot be recognised immediately". [. . .] He asserted that it was one's duty "to don an unrevealing mask"'.[27] Not only that, but while this showpiece was being built nearly sixty percent of the population, principally made up of the immigrants who laboured on the construction project, still lived in destitution in the suburbs. As Schorske puts it '[n]ot utility but cultural self-projection dominated the *Ringstraße*'.[28] The double life of Vienna expressed itself; the surface decoration, glitz and champagne enclosed the civil and nationalist unrest within. It also provides a physical representation of the changes in the waltzes musical and narratological signifieds over time. In the first two waves of construction, 1861–1873, there was a demarcation between the interior and the façade. There was a tendency towards smaller units with decorative classical uniformity in the façade, an aesthetic termed by Adolf Loos as *"Potemkimsche Stadt"* ("Potemkin City"), meaning, in Gartenberg's words 'the city of the noble façade with misery lurking behind it'.[29] Imposing stairwells with prominently placed statues reached the first floor whereupon they were replaced by utilitarian smaller staircases. In 1893, however, Otto Wagner won a competition for a new development plan. He denounced the masquerade of history over modernity and functionality and put forward a plan based around transportation as a key to growth based around Semper's motto *"Artis sola domina necessitas"* (Necessity is art's only mistress).[30] One of the clearest examples of this new style is a comparison between the opulence of Franz von Neuman's Reichratstrasse (1873) and Wagner's apartment buildings Linke Wienzeile and Köstlergasse (1898–1899) and Neustiftgasse 40 (1908–1909).

This marks the move to authenticity, one of the narratives outlined in chapter two, and, with the death of Strauss II in 1899, a marked alteration in the association of the waltz from *Wiener Schmäh* and immorality to laying out of just such immoral acts, an exposition of the truth and the uncanny nature of Viennese life.

Nationalism as 'Other' in the Austrian Narrative

To be able to discern the hermeneutic qualities of the waltz within a musical narrative it is important to be able to identify the other contemporary dances that may be set in opposition/juxtaposition with it. Two of the major topics (dance or otherwise) are the polka – the other high-class dance beloved in the Viennese ballrooms – and the *style hongrois* – the Hungarian and gypsy style representing the other half of the Dual Monarchy. Folk music in Vienna was used in two distinct ways, both to give the minorities a sense of independence and identity, and to highlight the contrariness of their culture to the Austrian German culture, and therefore the imbalance between the two nations. Judit Frigyesi writes that

> [i]n this context, nationalism appears to be a political force used in the discourse – or, better, struggle – between smaller and larger nations: it is a negative force when used to oppress the smaller nations and a positive one when used to liberate the oppressed ones.[31]

As such, nationalism is linked to the portrayal of Jews and Judaism in music as an exotic Other, meaningfully undistinguished from incongruent nations other than as in opposition to "Viennese".[32] Bartók similarly suggests the link between folk music and the peasant class, implying that the other nations were regarded as "uncultured" and therefore subordinate:

> folk music is the music of the class of population least affected by city culture, a music of a more or less great temporal as well as spatial extent, which is or sometime was alive as a spontaneous manifestation of musical impulse. According to this definition the peasant class, being the least affected by city culture, should be the carrier and propagator of folk music.[33]

The disparate nationalities stirred to patriotism by the inequalities of the time used folk music as a source of rebellion against the Empiric rule. Bartók, although living in Budapest at the time, announced in a letter to his mother in 1903 that he intended to 'carry on the nationalist struggle against Habsburg domination by scrupulously avoiding the German language and speaking only Hungarian'.[34] Hence, as the Czech and Hungarian universities were campaigning to educate and learn in their own language, so were composers writing in theirs. However, they continued to use the same source material as the German Austrians: the march. Patriotic marches are found throughout Viennese art music; for example, Act One of *Die Lustige Witwe* begins with a march that proclaims the sadness of the Pontevedrian people at being away from home, but the best illustration is the finale of Act Two of *Die Zigeunerbaron*. At this point Barinkay, Zsupán and Ottokar are leaving to join the Hussars to fight in Spain. The finale contains a recruiting march (taken from No. 12 ½), and also a cavalry march in compound time, which among other Hungarian characteristics uses fanfares on the clarinet rather than trumpet, the clarinet being the second solo instrument in Gypsy music after the fiddle.

The theatre composers instigated the use of folk music as a way of introducing the exotic and a sense of Other into their operettas. Crittenden states that Viennese operetta often features 'overt and specific reference to regions of the Habsburg monarchy in general and to Vienna in particular. This subjectified Vienna is often established in opposition to some Other', for example, Pontevedria in *Die Lustige Witwe*, or Hungary in *Die Fledermaus* and *Der Zigeunerbaron*.[35] Vienna itself is usually represented by a waltz or polka, both of which symbolise the ceremonial nature of the Empire and the aristocratic nature of the city. Songs alluding to the decadence of life, for example, 'The Champagne Song' from *Die Fledermaus*, or 'O Vaterland' from *Die Lustige Witwe*, also reference it.

The Polka

As mentioned above, the polka is associated with the aristocratic class, and by extension *Alt Wien*, despite the fact that the dance originated in Bohemia. This is because the polka was not a folk dance; it did not evolve from a nationalist dance in the way the waltz or mazurka (outlined below) did. Instead, the polka was an urban social dance dating no further back than the 1830s.[36] Gracian Černušák describes the trends rapid proliferation through the European upper classes:

> The polka was introduced to Prague in 1837 and appeared in print the same year in Berra's collection *Prager Lieblings-Galopen für Pianoforte*. In the following years innumerable polkas were written by such composers as Hilmar, Joseph Labitzky and Josef Neruda, and were published in collections of dances or in special series with picturesque or topical titles. In 1839 the band of a Bohemian regiment took the polka to Vienna, and that year it also reached St Petersburg. The Prague dancing-master Jan Raab introduced it to Paris in 1840, though it was not until 1843–4 that it became the favourite dance of Parisian society. On

11 April 1844 the dance was first performed in London by Carlotta Grisi and Jules Perrot on the stage of Her Majesty's Theatre.

Once in Vienna versions of this dance were composed and performed by Strauss I and Joseph Lanner, who developed two distinct forms: the *Polka française* and the *Schnell-Polka*.[37] In the words of both Andrew Lamb and Stanley Goscombe – in their biographies of Bohemian composer Joseph Labitzky and Hungarian bandmaster Josef Gung'l, respectively – the Viennese Strauss family 'overshadowed' the Bohemian composers, which perhaps explains the dance's subsequent association with the Austrian court and the Viennese upper class. However, the dance still retains its "notions of Czechness", and has been incorporated into "art" music, such as Smetana's String Quartet no. 1 JB 1:105 (1876), the second movement of Dvořák's *Czech Suite* Op. 39 (1879), and his *Slavonic Dances* Op. 46, No. 3 (1878). The sudden swell of popularity this dance enjoyed, leading to its adoption by the Strauss family, while still being "unconsciously Czech", as Černušák suggests, provides a multivalent aspect to this topic: it is, in essence, both Viennese and Other.

The polka is usually in ternary form with eight-bar sections, sometimes with a brief introduction of coda. It is in duple time, and played at a moderate speed, with the exception of the *schnell-polka*, which is similar in tempo to the *galop*. Characteristic rhythmic patterns are made up of quavers and semiquavers, generally without an upbeat (figure 3.1). These rhythms follow the distinctive "half-step" performed by the dancers. These characteristics can be found in Strauss's *Die Fledermaus*, initially as the ball theme, which Carl Dahlhaus suggests acts as 'a sort of musical emblem or leitmotiv for Falke's intrigue', a concept discussed below in chapter 4.[38] The polka also appears in Act Two, No. 11, when the guests at Prince Orlofsky's ball toast champagne as the King of all wines over a polka, which echoes the *Champagner-Polka* Op. 211, written by Strauss fifteen years before.

Figure 3.1 *Strauss II,* Die Fledermaus, *Act Two, No. 11.* **Polka.** (Leipzig: August Cranz, n.d., 1890).

Style Hongrois

The indications of the Other, exotic nationalities often cite the pastoral side of life, such as in Rosalinde's *csárdás*: 'die Sonne so klar, / wie grün deine Wälde, / wie lachend die Felder'.[39] This pastoral idyllic idea appealed to the Viennese imagination, symbolising 'freedom, nonconformity, and independence from the constricting mores of society'.[40] Because of the close relationship Austria had with Hungary over the other Slav peoples, which culminated in the Compromise in 1867 by which the Austrian Empire became the Dual Monarchy of Austria-Hungary, these references were often in Hungarian (or *style hongrois*) or Gypsy styles.[41]

In his book *The* Style Hongrois *in the Music of Western Europe*, Jonathan Bellman sets out a lexicon of individual gestures separated into several broad categories: imitations of the instruments most commonly used by the Gypsies; rhythmic figures derived from the Hungarian language and common ornamental and dance rhythms; melodic gestures, including coloured intervals; and harmony. Catherine Mayes claims that the origin of the *style hongrois* from dances, rather than the *hallgató* style – "to be listened to" – is unsurprising.[42]

The *verbunkos*, for example, drew on well-known elements of Hungarian social dances, such as would be performed at weddings which, through inclusion in Western composers' *Hausmusik*, became 'synonymous with Hungarianness'.[43] The association of Hungarian-Gypsy music with dancing, Mayes claims, was commercially sound, with hundreds of published collections appearing from the 1780s to 1820s.[44] In her analyses of these collections Mayes notices that, while the first half of the dances were 'jovial and flirtatious', the second half were often in the minor, had forte dynamics, with, on occasion, the indication *maestoso*, which acknowledged that, in addition to its purpose as dance music, this music aided military recruitment. Mayes explains that

> the primary character of most Western European representations of Hungarian-Gypsy dances is one of jovial or trifling simplicity rather than of 'warlike rage' [that] reflects the desire of Western Europeans to translate an impression of Hungarian-Gypsy music that served their own needs and tastes.[45]

It is, however, important to note Mayes' use of the phrase "Western European representations". The *style hongrois* detailed above is a representation. It is not Hungarian music, or Gypsy music, but a stylised version of what people perceived these musics to be. This is what Bartók railed against: that what Liszt and Brahms called "Hungarian" and Sárosi called "Gypsy" is in fact neither. In the same way that the military topic signifies nobility and medieval chivalry, rather than the bloody reality of savage warfare, the *style hongrois* has no basis in Hungarian music, as confirmed in particular by its most prevalent signifier, the Gypsy scale. The characteristics of this style instead derive from varied origins, such as the Turkish style (from which comes the use of percussion, particularly cymbals, the importance of the repetition of the third, upper neighbour notes, the drone and harmonic stasis), and the Hungarian-Gypsy folk dances such as the *verbunkos* and the *csárdás*.[46] Jonathan Bellman has categorised these characteristics and I have outlined them below illustrated with examples from relevant musical sources.

Similar to the waltz the instrument commonly associated with the *style hongrois*, characterised by rhapsodic elements, small, jangling ornaments and grace notes, non-melodic extremes of range and pizzicato, is the fiddle. The fiddle player was in the primary position within the ensemble, and acted in place of a conductor, who was never present. Hence, he performs the *friss* sections with virtuosity, and the slow *hallgató* style with rubato overwhelmed by improvised expression. At the end of these fiorituras the whole band plays chords and long notes, briefly grounding the soloist before he progresses to the next flourish. The *hallgató* style was not only the provenance of the fiddle, however; middle-range woodwind, such as the clarinet, oboe, or the more traditional *táragató* were also used for this type of expression.[47] The *táragató* is described by Bellman as 'a shrill, shawmlike instrument that dates back to the Hungarian independence movement of the late seventeenth century', although this instrument is now generally superseded by the clarinet or oboe (figure 3.2, including vocal and *táragató* improvisation).[48] The bagpipe was also important within Hungarian folk music, but like the *táragató* the instrument itself had all but died out, while the drone fifth characteristic of the bagpiper's style, now played by the double bass or cello, had lived on. This, Bellman suggests, is the possible origin for the propensity towards harmonic stasis in the style.[49]

One final instrument, which is fundamental to Gypsy bands as accompanist or soloist, is the cimbalom. A malleted string instrument, it initially had no sustaining pedal, although this was added in the nineteenth century. When evoking this instrument, usually on the piano, composers such as Liszt and Schubert used tremolo effects, for example, in the openings of Liszt's Hungarian Rhapsody Nos. 11 and 12.

Vocal imitation is evoked using parallel thirds and sixths, and grace notes, often falling from more than a fifth above the melody. The parallel "voices" descend from folk singing traditions in Eastern Europe and are voiced equally, with neither melody taking precedence. It is noteworthy, particularly in the methodological context of topic theory, that the commercial Gypsy bands never employed vocalists (although Bartók states that 'real, non-musician rural Gypsies' did have songs which were never performed in public); this is

Figure 3.2 *Vocal Improvisation.* Kálmán, Gräfin Mariza, No.1, bb. 52–56. (Wien: Josef Weinberger, 1924).

one area which Bartók uses as evidence that Gypsy and Hungarian music are so different.[50] He notes that

> in the folksong, text and music form an indivisible unity. Gypsy performance destroys this unity because it transforms, without exception, the vocal pieces into purely instrumental ones. This alone suffices to prove the lack of authenticity in Gypsy renderings of music, even with regard to popular art music. If a person were compelled to reconstruct our popular art music with the aid of Gypsy bands alone, he would find the task impossible because half of the material – the texts – is lost in the hands of the Gypsies.[51]

Consequently, the gestures that mimic the voice in the *style hongrois* are in fact stylised representations of what were already imitations of Hungarian folk-song by Gypsy instrumentalists.

Many of the rhythmic characteristics of the *style hongrois* derive from the angular traits of the Hungarian language. Others are ornamental rhythms used for effect and expression. In the former category lies the spondee, the choriambus and the Lombard, while the *alla zoppa*, dotted and triplet rhythms, and the *bókazó* originate more from dance rhythms than textual sources.

The spondee is a metrical foot consisting of two long notes which have the effect of halting quicker motion, an effect similar to the one a full stop has on a sentence (figure 3.3). Of all the rhythms outlined here, it is the least likely to appear in an operetta, and indeed no such use has been found, as it stops the music so suddenly. Within an operetta, designed to be danced to and for the public to be able to sing and play along with at home, this rhythm would not have been easy to assimilate into the exceedingly Western structures needed for maximum commercial viability. The choriambus, long-short-short-long, is commonly seen in Bartók's folksong settings, linking it closely to the Hungarian language. The accented short-long is the Lombard, while the accented short-short-long is termed the Hungarian anapest.

The *alla zoppa* rhythm is one of the most common in the style, and consists of a crotchet between two quavers, or a minim between crotchets, giving a syncopated flavour to the music. The *bókazó* – "capering" – rhythm is, Bellman states, one of the clearest indications of the style, and appears most frequently at the end of phrases; hence Liszt referred to this rhythm as the 'Magyar cadence'. This rhythm originated from a heel- or spur-clicking figure common in Hungarian dance. The Hungarian's history as equestrian nomads helps to explain the significance of this spur-clicking dance rhythm to the *style hongrois*.[52] This rhythm also has a melodic contour associated with it: a turn beginning on the upper neighbour note.

Figure 3.3 *Spondee. Schubert,* **Quintet, Op. 163,** *First Movement, Closing Theme, bb.* ***138–142.*** (Liepzig: Breitkopf & Härtel, 1888).

The *verbunkos*, a Hungarian term derived from the German *Werbung*, meaning "recruitment" or "courtship", is a dance played by Gypsies to lure village boys into the army. The recruiters would often force Gypsies to accompany their enlistment campaigns with this upbeat dance to give an impression of "jolly, carefree army life".[53] The characteristics of the *verbunkos* include duple meter, a gradual increase in tempo from very slow to very fast, and a profusion of instrumental ornamentation. An example of the *verbunkos* within *Gräfin Mariza* can be found in Mariza's entrance music, No. 4. Gypsy musicians, Sárosi explains, gravitated to places where there was a possibility of making money. This meant they often obtained patronage from aristocrats or minor nobles. Only in the larger towns and cities, like Budapest or Vienna, were they able to settle without patronage.[54]

The *csárdás* is possibly a later version of the *verbunkos*, although, Bellman claims, if so it incorporates elements of the *nóta* song style.[55] The *nóta* songs are a folk-influenced genre, combining aspects of both Viennese and *verbunkos* music. They were often composed by minor nobles, described by Bellman as 'people for whom professional musical performance and involvement would have been unthinkable, and were often sentimental in nature'.[56] These songs tended to be slow, with the marked rhythms of the Hungarian texts giving them a distinctive character.[57] The *csárdás* is a traditional Hungarian dance and has two sections: *lassu* or *lassan* (slow) and *friss* or *friska* (from the German *frisch*, fresh or fast). The opening section is a slow, measured, 4/4 dance, often resembling a "presentation step" or a 'metrically free, rhapsodic approach'.[58] The fast section consists of either one, or several songs, which represent a loss of control and emotional abandonment. The dance is still popular in Hungary today, and often takes the form of a medley of tunes progressing from slow to fast, rather than the traditional two-part form.

Signification

The 'impression of Hungarian-Gypsy music', cited above, translates to the manipulation, or evolution, of the topical signification of the *style hongrois* topic. The Gypsies' way of life, travelling as they did from city to city, picking up different cultural characteristics, had the result that, with relatively little transcription on paper, the musical gestures evolved to include many different styles, and consequently multiple layers of association. Bellman suggests that because of this lifestyle

> what the Gypsies and their music represented to the Romantic sensibility is encapsulated by Liszt's performance instruction at the beginning of the seventh Hungarian Rhapsody, which reads: 'To be played in the Gypsy style, defiant, and yet melancholy'. To the popular imagination, the Gypsy symbolized

freedom, nonconformity, and independence from the constricting mores of society.[59] [...] The parallels in Liszt's case are obvious: the self-conscious simplicity of his Magyar spirit and pietistic leanings sits in marked contrast to his cosmopolitan pretension and associations with wealth and aristocracy.[60]

Anna Piotrowska agrees that the image of the idealised Gypsy musician, constructed both in literature and within musical works, 'has been considered the embodiment of the inspired creator, possessing the specific features of the sensitive romantic artist. He was seductive while at the same time free and rebellious, and his separateness from bourgeois society was strongly emphasised'.[61] His music, therefore, signified similar qualities. 'The idealised concept of Gypsy music', Piotrowska goes on to explain, 'only loosely related to the musical practices of real Romanies, fulfilled the romantic hankering after exotic, charming, and highly emotional music'.[62] Freedom and defiance were not the only significations of the style, according to Warren. He identifies the misconceptions the Austrians held concerning the Magyars. Despite their political partnership, the Hungarians were viewed at times by the Viennese as 'savage, uncivilised foreigners from the East'.[63] Additionally, the memory of the Magyar allying themselves with the Ottoman Turks in the sixteenth and seventeenth centuries against the Austrians added to the mistrust.[64] Their refusal to assimilate into the culture, but instead to thrive as societal outsiders, added to the fascinating "defiant freedom" aspect the *style hongrois* signified, while simultaneously overlaying it with the fear of the unknown and Other.[65]

This ambiguity in the signification of the Hungarian-Gypsy musical style is discussed by Mayes in a comparison between the *alla turca* and the Hungarian-Gypsy musics.[66] She posits that 'that music *alla turca* and early representations of Hungarian-Gypsy music cannot, for the most part, be considered discrete topics from a stylistic point of view is due . . . to the fact that they were largely constructed by the same culture'.[67] Mayes explains that the perception of Eastern Europe as a cohesive whole during the Enlightenment meant that the Hungarians were classified along with the Turkish as Western Europe's 'barbaric Other *par excellence*'.[68]

Recent research on the differences between Gypsy music and the *style hongrois* is provided in Piotrowska's detailed history *Gypsy Music in European Culture*, in which she outlines the two models of academic consideration, the assimilative and non-assimilative models:

> In the period following the French Revolution right up until the beginning of the twentieth century, the assimilative model was based on the concept of the nationality propagated within the whole of Europe. As such, Gypsy music was presented as an integral component of European culture, a form that joined with local musical idioms to create national musical traditions in individual countries. Meanwhile, within the nonassimilative model, Gypsy music was

presented as belonging to a distinct culture, whose outlook was inherently alien to European civilisation. The nonassimilative model employed the concepts of exoticism (Orientalism) and race, weaving Gypsy origin, musical characteristics, and thinking on the culture of Gypsies into an interdependent web.[69]

Using specific dances and rhythms, such as the *verbunkos* or *csárdás*, the *style hongrois* represents Hungarian-Gypsy music in particular, rather than a generic Other, and has a particular significance in Vienna owing to the presence of a 'culturally learned recognition'. It is therefore part of the assimilative model outlined by Piotrowska. It is not the alien Other, the exotic presence used to provide the audience with a form of escapism, but a familiar Other, which, as suggested above, evokes familiarity, but also fear and dread of the unknown. It could therefore be understood as a manifestation of the uncanny: 'that class of the frightening which leads back to what is known of old and long familiar'.[70]

Fear was not the only negative connotation this style achieved. Shay Loya suggests that the authenticity of this 'much perverted imitation of older and more authentic' folk music resulted in 'an aesthetic depreciation of the value of Hungarian Gyspy-band music in scholarly discourse inside and outside Hungary'.[71] He further notes that Bartók deemed there to be a dichotomy in 'the aesthetic sympathy between peasant music and highbrow musical modernism and it's supposed opposite the unholy union between fake folklore and lowbrow romanticism'.[72]

The Hungarian style is obviously not the only national style that was common at this time, although it is the most prevalent. Another style worth investigating, made popular by Chopin in the Parisian salons of the nineteenth century, is the Polish mazurka.[73] There are three basic types of mazurka. The *oberek* is the fastest of the three, originating in central and western Poland; the mazurka (or *mazur*) is slower but still lively in character, while the *kujawiak*, a dance from the Kraków region, is of moderate tempo, with longer phrase lengths. All three variants are in triple meter; are usually accompanied by a drone on the tonic, or tonic and dominant; and feature a *tempo rubato* that lends the dances a rhythmic freedom.[74] The instruments most commonly used in this folk tradition consist of violins (which may play the melody or the drone), drum and harmonium.

The three dances are distinguished not only by their tempo but also by their varied placement of accented notes. In the *oberek* the accent falls on the last part of the second measure; in the *kujawiak* the main stress is placed on any part of the fourth bar of the phrase; and in the *mazur* the accents can be placed according to the composer's whim, creating an irregular character to the dance with its free pattern.[75] This dance has similarities with the German *Ländler* (the triple time and melodic diatonicism), and with the rhythmic freedom of the Hungarian *hallgató* style, but it is the inclusion of the tonic-dominant drone which places it apart from either of these, while at the same time associates it firmly with the more general pastoral folk topic.

It is important then to understand the pastoral topics in relation to the urban topics of the waltz and the polka and the how the *Ländler* bridges the gap between the two. Despite the waltzes derivation from the rural dances found in beer halls, its eventual signifieds are firmly entrenched in not only the city of Vienna, but that city's elite. Its upper-class associations however are due to the historical accounts available to us, which, just as the noble hunt, are written in general by the elite or their critics and so it is the perception of the waltz – actually enjoyed by all but not in the same ebullient manner – that is important. *And it is* perception that is important here. The artificiality of the aristocracy and the bourgeoisie masked the decline of the empire. Through the loss of territory, the stagnation of the monarchy, the repression of Metternich's laws, the abject poverty and, of course, the failure of the revolution, Vienna danced on. As Gartenberg states 'all congealed in a common nearsighted enjoyment of today [. . .] What better way to forget than to dance and eat?'.[76] The *Ringstraße* marks both the physical representation of this double life of Vienna and of the change that occurred around the turn of the century when Wagner and Semper introduced their art based on necessity and need. With the death of Strauss in 1899 the associations of the waltz also began to change from Strauss's sarcastic depiction of the aristocracy seen in *Die Fledermaus* to Lehar and Kalman's illumination of the moral choices their characters make, all of which will be explored in the next chapter. To do this they use the nationalist styles and dances of the other/"Other" countries of the empire described above, and other class-based topoi, placing them in opposition/juxtaposition to one another to create a narrative exploring immorality and the double – whether the double life of the Viennese or the *Doppelgänger*'s of Freud's Uncanny.

NOTES

1. Eduard Reeser, *The History of the Waltz*. Trans. from the Dutch by W.A.G. Doyle-Davidson (Stockholm: The Continental Book Company A.B., 1949), 7.

2. Reeser, *The History of the Waltz*, 14.

3. Reeser, *The History of the Waltz*, 15.

4. Egon Gartenberg, *Johann Strauss: The End of an Era* (Pennsylvania State: Pennsylvania State University Press, 1974), 34.

5. Andrew Lamb, "Waltz (i)", In *Grove Music Online. Oxford Music Online*, http://0-www.oxfordmusiconline.com.wam.leeds.ac.uk/subscriber/article/grove/music/29881 (accessed July 21, 2015); Mosco Carner, "Ländler", *The New Grove*

Dictionary of Music and Musicians, ed. Stanley Sadie, 2nd ed. (London: Macmillan, 2001), 223.

6. Derek B. Scott, *Sounds of the Metropolis: The 19th Century Popular Music Revolution in London, New York, Paris and Vienna* (Oxford: Oxford University Press, 2008), 118.

7. Scott, *Sounds of the Metropolis*, 223.

8. Micznik, 'Mahler and "The Power of Genre"'. The *Ländler* can be found in the second movement of Mahler's Ninth Symphony at bars 1, 369 and 523.

9. Titles taken from Josef Lanner's *Ländlers, Zauberhorn* (1829).

10. Allanbrook, *Rhythmic Gesture in Mozart*, 63.

11. Gammond, Peter and Andrew Lamb, "Waltz", in *The Oxford Companion to Music*, ed. Alison Latham, *Oxford Music Online*. http://0-www.oxfordmusiconline.com.wam.leeds.ac.uk/subscriber/article/opr/t114/e7260 (accessed July 21, 2015).

12. Eduard Hanslick quoted in Egon Gartenberg, *Johann Strauss*, 36.

13. Gartenberg, *Johann Strauss*, 198.

14. Scott, *Sounds of the Metropolis*, 126.

15. Scott, *Sounds of the Metropolis*, 127.

16. Joonas Jussi Sakari Korhonen, "Urban social space and the development of the public dance hall culture in Vienna, 1780–1814", *Urban History*, 40, 4 (Nov 2013), pp. 606.

17. Gartenberg, *Johann Strauss*, 7.

18. Steven Beller, *Vienna and the Jews, 1867–1938: A Cultural History* (Cambridge: Cambridge University Press, 1989), 176.

19. The Kings of Württemburg and Bavaria changed their regimes from absolute to constitutional monarchies in 1819 and 1818 respectively.

20. Gartenberg, *Johann Strauss*, 26.

21. Henry Schnitzler, "'Gay Vienna'—Myth and Reality", *Journal of the History of Ideas*, Jan 1954, Vol. 15, No. 1, pp. 99–100.

22. Gartenberg, *Johann Strauss*, 17–18.

23. A. J. P. Taylor, *The Habsburg Monarchy 1809–1918* (Middlesex: Penguin books, 1990) originally published by Hamish Hamilton, 1948, 64.

24. Hans Sassman, *Das Reich der Träumer; Eine Kulturgeschichte Oesterreichs vom Urzustand bis zure Republik* (Berlin: Verlag fur Kulturpolitik, 1932), 406.

25. 'The "museumish" was reserved for Vienna, indeed as a sign of its ruin, the sign of Austrian ruin. For in despondency decay leads to vegetating, but in wealth it leads to the museum. Museumishness [*Musealität*] is the vegetating of wealth, a cheerful vegetating, and Austria was at the time still a wealthy country'. Hermann Broch, *Hugo von Hofmannsthal and his Time: The European Imagination 1860–1920,* trans. and ed. Michael P. Steinberg (Chicago: University of Chicago Press, 1984), 61.

26. Hermann Broch, *Hugo von Hofmannsthal and his Time: The European Imagination 1860–1920,* trans. and ed. Michael P. Steinberg (Chicago: University of Chicago Press, 1984), 64.

27. Heinrich Jacob, *Johann Strauss Father and Son: A Century of Light Music*, trans. Marguerite Wolff (London: Hutchinson, 1940; originally published as *Johann*

Strauss und das neunzehnte Jahrhundert. Die Geschichte einer musikalischen Weltherrschaft, 1819–1917 [Amsterdam: Querido-Verlag, 1937]), 195.

28. Schorske, *Fin-de-Siècle Vienna*, 26.

29. Gartenberg, *Johann Strauss*, 223.

30. Heinz Geretsegger and Max Peintner, *Otto Wagner 1841-1918: The Expanding City, the Beginning of Modern Architecture*, Associate Author: Walter Pichler. Introd. by Richard Neutra; Translated (From the German) by Gerald Onn (London: Rizzoli, 1979), 12.

31. Frigyesi, "Bela Bartók and the Concept of Nation and Volk in Modern Hungary", 255.

32. It is obvious that the Jewish community in Vienna is an important part of the Viennese historical narrative. However, as this book is focussing on how the culture is mapped within the contemporary music, and Jewish music is such a broad and well-developed subject in and of itself, it will not be explored within this book unless it is pertinent to a specific narrative.

33. Bartók, *Essays*, 316.

34. Trumpener, *Music and the Racial Imagination*, 406.

35. Crittenden, *Johann Strauss*, 120. For extensive discussion of the exotic Other in Western music see Bellman, *The Exotic in Western Music* (Boston: Northeastern University Press, 1998); Georgina Born and David Hesmondhalgh, *Western Music and Its Others* (Berkeley: University of California Press, 2000); Matthew Head, *Orientalism, Masquerade, and Mozart's Turkish Music* (London: Royal Musical Association, 2000); Ralph Locke, *Musical Exoticism: Images and Reflections* (Cambridge: Cambridge University Press, 2009); Catherine Mayes, "Cultural Associations of Turkish and Hungarian-Gypsy Styles in the Late Eighteenth Century and their Compositional Implications", *Oxford Handbook of Topic Theory*; Derek B. Scott, "Orientalism and Musical Style", *The Musical Quarterly* 82, no. 2 (Summer 1998), 309–335.

36. Gracian Černušák, et al., "Polka" *Grove Music Online. Oxford Music Online.* http://0-www.oxfordmusiconline.com.wam.leeds.ac.uk/subscriber/article/grove/music/22020>, (accessed November 25, 2015).

37. Černušák, et al., "Polka". Capitals in original.

38. Carl Dalhaus, *Nineteenth-Century Music*, trans. J. Bradford Robinson (Berkeley: University of California Press, 1989), 231.

39. (The sun so clear, / how green the forests, / the laughing fields) from No.10 *Csárdás, Die Fledermaus*.

40. Bellman, "Toward a Lexicon for the *Style hongrois*", 214.

41. In 1867, after the shattering defeat at Könnigratz, Emperor Francis Joseph agreed to terms made by the Magyar leadership intended to turn the Habsburg Monarchy into a German-Magyar condominium, with the Magyars ruling Hungary and the rest of the Empire ruled by Austrian Germans. The result of this agreement was the *Ausgleich*, or Compromise of 1867. Beller, *A Concise History of Austria*, 142–143.

42. Catherine Mayes, "Turkish and Hungarian-Gypsy Styles", *Oxford Handbook of Topic Theory*, 221.

43. Mayes, "Turkish and Hungarian-Gypsy Styles", *Oxford Handbook of Topic Theory*, 221.
44. Mayes, "Turkish and Hungarian-Gypsy Styles", *Oxford Handbook of Topic Theory*, 226.
45. Mayes, "Turkish and Hungarian-Gypsy Styles", *Oxford Handbook of Topic Theory*, 226.
46. Bellman, "Toward a Lexicon for the *Style hongrois*", 218. Bellman's lexicon has been chosen over other more recent categorisations of *style hongrois* and Gypsy music because these are based predominantly on Bellman's research. For other lexicons for the *style hongrois* see Shay Loya, *Liszt's transcultural modernism and the Hungarian-gypsy tradition* (Rochester: University of Rochester Press, 2011); Bálint Sárosi, "Gypsy Musicians and Hungarian Peasant Music", *Yearbook of the International Folk Music Council* 2 (1970): 8–27; Sárosi, *Gypsy Music,* trans. Fred Macnicol (Budapest: Corvina, 1978); Jackson Eliot Warren, "The *Style Hongrois* in the Music of Johann Strauss Jr" (PhD diss., University of Arizona, 2012).
47. Jonathan Bellman, *The Style Hongrois in the Music of Western Europe* (Boston: Northeastern University Press, 1993), 103.
48. Bellman, *The Style Hongrois in the Music of Western Europe*, 103.
49. Bellman, "Toward a Lexicon for the *Style hongrois*", 227.
50. Béla Bartók, "Gypsy Music or Hungarian Music?" *The Musical Quarterly* 33, no. 2 (1947), 240–325, 252.
51. Bartók, "Gypsy Music or Hungarian Music?", 252.
52. Bellman, *The Style Hongrois in the Music of Western Europe*, 119.
53. Bellman, *The Style Hongrois in the Music of Western Europe*, 17.
54. Bellman, *The Style Hongrois in the Music of Western Europe*, 16.
55. Bellman, "Toward a Lexicon for the *Style hongrois*", 217.
56. Bellman, *The Style Hongrois in the Music of Western Europe*, 21.
57. Bellman, "Toward a Lexicon for the *Style hongrois*", 217.
58. Quotations from, respectively, Bellman, "Toward a Lexicon for the *Style hongrois*", 217; Bellman, *The Style Hongrois in the Music of Western Europe*, 21.
59. Bellman, "Toward a Lexicon for the *Style Hongrois*", 214.
60. Bellman, "Toward a Lexicon for the *Style Hongrois*", 216.
61. Anna Piotrowska, *Gypsy Music in European Culture* (Boston: Northeastern University Press, 2013), 1.
62. Piotrowska, *Gypsy Music in European Culture*, 1.
63. Warren, "The *Style Hongrois* in the music of Johann Strauss Jr." (PhD diss., University of Arizona, 2012), 38.
64. Warren, "The *Style Hongrois* in the Music of Johann Strauss Jr.", 38.
65. Warren, "The *Style Hongrois* in the Music of Johann Strauss Jr.", 38.
66. Mayes, "Turkish and Hungarian-Gypsy Styles", *Oxford Handbook of Topic Theory*, 215–236.
67. Mayes, "Turkish and Hungarian-Gypsy Styles", *Oxford Handbook of Topic Theory*, 217.
68. Mayes, "Turkish and Hungarian-Gypsy Styles", *Oxford Handbook of Topic Theory*, 217.

69. Piotrowska, *Gypsy Music*, 13.

70. Freud, "The Uncanny" *The Standard Edition of the Complete Psychological Works of Sigmund Freud*, ed. and trans. James Strachey (London: Hogarth,1964), vol. XVII, 220.

71. Shay Loya, *Listz's Transcultural Modernism and the Hungarian-Gypsy Tradition* (New York: University of Rochester Press, 2011), 118.

72. Loya, *Liszt's Transcultural Modernism*, 123.

73. Stephen Downes, "Mazurka", in *Grove Music Online, Oxford Music Online*. http://0-www.oxfordmusiconline.com.wam.leeds.ac.uk/subscriber/article/grove/music/18193 (accessed July 21, 2015).

74. Downes, "Mazurka".

75. Anne Swartz, "The Polish Folk Mazurka", *Studia Musicologica Academiae Scientiarum Hungaricae* 1, no. 4 (1975), 250–252.

76. Gartenberg, *Johann Strauss: The End of an Era*, 43.

Chapter 4

Narrative and Deception

With a firm grasp of the cultural context the waltz inhabits, I will now discuss how the topic reflects the historical and cultural transformation at the turn of the century. Through a narrative method, I have traced the signification of the waltz from depicting deception, immorality and the "gay apocalypse" in 1874 through a realisation of that deception but yearning for the cosy easiness of *Alt Wien* and to the waltz as a sign of high Viennese morals in juxtaposition to the simple, "heavenly" nationalist characters and in opposition to the lowbrow and low-class immoral characters. To make sure there is a certainty (or at least as certain as one can be when the analysis relies so heavily on the interpretant as Byron Almén tells us) about how the waltz acts within the narrative this chapter concentrates on texted operettas by "light" music composers. This provides a more solid notion of what the topics signified to the composers of Vienna 1900 and how they were used to illustrate or subvert the libretto.[1]

The editors of *Narrative in Music Since 1900*, Michael L. Klein and Nicholas Reyland, state that the convention when discussing musical narrative is to start with Jean-Jaques Nattiez's 'famous question, "Can one speak of narrativity in music?", and Nattiez's equally famous answer: "no"'.[2] The approaches to a theory of musical narrative have been as varied as the objections. Carolyn Abbate and Nattiez both argue that music is mimetic rather than diegetic, hence, as Abbate states, it has no past tense.[3] Lawrence Kramer also rejects the idea of a narrator: 'various elements of an instrumental piece may confront this presiding subject with agencies but not with agents, with personifications but not with persons'.[4] Music, Kramer states, is a supplement to narrative, it cannot be a narrative itself.[5]

These objections arose in answer to narrative theories put forward by Edward T. Cone and Fred E. Maus, and in subsequent decades the solutions have varied.⁶ Maus, for example, links music to drama, in that the action within a play is immediate and in the present, therefore negating the need for a past tense. Most notable is Klein's 2004 article 'Chopin's Fourth Ballade as Musical Narrative' in which he cites Paul Cobley:

> Recent work on narrative [. . .] has shown the difficulty of maintaining the distinction between mimesis and diegesis. J. Hillis Miller, for example, argues that Sophocles' Oedipus Rex fails as an example of mimesis, because the action in the play is 'made up almost exclusively of people standing around talking or chanting'.⁷ Paul Cobley argues that a telling is also a showing, because the creator of a narrative in any medium chooses to reveal some events, while hiding others. Accordingly, Cobley defines narrative as the 'showing or telling of these events and the mode selected for that to take place'.⁸ Under this definition, music's failure of the diegesis test ceases to impact its status as a narrative artform.⁹

Common to these approaches is the recognition of similarity between musical and literary discourse, and the definition of narrative as a transformation of semantically meaningful units over time, whether the units are themes, motives, figures, tonal events or topics. Anthony Newcomb refers to an analogy between literary and musical patterning. Byron Almén, led by Hatten's hierarchically structured "markedness" concept, defines narrative as 'track[ing] the effect of transgressive shifts or conflicts on a prevailing cultural system, as inflected by that which is important to the observer'.¹⁰ Almén is not the first to highlight the importance of the interpretant. Newcombe and Eero Tarasti also emphasise the listener's role in the creation of a narrative: 'it is subjective in that it depends on the education, intuition and talent of the individual critic-interpreter'.¹¹ Led by Tarasti's analysis of Chopin's Ballade in G Minor, Almén cites this as an important insight about musical narrative:

> *Musical narrative is fundamentally dependant on the listener's, analyst's, and/ or performer's interpretation.* [. . .] Of course, a successful – that is to say, persuasive – interpretation will be significantly guided by the phenomenal data, but a great deal of leeway remains with respect to the shaping and contextualising of these data.¹²

This is significant here because of the analytical process employed in the study of the music of *fin-de-siècle* Vienna. With each following case study, the first analysis has been prepared with no prior knowledge of the piece or any extant literature on the music. This somewhat corresponds to Cone's 'First Reading' of a detective story in his article 'Three Ways to Read a Detective Story—Or a Brahms Intermezzo' in which he advocates three readings of the story in order to fully comprehend it.[13] The first reading 'refers to any reading based on total or partial ignorance of the events narrated'.[14] This ensured that the initial topical analysis was unbiased, that is, that other interpretations, or previous interpreter's conventional perceptions, did not colour the eventual analysis put forward. With the "blind" analysis complete, an investigation into the surrounding literature shows a connection between the revealed topical narrative and the encircling contemporary culture and current literature. For example, the connections found to psychoanalysis in Schoenberg's works that is preceded by such scholars as Klein, Kramer, Richard Cohn, Michael Cherlin and Alexander Carpenter.

I began this project with a reorganisation of Hatten's topical hierarchy, designed to assign rank within the topical universe in order to create a musical narrative through markedness, as outlined by Hatten and Almén. The resulting diagram (table 1.1, found in chapter 1) is instead similar to a syntactic diagram, and therefore follows more closely a theory of musical narrative derived from literary sources – such as Gérard Genette, Seymour Chatman and Martin McQuillan – in which different levels of association can be navigated without necessarily connoting rank.[15] Chatman explains 'that [. . .] all narratives, in whatever medium, combine the time sequence of plot events, the time of the *histoire* ("story-time") with the time of the presentation of those events in the text, which we call "discourse-time"'.[16] Vera Micznik further explains how these two levels of narrative apply to music:

> [u]nder the heading 'Story', I abstract from the two works the 'musical events' themselves [the signifieds] and analyse their meanings from the simplest to the more complex – from explicit to implicit—semiotic levels [. . .] as a demonstration of what makes them 'events'. And under 'Discourse', I examine the particular mode of unfolding (the presentation) [the signifiers] of these events within the 'musical formal discourse' of the respective movements and the capabilities of the 'discourse' itself to produce meanings through 'gestural and intertextual connotations' and through 'temporal manipulations'.[17]

I have used a similar model of analysis in each case study throughout this book, that is, each begins with an identification of the signifiers within the piece and then an exploration of their position within the temporal and cultural/historical landscape of the work.

The above literature on narrative in music centres on what Susan McClary describes as 'the music that narrates by itself', the European canon stretching roughly from Vivaldi to Mahler (1700–1900).[18] Thus, despite her claim that 'even the most austere, apparently self-contained of the pieces produced within this repertory attain their coherence and effectiveness as cultural artefacts through processes aligned with narrative', McClary dismisses the notion that non-tonal music can resemble narrative.[19] In fact, she writes, 'beginning with Debussy, Stravinsky, and Schoenberg and extending to the experiments of John Cage, the avant-garde music of the twentieth century has been self-consciously ANTI-narrative'.[20] Jann Pasler, however, lists anti-narrative as one of 'three significant innovations' stimulated by 'twentieth-century composer's attempts to thwart listeners' expectation of narrative':[21]

> anti-narratives and nonnarratives both challenge important aspects of narrative, but still have narrativity (i.e. some organising principle). [. . .] Works without narrativity try to eliminate completely the listener's predilection to seek for narrativity.[22]

Anti-narrative relies on a frustration of narrative expectation through interruptions of the temporal processes, and 'change without narrative transformation'. Stockhausen's "moment form", or Jonathan Kramer's "moment time", exemplified in Pasler's chapter by Stockhausen's *Carré* (1958–9) and *Stop* (1965), produces this type of signification.[23] Therefore, there is still a degree of narrativity, rather than an absence of it. The frustration of narrative temporality in *Stop*, for example, is offset by the sense of narrative provided by the organising principle of the twelve-tone row.[24] Reyland's analysis of Lutosławski's *Livre pour orchestre* also explains anti-narrativity as a modernist structure that in *Livre*, and in spite of Lutosławski's original intentions, is 'ultimately subjugated to the classicist narrativity of its emergent symphonism'.[25]

Non-narrative works are 'works that may use elements of narratives but without allowing them to function as they would a narrative'.[26] These elements are related and derive from one another; however, the transformation through time that defines narrative does not occur. Klein outlines non-narrative as 'music with no tonality, no themes, no sense of causality or transformation, no organising principle whatsoever, in fact; just a set of independent sound worlds, textures, or blips of acoustic matter'.[27] He goes on to outline a fourth signification: neo-narrative. 'Here', Klein writes, 'is music in search of new ways to tell stories. Sometimes the rhythmic drive of this music is enough to give us a sense of musical plot, or the everchanging timbres of orchestral colour stand in for transformation, or the gradual motion through register lends us a sense of musical agency'.[28] Klein suggests that Schoenberg's music fits into this category, citing Boulez that Schoenberg's ambition was to 'create works of the same nature as those of the old sound-world which he had only just abandoned'.[29] While Schoenberg does indeed use new techniques in his music – twelve-note series and new timbres, a modernist view of embellishment and so on – I believe the narrative style of his works remains similar to that of Strauss and Mahler. This is demonstrated in the later chapters particularly through the uncovering of the similar utilisation and signification of the waltz that can be seen running through the narratives of the supposedly incompatible styles. In *Music and Narrative*, Almén and Hatten discuss twentieth-century narrative techniques such as developments in temporality, tropological or agential narratives, and myth, while Márta Grabócz also tackles temporality in opera.[30] The acceptance of narrative (in some form) is queried, however, by Lawrence Kramer, who suggests both that 'modernity does not make narrative disappear but instead renders it inoperable', and further, that 'modern narrative becomes a version of Lacan's *objet petit a*, the locus of a desire that at best must accept its endless deferral in lieu of fulfilment'.[31] Kramer, like McClary, cites Mahler as the last inherently narrative composer. With many other exemplars of narrative centring on Mahler's works, the discussion on how topics and narrative devices (changing associations, opposition and inflection) integrate to reveal subtextual "stories" begins with the art music composer's works and his contemporaries, such as Alexander von Zemlinsky. However, even before that one must look at the quintessential Viennese storytellers through 'light' music: Johann Strauss, Oscar Straus and Franz Lehár.[32]

On their own, topics evoke a specific signification, as explored in the previous chapters. When new topics are imported into an existing topical field, relationships form between the topics, creating narratives.[33] New meanings are generated by the interactions of the various topics, depending on the marked differences of each new affect. If the topics are relatively similar, the topical field will be largely unaffected; the narrative may be flavoured or distilled, but ultimately it will be the same. With markedly different topics, say the pastoral and learned styles, their juxtaposition will create a palpable narratological dialogue. Topics are not always imported as a whole: they can be fragmented so that not all their signifiers are present, and therefore only inflect the existing topical field. In this instance, new meaning is generated giving rise, perhaps, to a satirical or idealistic narrative. Additionally – and this was also highlighted in the previous chapters – topics often correlate with a specific period, so the composition date and cultural background of the work being analysed is important. As such, musical affects associated with each topic may change, or become stylised, as in Baroque dances or Classical symphonic devices like the *coup d'archet*.

To create a working narrative, whether in literature or music, meaning is often derived by oppositions between themes, characters or imagery; for example, between good/evil, light/dark or natural/supernatural. The topical narrative that emerges from the analyses of Strauss II's *Die Fledermaus* (1874), Lehár's *Die Lüstige Witwe* (1905) and Oscar Straus's *Ein Walzertraum* (1907) are no different, demonstrating established oppositions between high- and low-class ideals and protagonists and rural and urban concepts.

DIE FLEDERMAUS AND *WALZERTRAUM*: DECEPTION AS AUSTRIAN IDENTITY

Through the musical narratives discussed below, a polemical view of the aristocracy and nationalism inflects the waltz and polka in all four operettas discussed in this book but this topical subversion was explored first in Strauss II's *Die Fledermaus* (1874) and later, and in a far less nuanced manner, in Oscar Straus's *Ein Walzertraum* (1907). Based on the premise of a practical joke, it is no wonder deception is the strongest theme throughout the plot of *Die Fledermaus*. At every major development of the story – with each new intrigue – Strauss employs one of the two topics associated with Austrian national identity, the waltz or the polka. The first plot theme of *Die Fledermaus* is the juxtaposition of upper- and lower-class protagonists, a plot Strauss illuminates by means of a comic opera device: a masked ball in which the characters' real identities can be hidden behind costumes. The operetta encapsulates the hedonistic atmosphere of the pre-Lenten festival season, known in Vienna as *Fasching*, with which Strauss was associated. This celebration is marked by heavy drinking, masked balls and exchanging the "Du" form of address in disregard of the usual social barriers; the finale to the second act, particularly in 'Brüderlein und Schwesterlein', is a poignant acknowledgement of this environment.[34] The other theme employs duplicity in a narrative that is arguably reliant upon the main theme. It tells the story of a practical joke: the revenge of "the bat". As the prank plays out, the victim, Eisenstein, is convinced to go to a ball rather than prison by his old friend, Dr. Falke, in revenge for Eisenstein's previous joke which left the doctor wandering the streets of Vienna in a bat costume following the previous year's ball. Falke convinces him to go to the ball because he knows Eisenstein will be caught out by his bad behaviour. As expected, when he gets to the party, Eisenstein attempts to commit adultery (although, as events turn out, with his own wife) and becomes the best of friends with the prison director, who has already mistakenly incarcerated someone else in his place.

In contrast to the inner city setting of *Die Fledermaus*, *Ein Walzertraum* is set outside the city, where Niki, a Viennese Lieutenant, has been picked by a rural Princess to be her Prince. Where *Fledermaus* encapsulates the insular revelry of Vienna, *Walzertraum* yearns for it. The title song, No. 7 'Walzertraum', is a love song to Vienna performed by the new Prince Niki and his friend Moschi as they hatch a scheme to leave the princess and return to "gay" Vienna. Although it's his wedding night, he falls in love with Franzi, the leader of the orchestra playing Viennese music in the castle grounds. Un-shocked, as Niki had already made his feelings clear to her, Princess Helene invites Franzi back to the castle where the musician teaches her how to win Niki back with Viennese charm and pleasures. It would appear, then, that the composer was aware of the affected nature of the Viennese charms and that "gay Vienna" was something which could be faked or imitated. Contrastingly, in *Die Fledermaus* there is no suggestion that the characters are aware of the artificiality of their way of life as they all join in sincerely with the drinking round in the finale to Act 2, 'König aller Weine!', a song about champagne, the "king of all wine". Falke follows this with a gentle and sentimental waltz to brotherhood and sisterhood followed by the quick swirling *Fledermaus* waltz. Even once all the intrigues have all been uncovered in Act three, rather than any consequences, apologies or acknowledgment of morality, they simply blame the champagne ("O Fledermaus, O Fledermaus"). This could be due to the difference in time between compositions. *Die Fledermaus* was composed in 1874, which while it was just after the financial crash, was before the critical modernists began their onslaught of necessity and authenticity. *Ein Walzertraum*, on the other hand, was premiered in 1907, after the crucial cultural pivot had begun. While it was a success, it is possible that the nostalgic portrayal of *Alt Wien* mirrored the public's yearning for a return to their charmed but inward-looking escapist lifestyle. For example, in No 10, Franzi's song devoted to the waltz is mostly written as a polka – describing travelling the world with her violins and making 'even grumpy faces light up' – with moderate waltz interludes, the libretto of the second such interlude being: '*Die Welt, die dreht sich umadum und wird dabei net gescheiter/die Menschen bleiben schwindeldumm und kommen gar net weiter!*' ('The world is turning and is not getting any smarter in the process/people remain dumb enough to be fooled or scammed and don't get any further!').[35] Referring presumably to the stagnation of the Austrian Empire at the end of its monarchy's reign, only nine years from when this operetta was published.

As previously stated, in these two operettas the waltz, and less often the polka, accompanies the immorality of the characters. One such instance is in the finale to Act One, which begins with a minuet that acts as a counterpoint to the following *Ländler* at bar 13. At bars 66–73, the minuet separates the recitative (bars 59–65) from the *Ländler* (74–81). The recitative, a high-class theatrical topic, sung by an upper-class protagonist with seemingly moral intentions, is performed by Rosalinde as she wonders why Alfred will not "take the hint" and leave. The *Ländler*, a low-class dance, is sung by Alfred, a lower-class character, as he "forgives" her for being untrue to him in an attempt to persuade her to commit an immoral act (an adulterous affair with him): Alfred tells Rosalinde that love is an illusion, so she may as well enjoy herself. While the use of both of these topics is analogous to their historically sedimented meaningfulness, the minuet that separates the two is distorted. The elegant dance is used as Alfred implores Rosalinde to drink quickly so he can take advantage of her, therefore corrupting its high-class associations. The waltz then dominates the rest of the finale as Rosalinde resigns herself to her immorality, with the famous line: '*Glücklich ist, wer vergisst, was doch nicht zu ändern ist*' (Happy is the one who accepts what after all cannot be changed).

The possibility that Strauss was intentionally mocking the upper classes is suggested by the Act Two finale, No. 11. This is an insightful portrayal of the effects of social drinking, beginning with a polka that toasts champagne as the "*König aller Weine!*" (king of all wines!). The party continues in customary fashion with a hymn to universal brotherhood, utilising a round, resembling a drinking song. It begins with a slow waltz, but from bar 149 the entries become fugal, beginning with the main characters singing until, at bar 161, the chorus also joins in. The *alla breve* topic emerges between bars 183–191 and 207–221, adding to the hymnal effect of this mostly *pianissimo* tutti section.

The use of the waltz here – and the appearance of the *Fledermaus* waltz in the ballet that follows – becomes significant when considering the dance as the symbol of Viennese identity. In both these situations, the waltz accompanies text extolling the virtues of drink – in the first, it is implied by the feeling of goodwill to all that is the direct consequence of too much champagne, and the camaraderie that leads to drunken rounds which were often bawdy and lascivious.[36] In the second, however, the text is more blatant – "Liebe und Wein gibt uns Seligkeit" (Love and wine give us bliss) – and the waltz is preceded by national dances from Spain, Russia, Scotland, Bohemia and Hungary until the Austrian dance is performed by the guests themselves, rather than the dancers. The fact that the national dances were considered entertainment to be performed by employees (the ballet girls), whereas the waltz is danced by the guests themselves, highlights the class distinctions present here. The guests consider the national dances rustic, peasant, low-class affairs, but the Viennese waltz is associated with the aristocracy (society balls) and therefore danced only by them. Prince Orlofsky's call to dance (bars 512–515) separates the dances, providing an introductory fanfare to the Austrian section which serves as a dismissive act to the ballet girls and, as such, the national entertainment. This confirms the perceived status of the waltz as the Austrian national dance, and, combined with the class associations, the hedonistic implications of the topic seems to confirm that Strauss is trying to convey a satirical message to the audience. This could be due to his treatment after the revolution as he spent a good deal of time repairing the damage to his relationship with the court after his time on the barricades, leading him and his brother Josef to compose *Vaterländischer Marsch* of 1859 which contained quotes from his father's works the *Radetzky-Marsch* and the *Kaiserlied*.[37]

In Straus's *Ein Walzertraum* in addition to the love song performed by Niki to Vienna, the only other waltzes that appear in the operetta illuminate Niki's unfaithful acts: leaving the Princess to hear the Viennese singers with

Montschi and as he woos Franzi, the orchestra leader. What emphasises the waltz's unethical association is the topics it is placed beside in the narrative. In the Act One finale, Helene speaks truthfully to Niki about whether he loves her and her song is underscored by a gavotte integrated by pastoral allusions, such as an oboe drone at the start, wind melodies throughout and a horn fanfare to finish. There is also a moderate 6/8 section with a bassoon drone under a woodwind melody. The pastoral connotations integrated in the high-class gavotte suggest Monelle's heavenly pastoral topic, the idealised version of a simple idyllic paradise. Helene, the topic suggests, is offering him that paradise while simultaneously demonstrating her rural naivety and, Monelle posits, as it highlights the city dwellers' attitude of superiority over the peasant/rural population it sub-textually colours Niki with that same attitude, evoking the listeners' sympathy for Helene. This shows that *who* is singing is just as important as *what* they are singing about. The opening of Act One in *Die Fledermaus* offers an example of the high/low-class juxtaposition from the lower class viewpoint. It begins with the pastoral topic, in this case a rustic pastoral signified by a simple melody, bird call, a horn drone and triplet rhythm, however, rather than the heavenly pastoral signified it is an 'evocation of brute peasantry'.[38] At this point, it is a low-class singing teacher and a maid who are on stage, but when the maid Adele receives a letter from her sister inviting her to the ball a high-class topic – the ball theme polka – begins to play.

However, this high-class topic is still overlaid by low-class pastoral signifiers (associated with the low-class characters) such as the birdcall accompanied by the clarinet drone (bars 39–42) and the cadenza that introduces her character at bar 38 imitating a bird's song. The significance of the inflection of the pastoral allusions onto the urban polka is multivalent. Superficially, it merely continues the pastoral illustration of the low-class characters while introducing the ball theme that is the focal point of the operetta. Subjacent to this, the combination of the bucolic pastoral and the sophisticated ball theme opening the first act immediately presents the main storyline to the audience: the conflict between the classes, but without inducing an empathic response to the characters as is evoked in *Ein Walzertraum*. In fact, if any response is articulated it is of an immediate aversion to the lowbrow characters that are planning to dupe their superiors.

VERISMO AND THE DOUBLE IN LEHÁR'S *DIE LUSTIGE WITWE*

The topical narrative of *Die Lustige Witwe* (1905) reveals the transfer from escapism in Strauss's *Die Fledermaus* to the depiction of reality, in that rather than the narrative revealing a satirical subtext such as the high-/low-class division it follows almost exactly what is expressed in the text. The opposition seen so much through Johann Strauss II's and Oscar Straus's music, between upper and lower classes and rural and urban, is here, it seems, replaced by what is revealed to be simply a love story. That is not to imply that either the plot or the accompanying music is simplistic, but rather that they reflect Richard Traubner's suggestion that 'Lehár opted not for the galloping foolery of Offenbach and his Parisian and Viennese followers but for the heady romanticism of verismo composers like Puccini. [. . .] [He] was ultimately responsible more than any other composer for changing the course of Viennese operetta from its original dependence on satire and fantasy to romantic sensibility'.[39]

The term "verismo" describes realism in opera. A style developed in the 1870s in Italy, it includes compositions such as Pietro Mascagni's *Cavalleria Rusticana* (1889). Its stories typically followed people of the lower classes, moving away from the mythological or royal subjects of previous operas, and often using gritty storylines with unhappy endings. In this sense, *Die lustige Witwe* is not typically veristic; although its characters are not royal they are from within the upper echelons of their respective governments, and there is no real unpleasantness in the plot. What Traubner refers to, therefore, is the lack of contradiction between the music and the libretto. Lehár has used the music to echo the text, validating the characters' emotions and actions, and enhancing the audience's understanding of the drama, rather than adding other levels to it; Matteo Sansone describes this as the 'total consistency of form and content', that is, the topics present within this operetta are closely linked with the dramatic action.[40] Where in *Die Fledermaus* a song about how a wife would miss her husband while he was in jail is accompanied by an upbeat *schnell-polka*, here the romance topic accompanies a love song, a cavalry march illustrates a "silly cavalier" and a mazurka emphasises the Balkan nationality of the main characters.

Thus, it is the music rather than the libretto that demonstrates the verismo qualities of this operetta. Both Bernard Grun, in his biography of Lehár, and Richard Traubner, in his history of operettas, note that instead of the libretto describing a specific reality, it is instead a reflection of its period:

> Because toasts here dissolved in chansons, and mass demonstrations in vocal ensembles. Because castles turned into little arbors, the head of state suddenly appeared as 'silly, silly, cavalier', and the suffragette as siren of the ball. Because concern with scientific and technical problems made way for the study of women, women, women; the Pomp and Circumstance march for the waltz of silent lips and whispering violins. Because, in fact, all melancholy and solemnity turned triumphantly into sparkling exuberance.[41]

In addition to the "intoxicating glamour" of *fin-de-siècle* Vienna, the dramatic plot set out by the musical and textual narrative reflects the contemporary political issues inherent in the dissolving empire, for example, the friction between Austria and the Other countries, and the economic downturn.[42] Pontevedro is commonly thought of as a thinly veiled reference to the Balkan state of Montenegro, for various reasons including the use of the names Baron Zeta, whose surname is the name of a river in Montenegro, and an old name for the South of Montenegro; and Danilo, who takes his name from a Montenegrin Prince.[43] Moreover, the original Danilo costume was the full regalia of the Crown Prince of Montenegro.[44] However, other nationalities are also present, creating ambivalence within the Pontevedran identity. The topical language, that is the topics that are actually titled in the score (polonaise, mazurka etc.), are associated with Poland, Czechoslovakia, Russia and Hungary. The placement of the mostly Polish topics and the Eastern inflections suggest Pontevedro is both Poland and Montenegro; it is also similar to the fusion of the two names. The consequent duality of the national identity here introduces Freud's concept of the split personality, in which there is a second state of consciousness, a "double" consciousness. Claire Rosenfield suggests the double could be 'a juxtaposition of two characters; the one representing the socially acceptable or conventional personality, the other externalising the free, uninhibited self'.[45] Here, rather than there being two characters (although an argument could be made that Danilo and Camille respectively represent them), there are two distinct representations of character.

The son of a military bandmaster, Lehár travelled the Austro-Hungarian Empire as a child, collecting musical characteristics and folk songs from each place. At twelve, he studied composition under Dvořák, among others, at the Bohemian Conservatory of Music in Prague. As such, his music utilises the same nationalistic narrative types encountered in the previous chapter from Mahler and Zemlinsky. His musical narratives often place smaller Other nationalities in the position of an underdog to Austria, or more specifically Vienna, but none of Lehár's operettas demonstrate this more aptly than the plot of *Die lustige Witwe*. The Parisian (Western) characters portrayed in this narrative are morally underhanded: two are suitors after the widow's money, while another attempts to seduce a married woman. This view of the Parisians is demonstrated by a topical field containing marches, polkas and the *romanze*, while the Pontevedrian's topical field, including national topics, is shown as morally upstanding. 'Ich bin eine anständige Frau' The song itself is a contredanse, the Western dance topic forcing the serious subject of adultery into a light-hearted frame, while also confirming the high social status of the characters. The eastern topic is alluded to briefly as Valencienne realises the consequences of the proposal. An A♭ in the score gives the triplets a minor flavour to the words 'Ich kann nur verlieren, / und Sie nichts gewinnen'. (I can only lose, / and you win nothing). This links the national topic with ethics and morality and Western topics with unscrupulous behaviour from the beginning of the operetta.

The waltz is set against this dialogue as the signifier for real (ethical) love. Most significant are the oppositions throughout the operetta – Pontevedra/Paris, ethical/immoral, the respectable woman/the adulterous man, ballroom/Maxim's – but representing all of these oppositions are the relationship between the waltz and the mazurka, and the waltz and the march or polka. The mazurka represents not only the East, but a pragmatic naivety, particularly with regards to romance, as seen in Hanna's description of Pontevedrian men, and the wish of Baron Zeta that she marries a Pontevedrian for the fiscal good of the country. The march and polka represent the immoral gold diggers and adulterers of Western civilisation. The waltz is always set in opposition to one of these dances, acting as the point of repression or as a pivot between the immoral West and the naive East. It represents real, ethical love, exemplified most clearly in Danilo's actions. As a self-styled immoral man he frequents Maxim's, signified by the French can-can. The polka plays while he auctions Hanna's dance, but a waltz accompanies their dance and signifies the recognition of their feelings. Danilo's story of the prince and princess, in a way similar to Freud's dreams, uses an unrelated story to infer meaning to signify his own repressed emotions and is accompanied by a romantic waltz. Finally, the happy ending is also, without need of explanation, a waltz. As such, the waltz acts as the only true representation of love, in opposition to the falsity of marrying for money or practicality. This is in contrast to the way in which the waltz signified deceptiveness in the other two operettas, but similar to its signification in Schoenberg's Op. 16, which will be discussed later. Its signification of ethical behaviour is consistent with Schoenberg's view of the superiority of Viennese civilisation, and the struggle to impose authenticity and moral accountability on the Viennese people.

Through the use of the narratological method, and by adapting Edward Cone's "blind first read", the way in which the waltz was used by light music composers before and after the turn of the century can be understood, as well as how topics evoke empathic reactions to the narrative, here particularly sympathy or aversion to the characters using nationalist and pastoral inflections. The use of the waltz in *Die Fledermaus* is a signpost for immorality, but also an in-situ description of the associations the higher class Viennese saw the dance and the ballrooms. It depicts drinking, dancing, lasciviousness, wine, lust and laughter as well as the sense of "Brotherhood and Sisterhood" alcohol often eventually endorses. The suggestion in *Ein Walzertraum* that being Viennese is a characteristic that can be affected suggests awareness that only hindsight can bring and that

Strauss II, in 1874, did not have. Lehár, on the other hand, follows the critical modernist movement, in literary and musical narratives if not in musical style. *Die lustige Witwe* embraces a verismo style rendering of two love stories that run concurrently creating a narrative that expresses Freud's concept of the double while also opposing the minority nationalities (low class but principled) with the western nationalities, represented by the high-class but immoral Parisians. Finally, Lehár's use of the waltz concretes its move from decadent signpost to the signifier of real love and honesty through his representation of Danilo's character and his relationship with Hanna. In the next chapter this change will be shown in the "art" music of Mahler, Berg and Zemlinsky, in texted songs and operas as well as non-texted symphonies and tone poems.

NOTES

1. The terms "light" and "art" music do not imply a hierarchy in composition, although that is what Hanslick intended when he used the terms. Rather in this case they are used only to distinguish between the two as they would have been seen contemporaneously as the Viennese population would have been far more engaged with the operettas and Strauss's waltzes as they would have with Schubert, Mahler and Zemlinsky.

2. "Preface", *Music and Narrative since 1900*, eds. Michael L. Klein and Nicholas Reyland (Bloomington: Indiana University Press, 2013), ix.

3. Carolyn Abbate, "What the Sorcerer Said", *19th-Century Music* 12, no. 3 (Spring, 1989); Jean-Jacques Nattiez and Katherine Ellis, "Can One Speak of Narrativity in Music?" *Journal of the Royal Musical Association* 115, no. 2 (1990).

4. Lawrence Kramer, *Music as Cultural Practice 1800–1900* (Berkeley, CA: University of California Press, 1990), 187.

5. Lawrence Kramer, "Musical Narratology", *Indiana Theory Review* 12 (1991): 155.

6. Edward T. Cone, "Three Ways to Read a Detective Story—or a Brahms Intermezzo", *Georgia Review* 31 (1977): 554–574 and "Schubert's Promissory Note: An Exercise in Musical Hermeneutics", *19th-Century Music* 5 (1982); Fred Everett Maus, "Music as Drama", *Music Theory Spectrum* 10, 10th Anniversary Issue (Spring, 1988) and "Music as Drama", in *Music and Meaning*, ed. Jenefer Robinson (New York: Cornell University Press, 1997).

7. J. Hillis Miller, *Reading Narrative* (Norman, Oklahoma: University of Oklahoma Press, 1998), 10.

8. Paul Cobley, *Narrative* (New York: Routledge 2001), 6.

9. Michael Klein, "Chopin's Fourth Ballade as Musical Narrative", *Music Theory Spectrum* 26, no. 1 (Spring 2004): 26.

10. Byron Almén, *A Theory of Musical Narrative* (Bloomington: Indiana University Press, 2008), 40.

11. Anthony Newcomb, "Schumann and Late Eighteenth-Century Narrative Strategies", *19th-Century Music* 11, no. 2 (Autumn, 1987): 164; Eero Tarasti, *A Theory of Musical Semiotics* (Bloomington: Indiana University Press, 1994); Almén, *A Theory of Musical Narrative*.

12. Almén, *A Theory of Musical Narrative*, 21.

13. Cone, "Three Ways to Read a Detective Story".

14. Cone, "Three Ways to Read a Detective Story", 79.

15. Gerard Genette, *Narrative Discourse: An Essay in Method*, trans. Jane E. Lewin (New York: Ithaca, 1980); Seymour Chatman, "What Novels Can Do That Films Can't (and Vice-Versa)", *Critical Inquiry* 7, no. 1 (Autumn, 1980) and his book on narrative, *Story and Discourse: Narrative Structure in Fiction and Film* (New York: Ithaca, 1978); Martin McQuillan, *The Narrative Reader* (New York: Routledge, 2000).

16. Chatman, "What Novels Can Do That Films Can't (and Vice-Versa)", 435–436.

17. Vera Micznik, "Music and Narrative Revisited: Degrees of Narrativity in Beethoven and Mahler", *Journal of the Royal Musical Association* 126, no. 2 (2001): 199–203.

18. Susan McClary, "The Impromptu That Trod on a Loaf: Or How Music Tells Stories", in McQuillan, *The Narrative Reader*, 168.

19. Ibid. See also Leon Botstein, "Modernism", in *The New Grove Dictionary of Music and Musicians*, 2nd ed., vol. 16, ed. Stanley Sadie and John Tyrell (London: Macmillan, 2001); and Christopher Butler, *Early Modernism: Literature, Music, and Painting in Europe 1900–1916* (Oxford: Oxford University Press).

20. McClary, "The Impromptu That Trod on a Loaf", 167.

21. Jann Pasler, *Writing through Music: Essays on Music, Culture, and Politics* (New York: Oxford University Press, 2007), 37.

22. Pasler, *Writing through Music*, 37.

23. Jonathan Kramer, *The Time of Music: New Meanings, New Temporalities, New Listening Strategies* (New York: Schirmer, 1988).

24. Pasler, *Writing through Music*, 39.

25. Nicholas Reyland, "*Livre* or Symphony? Lutosławski's *Livre pour orchestre* and the Enigma of Musical Narrativity", *Music Analysis* 27, nos. 2–3 (2008): 282.

26. Reyland, "*Livre* or Symphony?", 41.

27. Michael Klein, "Musical Story", in *Music and Narrative since 1900*, 4–5.

28. Klein, "Musical Story", in *Music and Narrative since 1900*, 5.

29. Klein, "Musical Story", in *Music and Narrative since 1900*, citing Pierre Boulez, "Schoenberg is Dead", in *Stocktakings from an Apprenticeship*, collected by Paule Thévenin, trans. Stephen Walsh (Oxford: Oxford University Press, 1991), 212.

30. Almén and Hatten, "Narrative engagement with Twentieth Century Music: Possibilities and Limits", 59–85 and Grabócz "Archetypes of Initiation and Static Temporality in Contemporary Opera", 101–124, both in Michael Klein and Nicholas Reyland, eds., *Music and Narrative since 1900* (Bloomington, IN: Indiana University Press, 2013).

31. Kramer, "Narrative Nostalgia: Modern Art Music off the Rails", in *Music and Narrative since 1900*, 165.

32. See, for example, Robert Hatten, *Interpreting Musical Gestures, Topics, and Tropes* (Bloomington: Indiana University Press, 2004); Almén, *A Theory of Musical Narrative*; Micznik, "Music and Narrative Revisited"; Anthony Newcomb, "Action and Agency in Mahler's Ninth Symphony, Second Movement", *Music and Meaning*, ed. Jenefer Robinson (Ithaca: Cornell University Press, 1997); Robert Samuels, *Mahler's Sixth Symphony: A Study in Musical Semiotics* (Cambridge: Cambridge University Press, 1995) and "Narrative Form and Mahler's Musical Thinking", *Nineteenth-Century Music Review,* 8 (2011): 237–254.

33. Robert Hatten calls the relationships between topics "tropes", discussing the interaction between a topic and its new context in linguistic terms, e.g. as metaphorical, ironic or synecdoche. Hatten's terms work more as linguistic similes for the terms used here, which are more direct and tend towards the musical analysis rather than a linguistic or semiotic analysis. (Robert Hatten, "The Troping of Topics in Mozart's Instrumental Works", *Oxford Handbook of Topic Theory*, 514–538; Robert Hatten, *Interpreting Musical Gestures*).

34. Crittenden, *Johann Strauss and Vienna*, 133.

35. Own translation.

36. For example, Mozart's *Bona Nox, Difficile lectu mihi mars* K. 559, "Leck mich im Arsch" K. 231.

37. Scott, *Sounds of the Metropolis*, 76.

38. Hermann Jung, *Die Pastorale: Studien zur Geschichte eines musikalischen Topos* (Bern: Francke, 1980), 144–51, quoted in Monelle, *The Sense of Music*, 191.

39. Traubner, *Operetta: A Theatrical History*, 244.

40. Matteo Sansone. "Verismo". *Grove Music Online. Oxford Music Online*. Oxford University Press. http://0-www.oxfordmusiconline.com.wam.leeds.ac.uk/subscriber/article/grove/music/29210 (accessed July 27, 2015).

41. Bernard Grun, *Gold and Silver: The Life and Times Franz Lehár* (London: W.H. Allen, 1970), 105.

42. Traubner, *Operetta: A Theatrical History*, 249.

43. Raymond Knapp, *The American Musical and the Performance of Personal Identity* (Woodstock: Princeton University Press, 2006), 22.

44. Grun, *Gold and Silver*, 116.

45. Claire Rosenfield, "The Shadow Within: The Conscious and Unconscious Use of the Double", *Daedalus* 92, no. 2 (1963), 328.

Chapter 5

The Development of the Uncanny Narrative

Although numerous analytical links have been made between Schoenberg and Freud, there are not known to be any direct personal links; other than having met and commissioned the *Erwartung* text from Marie Pappenheim (the sister of one of Freud's more infamous cases, Anna O.), Schoenberg was not known to have read any of Freud's works or met him directly. Reinhold Brinkmann suggests that the reason why this link between the two is continually made is 'the central idea of introspection as the primary figure of thought' which 'characterise[s] the origin and the structure both of Freud's psychoanalytical theory and of Schoenberg's atonal compositions'. Thus, he continues, 'with an identical social and historical accentuation, "Freud's Vienna" could also be named "Schoenberg's Vienna", just as philosophers rightly call it "Wittgenstein's Vienna" and art historians call it "Schiele's Vienna"'.[1] To augment this sociocultural analysis Brinkmann cites the psychoanalyst Bruno Bettelheim from his essay "Freud's Vienna":

> In Freud's time, the cultural atmosphere in Vienna encouraged a fascination with both mental illness and sexual problems in a way unique in the Western world – a fascination that extended throughout society. [. . .] The origins of this unique cultural preoccupation can be traced to the history of the city itself, but most especially to the concerns and attitudes foremost in the minds of Vienna's cultural elites just before and during the period in which Freud formed his revolutionary theories about our emotional life. [. . .]
>
> The greatest of Freud's works [*The Interpretation of Dreams*] is one of introspection; in it all interest is devoted to the innermost self of man, to the neglect of the external world, which pales in comparison to the fascination of this inner world. That this turn-of-the-century Viennese *chef d'oeuvre* was indeed the result of desperation at being unable to change the course of the external world and

represented an effort to make up this deficiency by a single-minded interest in the dark underworld, is attested to by the motto which Freud put at the beginning: Virgil's line: "*Flectere si nequeo superos, Acheronta movebo*" ("If I cannot move heaven, I will stir up the underworld instead"). This motto was a most succinct suggestion that turning inward toward the hidden aspects of the self was due to a despair that it was no longer within one's ability to alter the external world or stop its dissolution; that therefore the best one could do was to deny importance to the world at large by concentrating all interest on the dark aspects of the psyche.[2]

Brinkmann's view, then, harks back to that of Janik and Toulmin, cited in chapter 2, that the link between the various disciplines, particularly in this instance music and psychoanalysis, is 'that they *were* all going on in this same place at this same time'.[3] The artificiality of liberalism and moral values effected repression, particularly of sexual desires within the upper classes. Eva Weissweiler has argued that Pappenheim's libretto for *Erwartung* is essentially an attack on the repression of the upper classes, represented by the Woman. Breuer's analysis, she claims, supports her argument in his speculation that Anna O.'s hysteria resulted from her upbringing as a typical upper-class Viennese girl. Bryan Simms summarises:

> She had been assiduously protected from life, kept in a monotonous, sheltered family routine. But her intellect and curiosity about the world could not be suppressed, and her only outlet was through daydreaming, [. . .] [which] began to dissociate her conscious from her unconscious faculties, inviting traumatic events and emotions in her life to be repressed into the unconscious.

Simms concludes, however, that Schoenberg did not embrace this subtext, asserting that the basic subject of the opera is the representation of emotions heightened by fear.[4] It is a combination of the opposition to bourgeois rationalism and the portrayal of emotions which brings Schoenberg to the representation of the unconscious. In a letter to Ferruccio Busoni in 1909, Schoenberg stated that

> [i]t is *impossible* for a person to have only *one* sensation at a time.
> One has *thousands* simultaneously. And these thousands can no more readily be added together than an apple and a pear. They go their own ways.
> And this variegation, this multifariousness, this *illogicality* which our senses demonstrate, the illogicality presented by their interactions, set forth by some mounting rush of blood, by some reaction of the senses or the nerves, this I should like to have in my music.
> It should be an expression of feeling, as our feelings, which bring us in contact with our subconscious, really are, and no false child of feelings and 'conscious logic'.[5]

It was "conscious logic", then, that Schoenberg contested; the 'classical notions of beauty and refinement', that the 'affluent Viennese middle-class music lovers' retained.[6] Schoenberg's defence, Botstein claims, was 'his assertion of artistic integrity [which] assumed a nearly puritanical façade of ethical superiority', summarised by the composer himself in "Brahms the progressive":[7]

> Great art must proceed to precision and brevity. It presupposes the alert mind of an educated listener who, in a single act of thinking, includes with every concept all associations pertaining to the complex. This enables a musician to write for upper-class minds, not only doing what grammar and idiom require, but, in other respects lending to every sentence the full pregnancy of meaning of a maxim, of a proverb, of an aphorism.[8]

Schoenberg's statement unites the above strands of cultural context and topical narrative – his superiority is apparent in the assumption that only an "educated listener" with an "upper-class mind" can comprehend his music, and the expectation that his music works similarly to topical association, in that, for example, a waltz signifies a 3/4 dance *and* a satirical commentary on the Viennese elite.

The idea of Schoenberg referencing Freudian psychoanalysis within his early music is not a new one, having been previously discussed by scholars such as Alan Street, Alexander Carpenter and Michael Cherlin.[9] However, the thrust of the aforementioned arguments have focused on the textual representation of anxiety, such as in Carpenter's comparison between the libretto of *Erwartung* and early psychoanalysis, or uncanny allusions within the music as exposed through the relationship between the music and the text, such as Cherlin's analysis of the "uncanny moon". Indeed, Cherlin does outline one particular musical device not predicated on text, the time shard, indicative of a moment of stasis outside of, or other to, the temporal axis of the existing musical narrative. This device will be discussed in further detail, as it undeniably exists within the works considered here; nonetheless, a device which works within a moment does not a psychologically referential piece make.

In contrast to my predecessors, I intend to outline the uncanny as a narrative rather than a topic as although there are musical events that point towards the uncanny, they are often ambiguous outside of the narrative context and as such, in keeping with Mirka's definition of a topic outlined in chapter one, cannot be topoi themselves. In order to make a clear and concise argument I will explore the development of the uncanny in Schoenberg's works only in this chapter before demonstrating the narrative across other contemporary works in the later chapters. This will allow me to define the narrative's functional units and prove their occurrence in the musical as well as textual system before linking them to the signification of the waltz in later chapters. As such, through detailed analyses of selections from Schoenberg's texted and un-texted music, I aim to show that the Freudian constructs of the uncanny and the unconscious are represented not just in the text of *fin-de-siècle* works, but in a recurring and encompassing musical narrative present throughout the fifty years following the premiere of *Die Fledermaus* in 1874. By identifying signifiers and their signified within the topical narratives of works with word settings or a documented program (in particular *Gurrelieder* and opp. 1, 3, 5, 15 and 17) a specific set of signs emerge which connote certain aspects of the uncanny: the unconscious, or "second state" and the castration complex. When these signs then reappear in non-texted music (e.g. Schoenberg's op. 16, Webern's op. 21 and Mahler's Seventh Symphony) the relation between the imagery and the text is implied, the music then "means" the same and thus informs an uncanny musical narrative.

This is not the first description of the uncanny in music; Susanna Välimäki provides a comprehensive survey of musical psychoanalytic signification in her book *Subject Strategies in Music*, in which she observes the uncanny in Tchaikovsky's Symphony No. 6, "the Pathétique".[10] Categories of the musical uncanny range from figurations of automata and ventriloquism, such as in Abbate's *In Search of Opera* and Klein's *Intertextuality in Western Art Music*[11] to Wojciech Stepiań and Joseph Kerman investigation of ogres, trolls and other magical grotesques. Richard Cohn, Klein and Peter Smith highlight uncanny tonal repetitions and progressions in nineteenth-century instrumental music and Cherlin focuses on tonal quotations in non-tonal works.[12] There have been various examinations of figuring the double, such as Kramer's "other-voicedness"; David Schwartz examines Schubert's settings of Heine's "Der Doppelgänger" and "Ihr Bild"; and Kurth similarly juxtaposes music against poetic text, and poet (Heine) against composer (Schubert) and two "philosopher-critics" (Derrida and Nietzsche).[13]

Returning to Schoenberg, Ethan Haimo states 'with little warning and with minimal precedent, Schoenberg went from writing intensely motivic music to writing music in which there were no repeated themes, no recurrent motifs, and a complete avoidance of learned devices'.[14] Despite this, in his essay "A Self-Analysis" Schoenberg writes, 'May I venture to say that, in my belief, even works of my third period, as, for example [...] the *Five Orchestral Pieces*, Op. 16 [...] are relatively easy to understand today'.[15] Further, in 'Brahms the Progressive', he posits, '*form in Music* serves to bring about comprehensibility through memorability'.[16] That is, the repetition of a musical idea (such as those in "Mother Goose songs" or "popular music") makes it comprehensible to 'the minds of simple citizens'.[17] He continues,

[o]n the other hand, one cannot talk to a trained mind in Mother Goose fashion. [. . .] In the sphere of art-music, the author respects his audience. He is afraid to offend it by repeating over and over what can be understood at one single hearing.[18]

The meaning must therefore come from a different learned tradition, rather than 'recurrent motives and devices'. Schoenberg instead repeats affects and styles in such a way that he expresses meaning through musical characteristics, which is where topic theory becomes a useful analytical tool.

FROM OMBRA TO THE UNCANNY

Writing about French and Italian music in the eighteenth century, Clive McClelland characterizes the *ombra* topic as generally of a high style, slow, somber, and sustained. It uses flat minor keys and shifting tonalities with "unexpected dissonances" which are bold and chromatic.[19] The melody is exclamatory with repeated patterns (ostinato) in the bass, tremolo effects and repetitive figuration. The rhythm is restless and syncopated, often with "ponderous dotted rhythms and pauses". The instrumentation is unusual, frequently including trombones with dynamic contrasts, sudden outbursts, and unexpected silences.[20] These musical devices are designed to signify fear, usually of the supernatural, to the audience. Although concentrating on the music of the eighteenth century, McClelland also discusses the pervasion of the *ombra* topic into the nineteenth century. The signification of *ombra* at this point still leans heavily on the use of tonality; the composers utilize minor keys and dissonances occurring over dominant pedals. Other signifiers based on rhythm, timbre, and melody are indicated, particularly the dactylic rhythms found in Schubert's Lieder *Der Tod und Das Mädchen* and *In der Ferne*.[21]

These signifiers appear regularly in eighteenth- and early nineteenth-century compositions, but, when faced with the emancipation of dissonance that occurred around 1908 in Schoenberg's compositions, some became obsolete. Strong harmonic rules were abandoned as motivic development overtook tonal progression in importance; as such, progressions can no longer "surprise", or can only surprise, amounting to the same thing. Not only have some of the signifiers changed, the meaning of the *ombra* topic in this context has also altered. The topic here is no longer only associated with the external fears of the supernatural: rather, through its interaction with other topics in the same musical syntax, the fear and terror portrayed is an internal struggle, perhaps, with the advent of psychoanalysis, between the conscious and unconscious. The audience is no longer expected to experience fear vicariously through the characters on a stage, as in an opera, but are instead subject to an anxious representation of their own psyche. An internalization of expression that began with works, such as Mahler's *Kindertotenlieder*, a piece in which the father's pain at losing his child is illustrated in detail within the music. Hence, this piece does not present the fear of the unknown or the supernatural, but fear both personal and universally understood by all.

Extant examples of the *ombra* topic signifying the terrifying aspects of dark forests are provided by McClelland from eighteenth-century operas, such as Act 2 of Gluck's *Alceste*, and most influentially, the Wolf's Glen scene in Weber's *Der Freischütz* (1821) (figure 5.1).[22] Used in this fashion it indexes an atmosphere for the coming action, as well as a time and hints at the psychological aspect of the characters, as such, it is unsurprising that Schoenberg uses this topic in a similar fashion at the beginning of many of his pieces.

The programmatic string sextet, *Verklärte Nacht* Op. 4 (1899), is set to a poem by Richard Dehmel, the opening stanza of which begins: 'Zwei Menschen gehn durch kahlen, kalten Hain/ Two people walk through a bare, cold grove'. The *ombra* topic is signified by the *sehr langsam* tempo marking, low pedal notes in the second viola and second cello parts, and the descending dotted melody in the first viola and cello. To the *pianissimo* dynamic marking an *immer leise* [always quiet] instruction is added ensuring the ethereal atmosphere persists (figure 5.2). McClelland writes that the appearance of repeated notes (such as the pedals seen here) 'in a supernatural context provide a firm foundation against which other features are heard as disruptive [. . .] At a psychological level there may well be associations with a heartbeat or footsteps, both of which are linked to a fear response'.[23] As drones are used both to suggest the pastoral (most often as a ground below a folk dance such as a musette) and to create suspense in theatrical settings, particularly when played in low-ranged instruments and with tremolo, the combination brings to mind Dehmel's opening line: the "bare, cold grove". The similarity of *Verklärte Nacht's* descending line to that in Weber's Wolf Glen's scene helps to concrete the symbolization. In *Gurrelieder*, (1901), the

Figure 5.1 *The Wolf's Glen scene in Weber's* **Der Freischütz *(1821): No. 10. Finale, bb 1–7.*** (Leipzig: C F Peters, 1986).

Figure 5.2 *Schoenberg,* Verklärte Nacht, *bb. 1–9.* (Berlin: Verlag Dreililien, 1905).

ombra topic is found in the opening of "Ross! Mein Ross!" Waldemar's ride through the forest is accompanied by low minim pedal notes in the F trumpet parts – significant here because of their lower range and darker sound. A *forte* dotted melody is played in the bassoon and cello accompanied by syncopation in the oboe and string parts. At 30, where the text reads: 'Sieh! Des Waldes Schatten dehnen/ Look! The forest shadows spread', the string's tremolando minims drop in both octaves and dynamics. The woodwinds' descending chromatic semiquavers fall only from *ff* to *f* over the course of the bar, before the bass clarinet and cello take over with a low tremolando melody.[24]

Pelleas und Melisande (1902/1903) also opens in a dark, mysterious forest where Golaud finds Melisande, lost and weeping by a stream. Once again, the *ombra* topic is presented through the low instrumentation and the drone-like syncopated rhythms. A solo English horn and viola play the chromatic main theme, giving it a darker timbre than if played by the oboe, accompanied by chromatic movements in the cello and bassoon lines and semiquaver swirls in the second viola and first bassoon parts. When the fate theme emerges in the bass clarinet at bar 3 the other movements stop, the clarinet a lonesome fanfare warning of what's to come.[25] Similarly, a ponderous chromatic melody in the bass clef which settles into a pedal note three bars before the voice enters introduces the first song from *Das Buch der hängenden Gärten*, Op. 15 (1908/09) illustrating the opening lines 'Unterm Schutz von dichten Blättergründen / Wo von Sternen feine Flokken schneien / sachte Stimmen ihre Leiden künden/ Under the protection of dense leaves / where fine flakes of stars snow / gentle voices proclaim their suffering'.[26] The abrupt dynamic contrasts (the *pianissimo* marking, sudden *sforzando* and return to *pianissimo* at bar 5) are also in keeping with the *ombra* topical signifiers as outlined by McClelland above.

Finally, in *Erwartung* (1909), the first scene is set at the edge of a high, dark forest, into which the Woman is scared to enter. The steady bass line is absent, but other *ombra* signifiers are present. The introduction is fragmented; the oboe has a melody with wide leaps, the other instruments play restless and syncopated fragments, and remain very quiet but with sudden outbursts from the celeste and French horn in bar 1 and the bassoon in bar 4. There are also harsh articulations, such as the tremolo and *am steg* marking in the lower strings and flutter tonguing in the bassoon.

As noted above, the *ombra* topic traditionally signifies fear, or awe, of the supernatural and/or deities and religious rituals and processions. However, in each of the examples cited above from Schoenberg's compositions the textual imagery is, in comparison, mundane. Two people walk into a wood, meet in a wood, are meant to meet at the entrance to the wood. This means, therefore, that this unit of signification not only indexes the forest (and all the implied psychological atmosphere), but also it informs the listener of the location and circumstance, as Barthes tells us 'the informant always serves to authenticate the reality of the referent, to embed fiction in the real world'.[27] This topic used in this narrative locale (i.e. at the start of the narrative system) provides the listener an image rather than a vague concept, as palpable as the set on a stage when the curtains roll back. The relation to the eighteenth-century *ombra* topic is the natural fear felt when in a dark forest; it is a psychological fear, one stemming not from a fear of the supernatural, but of the unknown: it is created by our subconscious to explain Waldemar's "forest shadows". As such, to explain how Schoenberg transforms the *ombra* topic from a fear of the supernatural to a natural fear of the unknown, I will turn to Freud.

CASTRATION COMPLEX

In *The Interpretation of Dreams* Freud ascribes symbolic signification to forests, suggesting that 'the female organ [is] symbolized by a landscape' – what he terms the "geography of sex" – and that a dense forest symbolizes female pubic hair, a representation he uses to analyze the dream of Dora in his *Fragment of an Analysis of a Case of Hysteria*.[28] Simultaneously, the multiplication of the phallic symbol, the tree, signifies castration. When a young boy first sees the female genitals, it appears as a void surrounded by hair. He believes that the woman has been castrated; he thinks that, as he has a penis, then so does everyone else. When he sees his mother/sister without one he believes their penis has been removed and therefore that his may be too. In the essay 'The Medusa's head', Freud explains that

> the hair upon Medusa's head is frequently represented in works of art in the form of snakes, and these once again are derived from the castration complex. It is a remarkable fact, that, however frightening they may be in themselves, they nevertheless serve actually as a mitigation of the horror, for they replace the penis, the absence of which is the cause of the horror. This is a confirmation of the technical rule according to which a multiplication of penis symbols signifies castration.[29]

In addition to the signification of castration through multiplication of phallic symbols, the forest locale also signifies, to Schoenberg at least, a specific theme: that of two lovers in a moment of crisis.

In *Verklärte Nacht*, the woman is terrified of telling her new lover that she is pregnant with someone else's child; in *Pelleas und Melisande*, Melisande is frightened, lost, and confused until she meets Golaud. Similarly, in *Erwartung*, the Woman is delirious, searching for her lover who has failed to meet her, and in *Das Buch der hängenden Gärten*, a man mourns the loss of his lover. This theme is significant because among the validations Freud provides for the association between the loss of eyes and castration

– both used as a punishment for desiring the Mother – is the intimate connection Hoffmann paints in his story 'The Sandman', between the anxiety about Nathaniel having his eyes taken and thrown into fire and his father's death. The Sandman appears each time 'in order to interfere with love'.[30] He separates Nathaniel from his betrothed, his best friend (Clara's brother) and Olympia. Freud goes on to say that

> elements in the story like these, and many others, seem arbitrary and meaningless so long as we deny all connection between fears about the eye and castration; but they become intelligible as soon as we replace the Sandman by the dreaded father at whose hands castration is expected.[31]

In light of the forest's symbolization of the castration complex, the movement from the indirect experience of dread to an intimate sensation of anxiety suggests that the signification of the *ombra* topic is no longer traditional. The *ombra* is now in the realm of the uncanny, which, Freud writes, 'belongs to all that is terrible – to all that arouses dread and creeping horror; it is equally certain, too, that the word is not always used in a clearly definable sense, so that it tends to coincide with whatever excites dread'.[32] Freud then defines the concept of the uncanny further as 'that class of the frightening which leads back to what is known of old and long familiar'.[33] To demonstrate the latter of these definitions Freud explores the two meanings of the word *heimlich*. The primary meaning is "familiar", "native" or "belonging to the home".[34] The secondary meaning of the word *heimlich*, is to conceal, keep, or do something secretly, which is to say something kept hidden behind the doors of the home. This ambivalent meaning develops, moving from something secret, like an affair, to something that is withdrawn from knowledge, becomes unconscious, and finally to something which is hidden and dangerous, until finally it coincides with its opposite, *unheimlich*.[35] Freud's uncanny, then, does not signify the supernatural in the way the *ombra* topic does, it signifies the distortion of something "familiar", hiding something more sinister. Consequently, the topical narrative that the *ombra* topic initiates is not associated with the external fears of the supernatural but, with the advent of psychoanalysis, the fear and terror portrayed is a very human, internal struggle between the conscious and unconscious.

TIME SHARDS

To further establish the transformation of the *ombra* into the uncanny in Schoenberg, the works cited also often include what Cherlin terms "time shards". 'These', Cherlin states, 'involve the use of a steady pulse-stream, set in contrast to its immediate musical environment, and expressing a sense of altered, "uncanny" time [. . .] Time shards are uncanny, at least in a large part, because their regular pulse-streams evoke a ghostly presence of the way that time "used to go"'.[42] Cherlin is here referring to the music's 'tonal precursors', the 'ghostly presence' of which, in post-tonal music, can be invoked through 'musical rhetoric, motivic development, even orchestration'.[43] Klein and Abbate both discuss a similar, but extended, idea: that of a mechanical repetitiveness, an automaton-like figure within the music. In a passage from the Wood Dove's song in Schoenberg's *Gurrelieder* (approx figure 108 onwards) Klein points to the ostinato staccato triplets in the wind and harp – including the bass trumpet and alto trombone – a signifier of the uncanny in its "mechanical aspect".[36] If one then adds the walking bass (the imminent approach of footsteps McClelland outlines as an *ombra* signifier), the syncopated sigh motif in the bass clarinets and horns, the tremolo in the strings and the drone in the trombone the listeners are submerged in an uncanny atmosphere. Abbate identifies the same phenomena when discussing Schumann's *Carnaval*, she describes the dramatis personae as "mechanical dolls" and "undead life" concealed behind the carnival masks. Automata are fearful objects, "rightly hidden from sight".[37]

A comprehensible parallel can be drawn between Freud's outline of hypnoid states from his *Studies of Hysteria* and these periods of suspension.[38] Josef Breuer, the co-author of this book, describes the hypnoid state as a 'second consciousness' caused by 'psychical traumas' or 'any experience which calls up distressing affects such as those of fright, anxiety, shame or physical pain'.[39] This state can take the form of a physical reaction, such as an uncontrollable rage, an epileptic-like fit or a sudden inability to speak or move. In the case of Anna O., on which *Erwartung* is supposedly based, the analysand loses the ability to speak her native German and becomes almost completely paralysed. Freud similarly links paralysis to the castration complex in his fragment 'The Medusas Head'. Freud writes that 'The sight of Medusa's head makes the spectator stiff with terror, turns him to stone', thus further associating the hypnoid state and its symptoms with the uncanny.[40]

Breuer associates the hypnoid state with hypnosis and dreams that occur while the patient is awake, suggesting that if a person is prone to daydreaming this can then lead to that person developing hysterical symptoms:

> the subject's longing thoughts about his absent loved one create in him a 'rapt' state of mind, cause his real environment to grow dim, and then bring his thinking to a standstill charged with affect. [. . .] Once this has happened, the

hypnosis-like state is repeated again and again when the same circumstances arise; and the subject.[41]

The hypnoid state returns, owing, Breuer claims, to the reminiscence or memory of the cause of the hysteria: the traumatic event that caused the psychological wound.[42]

Therefore, when Cherlin posits the concept of 'uncanny time', the temporal interruption signifies another level of the uncanny narrative: the 'double conscience', or second state as Breuer refers to it.[43] Freud describes the repression of the unconscious thoughts and feelings by the conscience as 'investing the old idea of a 'double' [doppelganger] with a new meaning'.[44] In the case of hysteria the unconscious thoughts are what the patients believe would be unseemly reactions to the circumstances in which they find themselves. Their ego represses these reactions as it represses the urges of the id and superego therefore creating the 'split' or 'second consciousness'. The ostinato therefore represents the second state: a traumatic event precedes a period of delusion, of daydreaming, in which the music is removed from its teleological surroundings.

Erwartung provides a clear example of the representation of the unconscious time shard from bars 110–125 (figure 5.3). The Woman seems delusional at this point, as she exclaims 'ich habe solche Angst. Liebster, mein Liebster, hilf mir.../ I have such fear. Darling, my darling, help me...'. Preceded by a traumatic demi-semiquaver crescendo to a fortissimo chord, an ostinato begins as the Woman descends into this dream state. The ostinato ends and the Woman emerges from the repressed state as she realises 'er ist auch nicht da/ he is not there either', an ambiguous comment which could mean simply that she cannot find him, or that she knows he is dead, the recognition of which may indicate the end of her delusion. The ostinato reappears at bars 149–164. The Woman finds a bloody body, and as the music climaxes she grasps that it is her lover. At bar 160 an ostinato accompanies the Woman's efforts to ignore the body, but the moonlight shines on the 'schreckliche Kopf...das Gespenst.../ the horrible head... the spectre....'. She wishes it would disappear, as it did in the forest.

There are numerous other examples of the time shard and the symbolisation of the unconscious state in Schoenberg's works. In *Erwartung*, it is the death or betrayal of a lover which acts as a traumatic event, and similarly each example deals with lovers and begins with a traumatic event, often a short climax to a sudden *fortissimo* preceding a time shard. A (not exhaustive) list includes 'Warnung', Op.3, BB. 41–45; *Pelleas und Mellisande* Op. 5, figure 25 when Mellisande dreams of Pelleas, 'Verlassen', Op. 6, bb. 38–54 and *Gurrelieder*, 'Stimme der Waldtaube', figure 108–109.

Figure 5.3 *Schoenberg,* **Erwartung** *bb. 110 – 114, string parts and voice only.* (Wien: Universal Edition, 1916).

Figure 5.3 Continued.

NON-TEXTED TOPICAL NARRATIVE IN OP. 16, NO. 1.

Having identified comparable signifiers of the uncanny narrative in multiple texted pieces, it is now possible to understand the narrative of non-texted pieces when analogous signifiers are present. What follows therefore is an analysis of the first of Schoenberg's *Fünf Orchesterstucke*, Op. 16, 'Vorgefühle'. This piece begins with the *ombra* topic (figure 5.4), signified by the sparse texture and instrumental combination of cello and low woodwind, the diminished intervals and chromaticism (particularly evident in the clarinets, contrabasss clarinet and contrabassoon figures), the lack of a regular pulse and the shifting of speed. This shifting temporality is achieved not just by the move from *sehr rasch*, to *langsamer* and back, but also by the variety of note lengths employed in the first 6 bars giving the impression of a different tempo every couple of bars. The dotted quaver rest leading into figure 1 combines with the slower note lengths to accentuate the change to the slower tempo. At bar 10, the topic changes to the *ombra* topic signified by the change

The Development of the Uncanny Narrative 97

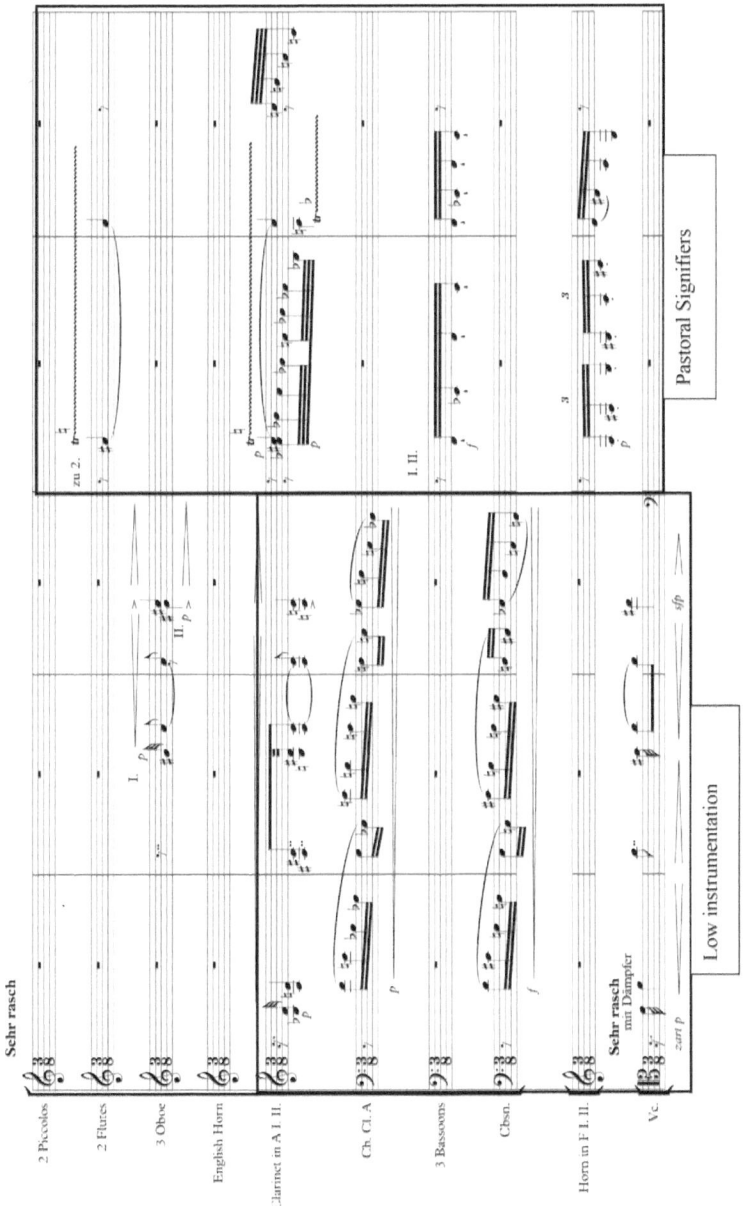

Figure 5.4 *Schoenberg, Fünf Orchesterstücke, 'Vorgefühle', bb. 1–14.* (Leipzig: C F Peters, 1912).

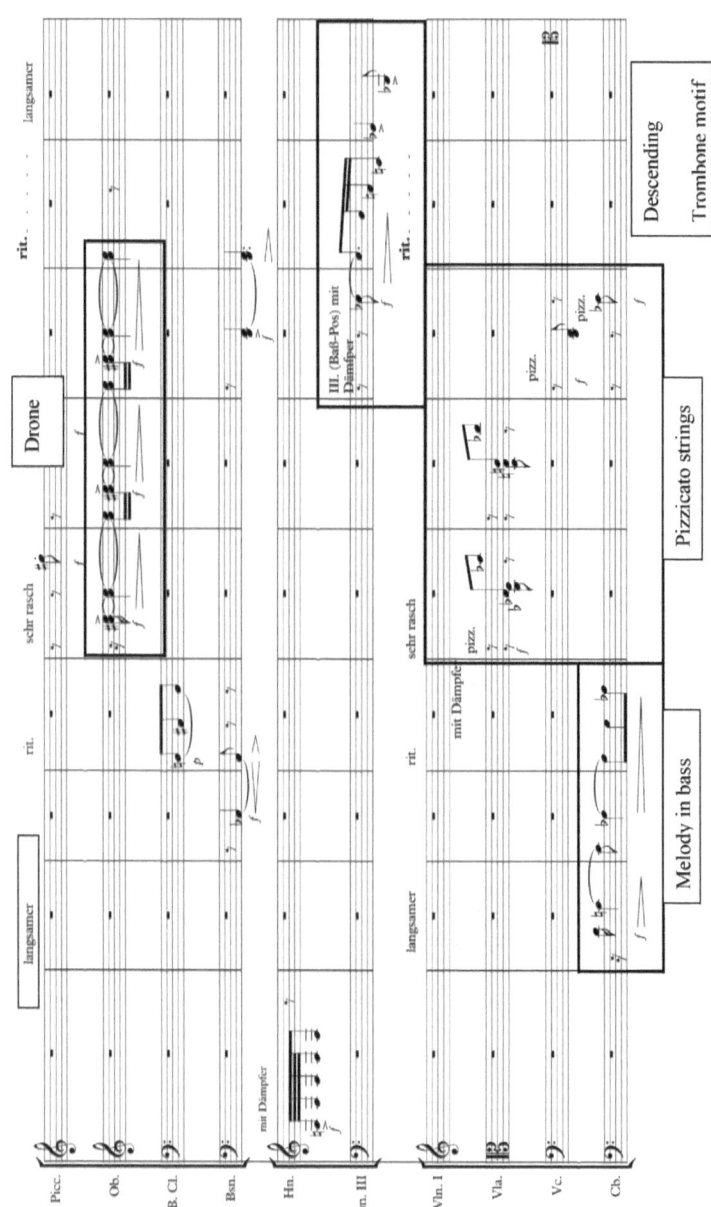

Figure 5.4 Continued.

in instrumentation: from the cello and lower woodwind, to tremolo strings and fast descending flurries in the oboe and clarinet. Particularly significant is the forte descending trombone *Hauptstimme* followed by low staccato demi-semiquavers in the trumpet. The dynamics become unpredictable, and the rhythmic pace changes, slowing down gradually under the instruction of *langsamer* markings and *rits*. Within these bars, then, the *ombra* signifies the multivalent forest: the location, the characters of lovers and the psychological uncanny. This is retrospectively confirmed at bars 24–25, when the traumatic event occurs: the descending forte semiquavers, which give way to the ostinato "second state" (figure 5.5). This fugue at bar 26 of the first piece, which signifies the learned style, takes the form of an ostinato-like quaver exposition starting in the cello. The exposition runs for 10 bars and is built on the intervals of the opening cello motive; the drone in the bassoons and bass clarinet contribute to the uncanny atmosphere while each new exposition entry is introduced by a violent outburst with strong dynamic contrasts. The learned style (signified by the fugue) particularly signifies the past; this topic, associated with composers such as J. S. Bach, and discussed as early as 1802 in Heinrich Christian Koch's *Musikalisches Lexicon*, is, as Elaine Sisman puts it 'the idea of an older, antiquated style dependent upon strict rules'.[45] Once again, there is the representation of 'the way time "used to go"', both symbolised by the fugue and the uncanny ostinato.

After 9 bars a solo cello figure descends into a mechanical repetition of the same three notes. Almost immediately, there is a restatement of the opening cello theme, now set in the oboe, clarinet and horn (hereafter termed theme A). Next, a restatement of the oboe and clarinet falling demi-semiquavers originally seen in bar 21 now appears in the flutes and clarinet in D (theme E). Elided with theme E is the syncopated repeated chords and quaver staccato leaps from bar 10 and the falling quavers – again with the same intervallic content as the inverted theme A – originally stated in bar 19. These restatements could be seen more as regurgitations. The 26 bar introduction acts as the "event" which the subject, or ego as Klein suggests, wishes to repress. The themes recur, spilling out of the subject's subconscious in a way similar to the dream images Freud uses to analyse his subjects. In Klein's discussion of the uncanny, he posits that 'in the wake of the uncanny, we may read narratives of the dissolution of subjectivity, the ego's heroic reintegration in face of that threat, or the ego's defiance in spite of it'.[46] In 'Vorgefühle', I propose it is the first of Klein's suggested narratives that is playing out. At first the restatements are whole lucid regurgitations of the original theme, but by bar 57 the ostinato dominates the texture and the regurgitations of the themes have retained enough of their characteristics to be recognisable, but altered enough for the narrative to be losing its lucidity.[47] Theme A and E are extended, E repeated three times at bars 60–62, and at 63 theme A is

100 Chapter 5

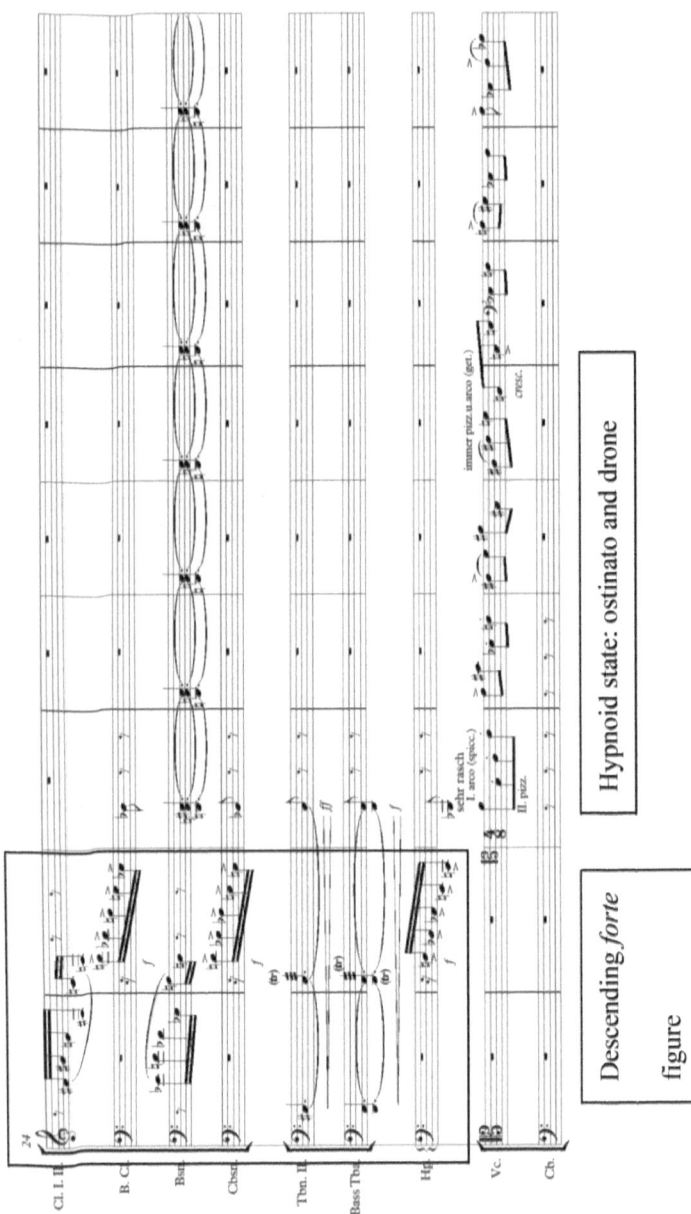

Figure 5.5 *Schoenberg*, **Fünf Orchesterstücke, 'Vorgefühle', bb. 24–32**. (Leipzig: C F Peters, 1912).

repeated twice, but rhythmically diminished and chromatically altered. These themes now sound grotesque: a parody of their former selves accompanied by repeated notes in the bass woodwinds and double bass parts as well as the ostinato played by almost the entire string section. The multivalent repetition at this point overwhelms the linear progression of the development of the themes so far, symptomatic of dissolution of the subject's subconscious and a signifier of the repression into a hypnoid state. The section climaxes with a repeated chromatic semiquaver figure that rises and falls providing an eddying, whirling motion that grinds to a halt with a *fff* cadence in the winds – containing all twelve tones – and a unison restatement of the fugue subject in the strings.

The climax precedes a bar and a half where only the low trombones and tuba sound a muted flutter tongue chord. The sudden quiet does not last long, however, as at bar 79 the bassoons, lower brass, strings and selected percussion re-enter with *fff* motifs, as if the subject continually strikes against a barrier to leave his unconscious state. While this section seems mechanical still, with its steady rhythmic tempo and walking bass, the motivic qualities endow the section with a more linear movement: it is progressing, not merely spinning in the same spot, like the current of the sea flowing beneath and around the static iceberg. The strings play the fugue subject, rather than repeating the three-note ostinato (although that is still present in the timpani and harp crotchets). The trombones and xylophones drive the movement with a rising crotchet motif with wider intervals than has been the norm up until now while the horns play a repeated syncopated rhythm based on a semitone interval, but again, at bar 86 the line begins to rise every bar. These two levels, the mechanical and the linear, create a narrative that gives the appearance of the subject attempting to return to the conscious, that is, to reverse the paralysis suffered while in the hypnoid state. It seems, however, that the subject fails. From bar 87 the trombones rising motif begins to fall in a repeated four-note series, the strings begin to repeat the first two bars of the fugue subject in a descending pattern and the ostinato in the harp augments from crotchets to minims before stopping alltogether. The strings dissolve into triplets in the lower strings only, and the forward momentum gradually disperses. Over the next 12 bars there are brief flourishes related to the opening themes – the semiquaver horn fanfare from bars 15–16; the demi-semiquaver repeated note motif that first appears in bar 6; the double bass theme from bars 7–9 – but they are accompanied by the re-emergence of the three-note ostinato in the harp.

The closing section begins at bar 113 with a *ppp* staccato quaver figure in the horn. The rocking motion of the semitone movement builds the suspense as the wind section (minus the clarinet) enters one by one every crotchet. An offbeat bassoon pattern struggles one final time at bars 120–124 before the subjects repressed state finally seems to overwhelm him as the last four bars consist only of the three-note ostinato and the drones that have been present throughout all but four bars since the ostinato began at bar 26. The presence of the drones throughout the subject's repression is significant. It provides a constant, letting the listener know the action is happening in one place, or one time, or involves only one character. It acts somewhat like the set on a stage, disappearing briefly only in the eddying current of passing time at bars 69–73, before it re-grounds us 5 bars before the climax at bar 77. There was a chance for reintegration into the conscious, it tells us, but that chance was lost. The uncanny, then, colours the entirety of this piece: the *ombra* topic sets the scene for the uncanny narrative, and the mechanical quality of the motivic regurgitations throughout the rest of the piece create the struggle of the character between his conscious and subconscious as he fights to emerge from, or perhaps not to enter in the first place, a hypnoid state. The 26 bar introduction sets out the character and the events, placing him in a specific situation – the dark forest with the sense of fear of the unknown that complements it – and introduces the events, the traumas, that his mind needs to repress. At first the subject tries to battle it, but by the climax at bar 77 the subject's unconscious dominates the ego and the mask of the uncanny is signified by the mechanical style of the music juxtaposed with the linear movement of the trombones at bars 83–87.

Within the other movements of Op. 16 there are three more significant occurrences of the hypnoid state: in the second piece, 'Vergangenes', the third, 'Farben', and the fourth, 'Peripetie'. The second piece is characterised by what Simms terms 'an unmistakable return to the earliest style of atonality'.[48] With allusions to D minor in the first and last sections of this ternary piece the singing style topic which begins the piece takes on a dirge-like quality, highlighted by the drones in the first three bars, the low pitch of the melodies and the overtly sparse texture – no more than five instruments at a time. These signifiers suggest a night-time pastoral topic; however, the legato style and melodic nature of the *Hauptstimme* lead to the conclusion that it is the singing style that is present here. The ambiguity between the presence of the pastoral and the singing style once again suggests that there is a character present within the forest, that the forest implies the psychological aspect of the narrative as much as, perhaps more, than the physical location. The singing style invokes the concept of a person – a song must be sung by someone – with the night pastoral signifying the forest.

The developmental B section, from bar 151, introduces seemingly new material, a characteristic melody containing either a quadruplet or sextuplet (figure 5.6).

Despite the new rhythmic groupings, the topical and intervallic content are familiar. The *Hauptstimme* (containing the quadruplet rhythms) are

Figure 5.6 *Schoenberg, Fünf Orchesterstücke, No. 2, bb. 151–154.* (Leipzig: C F Peters, 1912).

reminiscent of the slow lyrical lines from the first part of the A section, while the *Nebenstimme,* and interjecting cadenza passages in the flutes and clarinets (bars 156–7 and 165–9), resemble the short birdsong phrases of the second part. The intervallic content of the two themes, which has until now remained mostly within the confines of the major third, begins to develop to include fourths and fifths. Within the lyrical themes, however, this seems to be because the pitches have been displaced up or down an octave. If the pitch were to be replaced within the same pitch range as the rest of the melodic line the intervals would more closely resemble the original A section. This displacement of familiarity adds to the feeling of the uncanny, the sense that the material that is being presented is simultaneously familiar and unfamiliar (figure 5.7). By displacing these pitches climactic moments are fashioned, tensions are created and released through the wide leaps in the melody, particularly the rising lines in the E♭ clarinet and first violin at bar 162 which, after reaching the apex of the melodic arch, relinquish the melody to lower

Figure 5.7 *Schoenberg, Fünf Orchesterstücke, No. 2, bb.174–178.* (Leipzig: C F Peters, 1912).

instruments. The E♭ clarinet and violins give way to clarinets, oboe, cello and trumpet then to the bass clarinets, horns and bassoons. The first violins begin to climb again at bar 173, but interrupting their ascent suddenly at bar 175 is a celeste and flute ostinato.

The piece's momentum, caused by the intervallic development, abruptly stops and is instead held in a dream-like stasis for ten bars. The use of the celeste adds to the dreamlike quality, associated as it is with lullabies – and more recently dream sequences – as the overlapping, incessancy of the figure creates the sense of temporal suspension. These ten bars represent the hypnoid state, the period of time when the character is in a "hypnosis-like" or dream-like state. Bars 182–184 are the only instance in the piece where more than five instruments are playing rhythmically in unison until the dream dissolves at bar 184 with triplets, quadruplets and sextuplets all competing as the first violin and viola perform a demisemiquaver cadenza.

As suddenly as it appeared the dream disappears at bar 185 as a fugue once more drives the piece's momentum forward. The fugue now has another level of signification to it, that of the rational topic. The rational topic centres around the moralistic virtues displayed by the older generation of Viennese, the idea that emotions should be repressed in favour of morality and disciplined conformity. Classical forms, diatonic harmony, the learned style and the chorale style signify this topic, which is meaningful as the psychological trauma is seemingly "repressed" by its presence. This is similar to Freud's theories on civilisation. In his "Civilisation and its Discontents", Freud writes that the entry into civilisation comes at the cost of repressing human natural instincts, that to be accepted as part of society one must suppress all urges that do not conform. Once again, this links with the castration complex, as, according to Freud, one of the first instincts a boy must suppress is the desire to kill his father, whom he believes will castrate him as punishment for desiring his mother.

Set against this momentum, however, is another ostinato in the second clarinet and first bassoon. The earlier lyrical quadruplet motif is now set alongside a memento of that dream, the ostinato all that remains of the previous episode, a lingering reminder of the repressed trauma. The interrupted climax begins to build again, reaching its peak at bar 194 in not only the high pitch range and utilisation of large intervals, but also the orchestration. For the first and only time within this piece all the instruments play simultaneously for four bars. However, the singing style that has pervaded the rest of the piece remains, signified by the *Hauptstimme* marking on the first violin part, the statement of the fugal subject at bar 190 leading the other instruments, nearly all of which are marked *Nebenstimme* and therefore seen as accompanying the violins. After the climax the fugue dissolves, but the ostinato remains, a reminder of the unconscious.

The A section returns at bar 205 with a solo statement of the main theme in the oboe over a horn drone, reconfirming the pastoral signifiers of the original A section. The second part of the A section then returns with stretto entries of the main lyrical theme, the quadruplet fugue subjects all appearing in the same order as they appeared earlier in the piece. The "dream" ostinato in the celeste and flutes and a drone in the cor anglais provide a cohesive background over which each of these themes can be heard. The hysteric has returned to his normal life, but the traumatic event still hovers in the background.

The third piece, "Farben", is an extended dream sequence, a slow-moving fugue in the outer parts with a faster moving, sensibility-style centre. As discussed in chapter 1, Matthew Head posits that '[c]onsciousness, subjectivity, and reflexivity are key terms in conceptualising sensibility, which referred not simply to a capacity to be moved but also to an awareness of that capacity and its moral obligations'.[49] It served as an early defence of sense (in this instance referring to the senses and emotions) over reason and rationalism, and was therefore a reaction to the "strict" or "learned" style.[50] As the fugue is a subset of the learned style, the signification of anti-rationalism in the central section of this central movement gives the listener an advanced diagnosis of the subject's psyche: the rejection, or struggle against, societies constraints and morals, or, considering the era in which it was written and the precursor of the uncanny in Mahler's music (chapter 6), the struggle against the staid monarchy and its pre-war stagnancy.

Burkhart demonstrates that the void created by the insertion of an emotionally unstable section into a linearly driven fugue is not only present in regards to the temporal stasis of the piece when compared to the surrounding pieces, but also within the piece itself. In his analysis of the fugue he shows that the first and eleventh chords are held for several bars; 'thus', he posits, 'the statement

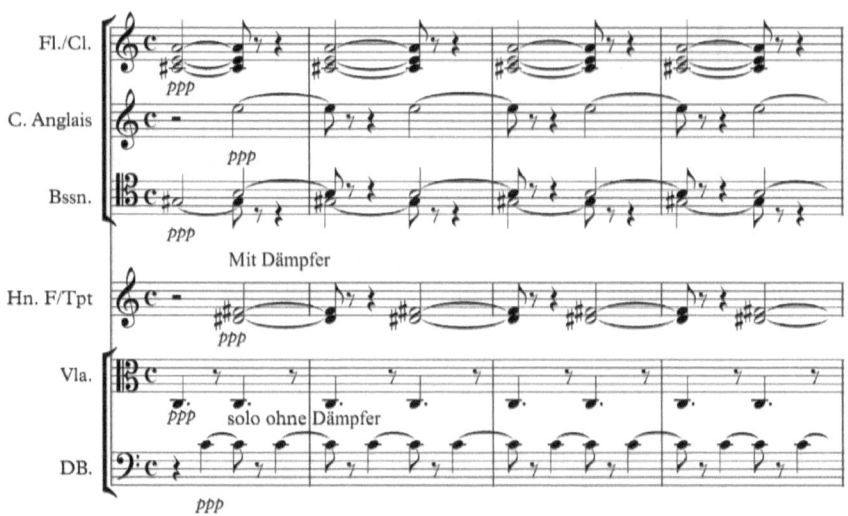

Figure 5.8 *Schoenberg, Fünf Orchesterstücke, No. 3, bb. 1–5.* (Leipzig: C F Peters, 1912).

of the canon is set off by absence of motion at its beginning and end'.[51] The third piece, therefore, creates a void at the centre of the work (figure 5.8). With regards to the castration complex this is a significant image, symbolising the void in the centre of a female's genitals, the space where the penis should be. The principal representation of the primal trauma is now placed at the centre of both the work and the musical representation of the uncanny.

The pastoral topic is present here, as indicated by the title often given it: 'Summer Morning by a Lake'. The overlapping rhythmic nature of the chord creates a constant movement, similar to the relentless movement of a river, as seen for example in Mahler's 'Des Antonius von Padua Fischpredigt'. This piece, more than any other, provides the link between the *Fünf Orchesterstücke* and *Erwartung*.

The combined symbolism of feminine sexuality and the scene of the lake are synonymous with the events that precipitated Dora's anguish, the inappropriate sexual proposal by Herr K, the husband of the woman who nursed her father while he was ill, and with whom he had an affair. In *Erwartung* it is Dora's dreams which are interpreted in the music – the burning house and the woods – while here the original real event is figured. This suggests that the connection between *Erwartung* and the *Fünf Orchesterstücke* is less than coincidental, the five pieces representing an event that led to the case of hysteria, diagnosed through the succeeding monodrama.

The fourth piece, 'Peripetie', demonstrates the acceleration of the changes between the normal/conscious and hypnoid/unconscious states of the hysteric through sudden changes in instrumentation and an alternation between the *tempesta*-inflected fanfare topic and the *Lied* style. 'Peripetie' begins with inflected fanfares: the dynamics and style of attack are a marked contrast to the strictly controlled second piece. This piece uses the instrumentation in blocks of colour to create demarcated characteristics by which the fanfares are presented. The woodwind uses wide interval leaps with a traditional triplet form, the trumpets and trombones play a semiquaver chromatic wedge figure and the trumpets and upper strings a demisemiquaver repeated chord, echoed at a slower pace by the upper woodwind. It is the horn triplet ostinato-style fanfare at bar 267 which is marked as the *hauptstimme* suggesting that this fanfare topic signifies the nobility and chivalry associated with the hunt call as much as the call to war, which is signified by its association with the military and *tempesta* topics. The association with the hunt topic here links the fanfare section with the calmer, but still dark pastoral style, signified by the horn drone and the chromatic bassoon accompaniment to the clarinet melody beginning at bar 271. It also once again highlights the desire to conform to the morals of the civilised world. Given the limited use of the *hauptstimme* in this piece – emphasising only one instrument at a time, rather than several as in the previous pieces – and the soloistic treatment of the themes in the calmer periods, this piece appears to be in the *Lied* style. This gives the piece a personal atmosphere, a feeling of internalisation in which the calmer solo parts seem to represent a solo voice, one person, whose emotional control slips and returns to create the rondo form of the piece. With each return of the stormy fanfare ostinato the person seems to have less control.

As detailed above, the first section, from bar 265–270, splits into clearly separated blocks of colour. The third section mirrors the first section initially, with bars 283–299 beginning with three blocks, the woodwinds and strings forming one block, the brass forming the other. However, the blocks quickly disintegrate, with the texture thickening as the instrumental sections become independent of each other while continuing to work cohesively within themselves. The best example of this comes between bars 292–298 where the three different types of fanfare play simultaneously, their frequency increasing to a climax at bar 299.

The *Lied* style attempts a return at bar 299 but the dynamic attacks and the continuation of the fanfare topic suggest that the control has slipped completely as, despite the sudden change in orchestration, the calmness does not return. From bar 312 instruments enter canonically, causing the orchestration to thicken gradually. However, despite the stabilising structural implications of the canon, the lack of a uniform time between entries – some have 1 beat, others 2–3 – denies the stabilising effect until even the introduction of ostinato figures at bar 323 fails to steady the anxiety that is being projected, as eventually four different ostinatos are running concurrently.

THE ANXIETY OF ALIENATION, OR 'ENTRY INTO CIVILISATION'

Bryan Simms posits that the final piece, 'Das obligate Rezitativ', is a waltz, Alan Street identifies it as the earlier *Ländler*, but if either of these interpretations is correct (and there are certainly signifiers present which would indicate they are) then the triple time dance has been distorted almost beyond any point of clear-cut recognition.[52] Certainly just from listening to the piece it is hard to pick out the waltz time or the entries on the second beat which would signify the *Ländler*; the strong beats on which the dance is traditionally built are obscured by the two-bar hypermeter of the small motivic line. However, from bar 42 in particular, the waltz signifiers subsume any *Ländler* signifiers. Employing a solo violin melody along with the solid dotted crotchet beats in the clarinets, trombones and cellos (rising an augmented sixth: the Viennese interval associated with the yodel) combined with the violins, flutes and bassoon figures starting with a semi-quaver rest it creates a singing melody with an oom-pah-pah waltz accompaniment. Schoenberg juxtaposes the waltz with the sensibility topic which evokes emotional tensions and releases using dynamics and rising and falling lines. The appoggiatura, which is a mark of this topic, is obviously moot in such an atonal piece. However, the constant tension and release that is the mark of the suspension is created with dynamics, particularly quick crescendo and decrescendo; rhythm, using dotted rhythms; and rests, so that the instruments come in on the off-beat, and sigh motifs coupled with wide leaps up that emphasise the higher note. The association of the sensibility topic with the middle-class chamber style suggests that it is the waltz, the more civilised of the two dances, which is presented; however, there is no certainty, which in itself is significant.

As in 'Farben', the waltz signifies Viennese society; the *Ländler* signifies the peasant dance, the rustic version of the triple dance, before it became civilised. The dissolution of the dance's rhythmic and harmonic signifiers therefore symbolise the character's psychological state in two ways. First, the liquidation of the dance's strong beat, the loss of a steady and secure base rhythm symbolises the loss of the character's conscious ability to order and control his thoughts/unconsciousness. Second, it represents the uncanny in the same way the rational topic did in the second piece. The repression of the uncivilised *Ländler* by the civilised waltz symbolises the man's entry into civilisation at the expense of the repression of his simpler, freer life, the liquidation of the waltz symbolising the dissolution of that society in the decline of the monarchy. The obligation in the title could then refer to the obligation of conforming to societal rules, the repression of basic human instincts. The dissolution of the dance's signifiers, combined with the interaction of the two dances with the sensibility topic, represents the character's total loss of control; the affected normalcy needed to ingratiate oneself into society has dissolved, leaving him alienated. As such, this signification is multivalent. On one level it represents the subject's status within his society: that of an alienated Other, perhaps because of the composer's Jewish faith, or more generally the concept of alienation that pervaded Vienna as the different countries (Czech, Hungarian, Bohemian etc) vied for equality. In this regard, the waltz and the *Ländler* form a relationship akin to Freud's "double". The waltz represses the *Ländler*, the symbol of the lower classes and rural Other nationalities, but the similarity of the signifiers for each dance mean that they are simultaneously present. On another, more personal level, this could symbolise the loss of the character's sense of belonging to his chosen society, that of the Viennese musical circle.

Schoenberg felt he was becoming isolated from the modern composers he admired because of his new methods. He looked for support from Richard Strauss, who then remarked to Alma Mahler, '[i]t would be better for him to shovel snow than to scrawl on music paper'.[53] The inflection of the waltz by the sensibility topic supports both these levels of signification. The sensibility topic denotes a personal emotional impression, supporting the interpretation that the character is in isolation, an interpretation also supported by the title 'Das Obligate Rezitativ'. A recitative is a solo vocal line with continuo accompaniment that traditionally connected the arias of an opera or oratorio, pushing on the dramatic action. In the eighteenth century the recitative was often accompanied by the orchestra and became more elaborate. This device was used to illustrate 'moments of intense dramatic crisis (disasters, irreconcilable decisions, general stress), mental confusion (particularly madness), magic scenes and other suitable moments'.[54] It therefore seems appropriate that Schoenberg chose this title for this piece, in which 'mental confusion', or hysteria, has completely taken over the character. He has not, however, used that term precisely; rather, he has called it "The Obligatory Recitative". In melodic terms, the obbligato is a musical line that is in some way indispensible, but it can also indicate an obligation to something, a self-imposed duty. In this case, this refers once again to Schoenberg's sentiment that his "destiny" has forced him towards his compositional style.

The traditional *ombra* topic relies to a certain extent on tonality, specifically the subversion of harmonic expectation. With the advent of the emancipation of dissonance came a change in signifiers, and subsequently a transformation in the signified itself. Where the eighteenth-century *ombra* topic represented the fear of the supernatural, the move towards a more private signification in the nineteenth century led to the topic signifying an internal expression of anxiety. This personalisation of fear parallels the concept of the sublime, which Kant describes as a duality of perception between the attractive and the repugnant. The intimate sensation of anxiety, however, also denotes the psychoanalytic theories of Freud, in particular the uncanny.

Alexander Carpenter, who suggested that this work is a representation of Schoenberg's neurosis owing to his wife's affair, grouped the *Fünf Orchesterstücke* under the heading of the psychoanalytic. Others, such as Friedheim and Street, suggest it was a reaction to his alienation from contemporary composers owing to his new compositional method. The scholars agree, however, that there is a strong link between the work and Freud's theories of hysteria, dreams and the uncanny.

The topical narrative of the *Fünf Orchesterstücke* reveals a correlation with the castration complex, signified by the representation of the forest, and the link between this and the plot of distressed lovers – suggesting that Carpenter's theory that the work denotes Schoenberg's marital problems is possible. The use of ostinatos and repeated figures, Cherlin's "time-shards", symbolise hypnoid states and introduces the concept of the double or second consciousness. The opposition of these states with the rational topic suggests a parallel conflict, that of man's struggle to repress his natural instincts in order to enter into civilisation, a narrative demonstrated particularly in the fifth piece. In this finale, civilisation is represented by the waltz, the dissolution of which is combined with the sensibility topic to represent on one level the anxiety of the character as he is alienated from society by his obligation to his composition methods – his "forced destiny". On a larger level, it symbolises the different nationalities feeling of being the Other, their alienation from the central government and therefore their separation from the Viennese "Society" of government and empire.

The duality presented throughout this work is, therefore, not only within the concepts of the split consciousness, or the doppelgänger, but also in the anxiety presented by the dramatic action of the narrative. Both readings by Carpenter and Street et al – that it represents Schoenberg's marital problems or his lack of musical acceptance – are apparent within this work, neither subsuming nor overbearing the other. What is clear, however, is that with the release of the tonal structure and the internalisation of fear and anxiety an uncanny narrative is now figured within this work. That it is definitive or unique, however, is certainly not true as will be demonstrated in the next chapter and in the analysis of Mahler's symphonic Scherzos.

NOTES

1. Reinhold Brinkmann, 'Schoenberg the Contemporary: A View from Behind', in *Brand,* Juliane and Christopher Hailey, ed., *Constructive Dissonance: Arnold*

Schoenberg and the Transformations of Twentieth-Century Culture (Berkeley: University of California Press, 1997), 196–197.

2. Bruno Bettelheim, *Freud's Vienna and Other Essays* (New York: Alfred A. Knopf, 1990), 3–17, and 14–15, quoted in Reinhold Brinkmann, 'Schoenberg the Contemporary', 196.

3. Janik and Toulmin, *Wittgenstein's Vienna*, 18.

4. Eva Weissweiler, "'Schreiben Sie mir doch einen Operntext, Fräulein'", *Neue Zeitschrift für Musik* 145 (1984), 4–8, in Bryan Simms, "Whose Idea was Erwartung?" in *Constructive Dissonance*, 103.

5. Schoenberg, Letter to Ferruccio Busoni, c. August 18, 1909, quoted in Joseph Auner, *A Schoenberg Reader: Documents of a Life* (New Haven: Yale University Press, 2003), 71.

6. Leon Botstein: "Music and the Critique of Culture", in *Constructive Dissonance*, 4.

7. Botstein: "Music and the Critique of Culture", in *Constructive Dissonance*, 7.

8. Schoenberg, "Brahms the Progressive", *Style and Idea,* ed. Leonard Stein, trans. Robert Black (Berkeley: University of California Press, 1975), 72.

9. Alexander Carpenter, "Schoenberg's Vienna, Freud's Vienna: Re-examining the Connections between the Monodrama Erwartung and the Early History of Psychoanalysis". *Musical Quarterly* 93, no. 1 (2010); Michael Cherlin, *Schoenberg's Musical Imagination* (Cambridge: Cambridge University Press, 2007); Alan Street, "Narrative and Schoenberg's *Five Orchestral Pieces,* Op. 16", in *Theory, Analysis and Meaning in Music,* ed. Anthony Pople (Cambridge: Cambridge University Press, 1994).

10. Susanna Välimäki, *Subject Strategies in Music: A Psychoanalytic Approach to Musical Signification* (Helsinki: The International Semiotics Institute, 2005), 267–299.

11. Abbate, *In Search of Opera* (Princeton: Princeton University Press, 2001); Michael Klein, *Intertextuality in Western Art Music* (Bloomington, IN: Indiana University Press, 2005).

12. Wojciech Stępień, "Musical Categories of the Uncanny in Edvard Grieg's "Troll Music", *Studia Musicologica Norvegica* 38 (2012): 47–65; Joseph Kerman, "Beethoven's Op. 131 and the Uncanny", *19th-Century Music* 25, nos. 2–3 (2002): 155–164; Richard Cohn, "Uncanny Resemblances: Tonal Signification in the Freudian Age", *Journal of the American Musicological Society* 57, no. 2 (2004), 285–323; Peter H. Smith, "The Sorrows of Young Brahms? On the Intersection of Structure and Tragic Expression in the C-Minor Piano Quartet" cited in Klein, *Intertextuality in Western Art*; Cherlin, "Schoenberg and *Das Unheimliche*: Spectres of Tonality", *Journal of Musicology* 11, no. 3 (1993): 357–373.

13. Kramer, *Music as Cultural Practice 1800–1900*; David Schwartz, *Listening Subjects: Music, Psychoanalysis, Culture* (Durham: Duke University Press, 1997); Richard Kurth, "Music and Poetry, A Wilderness of Doubles: Heine–Nietzsche–Schubert–Derrida", *19th-Century Music* 21, no. 1 (1997): 3–37.

14. Ethan Haimo, *Schoenberg's Transformation of Musical Language* (Cambridge: Cambridge University Press, 2006), 318.

15. Arnold Schoenberg, "A Self-Analysis", in *Style and Idea*, 79.
16. Schoenberg, "Brahms the Progressive", in *Style and Idea*, 54.
17. Schoenberg, "Brahms the Progressive", in *Style and Idea*, 55.
18. Schoenberg, "Brahms the Progressive", in *Style and Idea*, 55.
19. McClelland, *Ombra*, vii.
20. McClelland, *Ombra*, vii.
21. Clive McClelland, "Death and the Composer: The Context of Schubert's Supernatural Lieder", in *Schubert the Progressive: History, Performance Practice, Analysis*, ed. Brian Newbould (Aldershot: Ashgate, 2003), 30–33.
22. Many thanks to Clive McClelland for pointing me to these examples.
23. McClelland, "*Ombra* and *Tempesta*", *Oxford Handbook of Topic Theory*, 286.
24. Own translation.
25. The themes of *Pelleas und Melisande* are all identified in Danielle Hood, "Schoenberg's *Pelleas und Melisande:* Hidden Agendas of the Sonata Form", *Musicology Review* 8/i, 2013.
26. Own translation.
27. Roland Barthes, *Image–Music–Text,* trans. Stephen Heath (New York: The Noonday Press, 1977), 96.
28. Freud. The Interpretation of Dreams, *The Standard Edition*, vol. IV, 91.
29. Freud. "The Medusa's Head", *The Standard Edition of the Complete Psychological Works of Sigmund Freud.* Vol. XVIII, ed. James Strachey (London The Hogarth Press, 1964), 273.
30. Freud, "The Uncanny", *The Standard Edition*, vol. XVII, 232.
31. Freud, "The Uncanny", *The Standard Edition*, vol. XVII, 232.
32. Freud, "The Uncanny", *The Standard Edition*, vol. XVII, 219.
33. Freud, "The Uncanny", *The Standard Edition*, vol. XVII, 220.
34. Freud, "The Uncanny", *The Standard Edition*, vol. XVII, 222.
35. Freud, "The Uncanny", *The Standard Edition*, vol. XVII, 225.
36. Klein, *Intertextuality in Western Art Music*, 87.
37. Abbate, *In Search of Opera*, 242.
38. Sigmund Freud and Josef Breuer, "Studies on Hysteria", *The Standard Edition of the Complete Psychological Works of Sigmund Freud.* Vol. II, ed. James Strachey (London The Hogarth Press, 1964).
39. Freud and Breuer, "Studies on Hysteria", *The Standard Edition*, vol. II, 6–15.
40. Freud, "The Medusa's Head", *The Standard Edition*, vol. IV 273.
41. Freud and Breuer, "Studies on Hysteria", *The Standard Edition*, vol. II, 15.
42. Freud and Breuer, "Studies on Hysteria", *The Standard Edition*, vol. II, 15.
43. Freud. "The Uncanny", *The Standard Edition*, vol. XVII, 235.
44. Freud and Breuer, "Studies on Hysteria", *The Standard Edition*, vol. II, 12.
45. Sisman, *Mozart: The Jupiter Symphony*, 68.
46. Klein, *Intertextuality in Western Art Music*, 87.
47. This is meant in the secondary usage of the transitive verb, that is, to repeat or reproduce what has been heard, read, or taught, in a purely mechanical way, with no evidence of personal thought or understanding. This follows the premise of Freud's

Interpretation of Dreams in that the imagery produced when dreaming is not often understandable by the analysand – it needs an analyst to decipher.

48. Bryan Simms, *The Atonal Music of Arnold Schoenberg, 1908–1923* (Oxford: Oxford University Press, 2000), 76–77.

49. Matthew Head, "Fantasia and Sensibility", *Oxford Handbook of Topic Theory*, 264.

50. Daniel Heartz and Bruce Alan Brown, "Empfindsamkeit".

51. Charles Burkhart, "Schoenberg's Farben: An Analysis of Op. 16, No. 3", *Perspectives of New Music* 8, no. 2 (Autumn, 1973–Summer, 1974): 146.

52. Street, "Narrative and Schoenberg's *Five Orchestral Pieces*, Op. 16", 176.

53. Simms, *The Atonal Music of Arnold Schoenberg*, 72.

54. Dale E. Monson et al., "Recitative", *Grove Music Online. Oxford Music Online*. Oxford. http://0-www.oxfordmusiconline.com.wam.leeds.ac.uk/subscriber/article/grove/music/23019 (accessed July 27, 2015).

Chapter 6 Part 1

The Waltz and the Uncanny in Mahler's Seventh Symphony

Despite Schoenberg's Op. 16 gifting one of the purest examples of the uncanny narrative, it is not the first place in which the story is told. An earlier example (and I am in no way suggesting this is the first) can be found in Mahler's Seventh Symphony, particularly in the Scherzo but also in the outer *Nachtmusik*, when one analyses the structure and themes of the Symphony as a whole. Moreover, within Mahler's music many narrative systems reflect 'a world alienated and broken, which was never going to regain its former unity and coherence', through what La Grange terms 'intrusions of the popular'.[1]

> The popular or pseudo-popular elements carry within them strong emotional and social connotations, which enable Mahler to combine and juxtapose laughter and compassion, tenderness and terror, death and mockery, coarseness and refinement. Introduced 'as a leaven into noble music',[2] these allusions to the 'inferior' sphere create tensions and shock effects that are already modern. Ceaselessly torn between mockery and nostalgia, these episodes also reflect the multicoloured spectacle of everyday experience, of its ambiguities and contradictions – a true image of life in all its heterogeneity.[3]

In Mahler's own words: 'the symphony is the world, it must embrace everything', including waltzes and *Ländler* which are often used by the composer as representations of the upper and lower class tensions abounding in Vienna at the time. Donald Mitchell, for example suggests the juxtaposition of the waltz and *Ländler* creates a 'conflict [. . .] between the two styles, one the primitive, peasant forerunner, the other, its brilliant, worldly successor, of the city, and sophisticated to a degree'.[4] Moreover, Joan Grimalt postulates that 'the "*Ländler*" might represent the rural traces of an upper social class that is trying to fit into urban life, without adapting to new modern social rules'.[5] Elsewhere he adds that 'Mahler, looking back to his origins from the distance, tends to stress its boorishness ironically, as in the Scherzo of the First symphony'.[6] Mahler's deliberate signification of the *Ländler* as "boorish" in fact continues throughout the Scherzos of his symphonies, however, the nature of the interpretation of satire changes. 'Scorn', Grimalt adduces, 'can be seen as an offensive element that can be contained in Parody or Satire; they can both use Irony as a way to express things just as they are not; and Humour is the comprehensive term that includes all of them. In Mahler's music, Irony is the main humorous tool, used in Parody and Satire, seldom in Scorn'.[7] When analysing the narrative arc of the Scherzos from Third to Ninth it appears that scorn does play a part in Mahler's musical language, particularly when viewed in light of an historical trace that follows Johann Strauss and Son rather than Richard Strauss and Wagner.[8] While both of these composers, along with many others, certainly influenced Mahler in his musical language and style, they will not be offered in evidence here as other scholars have discussed them in detail elsewhere.[9]

Whether it can be justifiably qualified as "Scorn" is arguable; however, the idealisation of nature and, consequently, the rural *Volk* in Mahler's symphonic narratives situates the urban – consequently "society" and, to a degree, "high-class" – as in opposition to this idealisation/idolisation lending it a parodic force within the paradigm. Mahler's manipulation of the class associations of the waltz and *Ländler* has also been illustrated by Vera Micznik in her analyses of the Ninth Symphony where she comments on 'the aggressive infringements of the established laws of order of "high art" [the waltz and minuet] through the intrusion of "low" genres [the *Ländler*] in the middle movements'.[10] In Micznik's article the idea is only taken as far as the opposition between 'high' and 'low', but, with the added connotations discussed above, a further layer of signification is exposed. Where Strauss utilised both the *Ländler* and the waltz as indicative of *Wiener Schmäh*, Mahler appears initially to return the associative value of the dances to their superficial significations: the former indexing a low-class, pastoral character and the latter a high-class noble dance often in conjunction with the older, but no less dignified, minuet. This is only superficial though, when the narrative is set out and all its layers exposed the deceitful artifice of the waltz's symbolisation is laid bare. Initially it represents the insincere morality of the aristocratic class, but as the century turns, it deepens to a symbol of the psychological anxiety felt by the populace as the Hapsburg Monarchy and the Empire fail to modernise and acculturate to their "Other" nationalities. Monelle argues that this change was possibly because of the emergence of the new bourgeois class:

> 'High pastoralism' was aristocratic, and there was no pretence of any real interest in the peasantry. The bourgeois, however, liked to imagine that his

cultivation of the folksong betokened a true love of the ancient, the simple, the collective, and a sentimental respect for the unlettered rustic. Unfortunately, 'folksong', both in Germany and Scotland, was vitiated by a desire to civilise and tame its oddities. [. . .] The aristocratic pastoral was purely conventional, and came clean about this. The bourgeois pastoral was earnest, spiritual, and a little dishonest.[11]

Grimalt agrees with Monelle, claiming that 'in Mahler's *Wunderhorn* songs, Pastoral references such as "Siciliana" or "Waltz" are often used meaning "False Appearances" and "Deceitful Love"'.[12] This would then place the signification firmly back in line with an historical trace leading directly to Strauss II and *Die Fledermaus*.

An example of one such musical narrative in Mahler's works is found in 'Rheinlegendchen' and 'Des Antonius von Padua Fischpredigt' from *Des Knaben Wunderhorn* (1892–1898). 'Rheinlegendchen' begins on the banks of the German river Neckar, narrated by a reaper who, distraught at losing his sweetheart, imagines throwing his ring into the water to be carried from the Rhine into the ocean, there to be eaten by a fish. The character appears naïve; he will offer a gold ring to his love and she will return. A pastoral *Ländler* accompanies his musing, the 3/8 meter with the accent on the second quaver and arpeggio figures throughout confirming the topic. However there is, as Julian Johnson suggests, 'a disjunction between the naïveté of their texts and sophistication of their musical setting'.[13]

The imagined fish is headed for the King's table, where his majesty will inevitably find it, the discovery of which will send the reaper's sweetheart hastening back, bringing with her the ring to reunite them. This fairytale, of course, depends upon the stereotyping of the characters: the low-class reaper and the sweetheart as "good", "loyal" and "in love"; the King as initially "bad" for "stealing" the sweetheart, but ultimately repentant and lets the girl go. A classic storyline of bad guy turns good.[14] Hence, as the fish reaches the King, the *Ländler* becomes a Viennese waltz, despite the tempo slowing slightly, and the instrumentation changes with the strings dominating the texture. The significance of the Viennese waltz here, then, is multivalent. It could signify the city Vienna itself, or the Viennese aristocracy (both the King and his court) as it does in Strauss' *Die Fledermaus*, and in addition, the feelings the reaper holds for his sweetheart, both good and bad. The sweetheart is held in high esteem by the reaper – one of high enough class to be dining with a king – yet who hastens back to the fisherman while the Viennese waltz continues, indicative of hope that he is seen as akin to the King in the maiden's eyes also, in contradiction with the lowly *Ländler* that illustrated his plight up to bar 70. The contrast between the reaper and the King, between the *Ländler* and the Viennese waltz, also calls to the opposition between rural and urban.

The country is portrayed by the "good" reaper whose sweetheart is stolen away by the shallow urbanity of the city. The continuation of the Viennese waltz when his love returns, however, suggests this "goodness" is no longer relevant. The shallowness of both the imagined actions of the sweetheart, and the connotations explicit in the expectation of the reaper of what is needed to win her back (i.e. a golden ring), is scorned by Mahler, demonstrated by the continuation of the waltz to the end of the song.

The way in which Strauss I, his son, and then Mahler, used the *Ländler* demonstrates the way in which a topic's signification can change. Monelle suggests this change parallels the changing class structure of the period, with the idealism of the aristocracy giving way to the earnest but dishonest bourgeois view of the lower classes. As shown in previous chapters, and will again be demonstrated in the below analyses, the bourgeois disregarded the uncouth aspect of the peasantry so it is the idealism and perception of the simplistic, rustic life of the lower class that is being signified, rather than the oppressive poverty and lack of basic amenities and rights that was the reality.

The *Ländler* changes from the simple rustic dance of Strauss I's ballroom, to the representation of the lower class's dwindling morality in Strauss II's *Die Fledermaus*. Mahler appears to return the *Ländler* to its original signification: from the low-class narrator's view the waltz represents the immoral King, while the *Ländler* signifies the good, simple reaper. However, the narrator's morality is also questionable. "Grasen" used to be a euphemism for having an amorous adventure, or "sowing wild oats", in which case, it would seem the reaper yearns less for a lost sweetheart than merely for one who will stay with him. Consequently, while the *Ländler* seems on the surface to be a low-class dance in opposition to the high-class waltz, returning to the innocence of Strauss senior's time, it still carries the taint added by his son.

'Fischpredigt', rather than emphasising the high/low-class conflict, concentrates on describing the inner struggle of St Antonius of Padua's hubris as he preaches to sea creatures expecting them to change. Once more, the text is set to a pastoral *Ländler*, marked *Behäbig. Mit Humor* (Sedate. With humour). To add humour to the song, Mahler employs the *Rute* a bundle of thin birch dowels or thin canes attached to a drumstick handle used to beat the bass drum and imported from Janissary music. It is employed here in a similar fashion to its use in Mozart's opera *Die Entführung aus dem Serail* (1782) where he portrayed Turkish inferences as a comic counterpoint to Osmin's rage. This counterpoint undermined the character of Osmin, his rage – his actions and emotions in general – painted as inconsequential, his perception of his position shown to be greater than the reality. Nasaar Al-Taee posits that

> Mozart clearly highlights Osmin's anger toward the end of his aria by speeding up the notes and adding 'Turkish music'. Prior to his coda, the gradual

uncertainty of the music establishes Osmin as a man devoid of rationality. The first section is highly unstable, a reflection of an erratic personality who is about to overstep the boundaries of logic.[15]

Mozart himself, in a letter to his father stated that 'just as a man in such a towering rage oversteps all the bounds of order, moderation and propriety and completely forgets himself, so must the music too forget itself'.[16] In 'Fischpredigt', in addition to the *Rute* there are allusions to the gypsy scale in the clarinet part (that Joan Grimalt names the "drunken clarinet" in reference to Bauer-Lechner's memoires) and oboe thirds further on. As such, Mahler has framed the *Ländler* as simplistic, rural and idealised. It signifies the peasants as generically lacking, undeveloped in terms of the civilised waltz, deficient of the self-awareness the waltz and its dancers boast of the government-made artificial world in which they spin and whirl. The topical narrative of this song then fits well with the hubris of Antonius shown as he preaches to fishes, but becomes more sophisticated as his surprise/disappointment/disillusionment/dejection turns inward and emerges as an early demonstration of the uncanny narrative's commentary on civilization. This narrative is acknowledged by Mahler, as he remarks that 'not one of them is one iota the wiser for it, even though the Saint has performed for them! But only a few people will understand my satire on mankind'.[17] In the final two stanzas, as the sermon ends and the fish return immediately to their natural instincts the musical language changes. The flowing river topic and drunken clarinet collapse in a descending chromatic scale, from *fff* to *pp* accompanied by *ff* cymbals and *pp* bass drum rolls. They are replaced by staccato repeated notes and a rising scale in C minor in the cello reminiscent of the "hypnoid state" ostinatos seen in Schoenberg's Op. 16. The clarinet attempts to reform its long lines but fails to surface to the conscious from the unconscious and fragments. The violin's river figure is similarly fragmented until at b. 177 an attempt at unification is attempted with a unison figure lasting just three bars before it too fragments. The chamber affectations of the sermon have now disappeared with full orchestral participation performing wide leaps and syncopated rhythms (bb.185–190) before a final collapse into a chromatic scale and low horn and bass drum note conclusion indicating the finality of St Antonius's despair.

When discussing Mahler and the *Ländler* and waltz most scholars look towards his symphonies, in particular the Scherzos where Mahler has not only adopted the dance as a major feature but caused this feature to overwhelm the Scherzo itself. Therefore, to begin with, I will explore the narrative of the Scherzo from Symphony VII, demonstrating the uncanny narrative in Mahler's topical soundscape before demonstrating how that narrative expands over the entire Symphony. I will then illustrate how this 1905 piece concludes a narrative formed through the Scherzo's of his Symphonies (Three to Nine) that plots the story of the Viennese dance halls from the aristocratic minuet, the emergence of the waltz and its opposition to the *Ländler* and its eventual correlation with the artificiality, stagnancy and eventual demise of the Habsburg Monarchy. The Ninth Symphony will be included as a conclusion to the account as it summarizes the interpretation developed out of the topical analysis of the preceding Scherzo's.

SEVENTH SYMPHONY SCHERZO

The movement begins with what William Ritter describes as a "game of iambic burps", a stuttering start reminiscent of Paul Dukas' awakening of the animated broom in the subtitled 'Scherzo after a Ballad by Goethe' from *The Sorcerer's Apprentice* written in 1819. Marked '*Fließend, aber nicht schnell; in den Anfangstakten noch etwas zögernd*' (fluent but not fast; somewhat hesitant in the opening bars), an image is created of timorous first footsteps of an automaton (theme A) (figure 6.1). The beats get closer together as the mechanical doll finds its confidence; the bass and Bb clarinets join in and the dynamics grow. After a climactic forte bar they drop back down to *pp* and a progression of triplets and dotted quavers develop and augment in range in the first violin (theme B). Meanwhile, the footstep ostinato continues around it as if the automaton matures with each step.

At b. 24 a new theme appears in the first violin, accompanied by a dotted thirds figure in the oboe. The violin theme is characterised by large dynamic contrasts and sigh motives. Staccato triplet scales continue in the viola and cello and an *ff* glissando, descending four octaves in the Bb clarinet over a loud chord in the trumpets, confirm the *tempesta* topic. Although this topic is symbolic of cataclysmic events such as storms, floods and fire, McClelland, the author of this topic, also correlates these characteristics with emotions such as rage, flight, conflict or madness.[18] As the narrative has identified the character of an automaton, it would be natural to assume that the emotional side of this topic is being represented. Joan Grimalt also posits 'Storms [. . .] tend to take a psychological slant, for instance in Shakespeare. In *King Lear*, the protagonist's inner torment finds in a horrid storm its correlate'.[19] He adds that 'romantic poetry abounds in a metaphorical use of nature in general and storms in particular to relate it to inner subjective states'.[20] This rage is countered, but not suppressed, by a lamenting theme (C) in the winds based on the sigh motif of the theme B. The triplets rage on under the lament, gradually receding from full octave scales to minor thirds.

A change of tempo and key introduces a waltz at b. 54 (theme D). Although this dance begins traditionally, at b. 66 the horns return to the sigh motif

The Waltz and the Uncanny in Mahler's Seventh Symphony 121

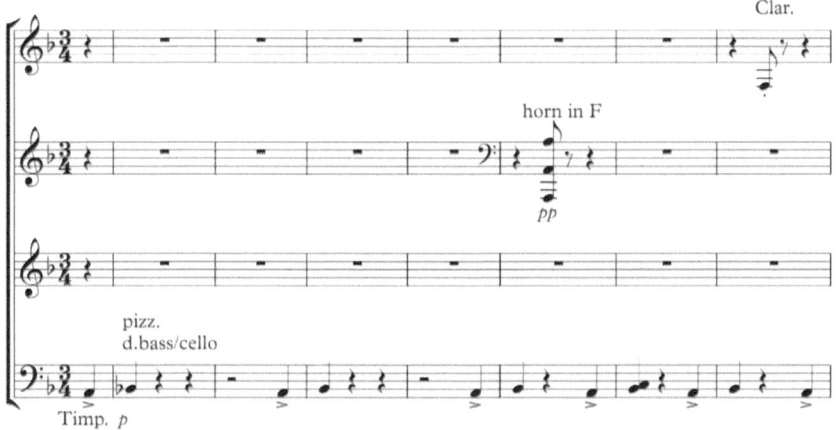

Figure 6.1 *Mahler,* **Symphony 7,** *movement 3, bb. 1–19.* (Berlin: Bote & Bock, 1960).

theme and two bars later the violins trade ascending and descending glissandi. The minor triplets re-emerge in the bass strings, oboe and clarinet, as if an attempt was made to return to "before" – the use of the waltz here indicates the "before" of *Alt Wien*, of blissful ignorance and lack of fear – but was quickly subsumed by the undeniable presence of the uncanny automaton.

Horn and violin glissandi take the listener into a recapitulation of the introductory footsteps. They are no longer hesitant and even include a hop-like movement in the bass and cello. The cello line develops into a solo line based on the lament theme (C) moving chromatically and is accompanied by a timpani roll beginning on the first beat and a *sfp* tuba sounding on the second, as well as a sigh motif in the bassoon and contrabassoon. The bassoon repeats the cello's chromatic descent falling back onto the sigh motif at b. 86. The

Figure 6.1 Continued.

triplets drive the tempo as the emotional *tempesta* topic returns climaxing as before on the dotted figure, this time sounding as more of a rage-filled fanfare in the trumpets and violins, than when in the oboe. The lament theme returns in the oboe, however, the orchestration is far sparser than at b. 37 with only the viola and the oboe playing the theme and the triplets emphasised only by long chords in thirds by the clarinets until the violins enter strongly with a fragment of the waltz. The waltz does not develop, however, a fragment is all the listener hears as themes A, B and C flicker in and out of view until b. 116 when the waltz returns and once again changes the mood. Unlike its first incarnation, this is a dark waltz, an uncanny version of the original. It has been displaced down an octave in the violins, the oom-pah quaver accompaniment in the horn and bassoon has been replaced by the horn, trombone and tuba, and the bass and cello walking accompaniment instead begins with a dynamically expressive chromatic *pianto* around its original hopping motif. It is familiar material presented in an unfamiliar way creating a shadowy atmosphere from the usually lively dance. The tense atmosphere is enhanced from b. 133 as the theme is placed up two octaves, employing harmonics in the violin against the turbulent triplets that reappeared at b. 131. The waltz, the lament and the *tempesta* topics all continue, winding around each other as the orchestration increases to a climax at b. 150 which leads to a dissolution led by the oboes *kreischend* ("screeching") "collapse".[21]

At b. 179 the Trio begins with a dysphoric waltz (theme E) featuring a chromatic neighbour note movement and combined with *ombra* allusions in the atypical waltz accompaniment by the viola and the violins, playing in their lowest range while the bassoon provides a countermelody in its highest range, and the trilled drone in the horn. The solo violin and flute replicate the *kreischend* figure from the end of the scherzo as a chromatic ascent leads to a rhythmically altered repeat of the waltz theme E. Moreover, the pastoral connotations of the section add a multivalent significance to the waltz:

- the high-class waltz topic, associated with the city and nobility;
- the pastoral connotations of the horn drone playing in fifths with the flute and clarinet drones, and the wind quintet melody and countermelody associated with rustic simplicity;
- *ombra* represented by the unusual pitch of the instruments and rhythm/articulation of the waltz oom-pah symbolising fear and awe.

As shown in the previous chapter, the juxtaposition of the pastoral and the *ombra* topics causes an uncanny narrative as the beauty of nature is coloured by the fear of the unseen and unknown to create a psychological fear in the subconscious. The solo violin punctuating the dysphoric waltz with the *kreischend* figure suggests an individual whose consciousness is collapsing when presented by whatever spectres are dancing afore them. William Mengelberg writes that

> this is a Dance of Death, as seen in old frescoes . . . Death plays the violin, inviting people to dance, as sooner or later all of them must . . . . The clattering of bones, baleful laughter, ghostly dancing, all can be recognised here. Mahler has painted a fragment of medieval legend with the colours of the modern orchestra. In this movement there is nothing real; it is a reflection of yesterday's world, peopled with ghosts.[22]

"Yesterdays world" is represented by the waltz narrating the collapse of the Viennese society and the ghost of a monarchy that used the craze surrounding the dance to amuse the people and divert their attention from the draconian police state, economic demise and loss of territory. The dance so traditionally full of the joys of spring, love, laughter and wine is minor, disjointed and interrupted by the *kreischend* figure, played *ff* and *f* in the surrounding *p* and *pp* waltz, that elongates the phrases to ten bars rather than the normal eight. Even the beginning of the waltz is intentionally jarring as a sudden change in key and mood – from the tempestuous triplets to a waltz in crotchet movement, confirmed by Mahler marking the second phrase of the theme as *Wie vorher (ebenso plötzlich)* (as before, just as suddenly). All of these signifiers indicate the topic being used now has moved firmly from the *ombra* of the early scherzos to the uncanny narrative described in the previous chapter.

The uncanny continues at b. 210 as a grotesque parody of the scherzo waltz (D) emerges (also developing the opening tenor horn motive of the first movement) employing an imitative narrative, with a lower instrument imitating and mocking the sweet waltz melody played by the viola and later the violin.

The waltz accompaniment in the low wind (contrabassoon, horn, timpani and double bass) alternates between D diminished and D major chords, seen most obviously at bb. 219–224 when the second violins and viola take over, but occurring at each reincarnation of the dotted theme. At this point, the horns imitate the violin melody, until, at b. 226 it accompanies the violins and oboe developed theme, with the original three-note theme played by the low strings and low woodwind imitated by the trombone and trumpet. Even this parody eventually collapses, however, as descending scales supplement the *kreischend* figure to a further developed theme in the violins with the trombones, contrabassoon and horns playing the theme. Interrupted at b. 243 by three *sf* chords with cymbals and triangle emphasis, the waltz collapses to its lowest rendition with arpeggios in the bassoon and bass clarinet accompanying the horn and cello with drones in the bottom range of the clarinet, English horn, viola and contrabassoon. Once again, it is suddenly interrupted by faltering dance steps in the clarinet dissolving rhythmically over the four bars to lead back to the *tempesta* triplets from the scherzo at b. 261. This proves to be a false recapitulation, however, and the scherzo proper returns at b. 293 with the automaton's now self-possessed footsteps. Significantly, the collapse of the waltz and the sudden stasis of the instruments surrounding the waltz at b. 252 (figure 6.2) are at the centre of the movement (and therefore the Symphony) indicating that the waltz and its attendant signified, both superficial and uncanny, are at the heart of the unconscious trauma implied by the plot of this and the *Nachtmusik*'s narratives.

The mechanical ostinato created here resembles the hypnoid, or second, state found in the uncanny narrative of Schoenberg's op. 16. Fragments of previous motifs interject over the almost constant beats in the timpani and low strings, each time attacking with a *sfp or fp* dynamic, and on occasion rising to the surface of the consciousness enough to stop the ostinato briefly (bb. 311 and 319–320). The interjections are placed almost entirely in low instruments: horn, bass clarinet, tuba, viola, cello and double bass, or in the low range of the flute and clarinet. The ostinato only stops when the initial climax and first sigh motif theme from b. 24 recurs, played this time by the violin and trumpet rather than the oboe, accentuating the climax and retrospectively confirming this as the cardinal act which forced the analysand into the hypnoid state. This shock forces the transference of the triplets and the sigh motif from the strings to the woodwind, where it has so far never been. The triplets now act as the ostinato under a recapitulation of the lament theme in the strings as the timpani and double bass attempt to reinstate the automaton's footsteps but are ultimately subsumed by the waltz (D) at b. 361.

The jovial waltz changes the mood suddenly, as it did at b. 54, but without the alternation between D major and D diminished chords. The cello and woodwind play the theme as the violin I, trombone, tuba, bassoon and double

Figure 6.2 *Mahler,* **Symphony 7,** *movement 3, bb. 247–256.* (Berlin: Bote & Bock, 1960).

bass accompany changing the atmosphere slightly by adding an uncanny tone to the dance with the unexpected timbre. When the trumpets attack their eight-bar drone on the tonic, the jovial nature dissipates and the violins takes the melody once more at a high pitch, highlighting the Otherness of their part in opposition to the rest of the orchestra. This occurs again at b. 389 when the violin enters with theme D after a return of the lament theme and leaps up to C4 followed by a chromatic staccato descent to a powerful full-orchestral discordant strike. After the chord liquidates into descending scales and declamatory fanfares in the horn, the *kreischend* figure causes the waltz to collapse once more into the rage-filled maturation of the automaton. A wild waltz combining the scherzo's waltz (D) and the trio's waltz (F) disrupts the *tempesta* triplets. With the tuba and trombones playing the trio waltz with accompanying horns, and the wind playing the scherzo waltz (further adding a piccolo playing extremely high) the overall impression is that of street music, a bastardisation of the dance normally symbolising the joy of spring. It doesn't endure, however, as the *kreischend* figure dissolves into the trio waltz, but this time performing it as a *Ländler* as the tempo drops slightly and the bass clarinet, bassoon, trumpet and finally cello and bass accompany with *Ländler-esque* arpeggios. A dominant drone in the trombone and tubas add to the pastoral feel of the dance which gradually combines with the romance topic which dominates from b. 434–438 but which also collapses. The last 60 bars of the piece are characterised by importunate attempts at returning the themes to their conventional significations (the themes have been diverted from their typical signification from the start of the movement) only to have them determinedly collapse before they can establish a firm hold. At b. 474 the collapsed figure is marked *grell* (piercing) and interrupts the timpani's attempt at the scherzo waltz, but after that, despite brief instances of the waltz oom-pah-pah, the movement finishes as if a clock is winding down, the automaton is running out of energy and takes its last few steps.

Nachtmusik II and IV

The horn begins with a rising major call echoed by a second horn, stopped in order to give it the illusion of distance and playing a minor arpeggio. This major/minor alternation continues until the clarinet (staccato) and oboe (legato) interrupt with pastoral triplet birdcall-like lines. The English Horn reiterates the minor call at b. 12 and the bassoon at b. 18. The wind becomes static, as if stuck while the tuba reiterates the horn call at bb. 22 and 24 suggesting the hypnoid state with regurgitations of theme A slipping from the subconscious. The janissary instrument, the rute, plays at bb. 26-7 (*pp-ff*) combining with the horn fifths from 24 to add a low-class affectation to the pastoral topic. The wind collapse in a chromatic flurry down 4 octaves, leaving only the contrabassoon and double bass to complete the last half bar.

At b. 30 Theme A reappears in the horn developing the introductions horn call. It begins a canon with a cello countermelody while the strings play the rhythm found in "Revelge" from *Des Knaben Wuhnderhorn* with the back of the bow on strings (*col legno*). The song tells of a drummer marching away from his sweetheart to battle, where he and his brothers die, returning as skeletons to the alley from whence they left. Theme B in violin 1 is a funeral march accompanied by timpani playing tonic-dominant-tonic, adding to the funeral march atmosphere until at b. 44 the minor horn call from the introduction is played in isolation strongly resembling Chopin's "Funeral March" from Piano Sonata No. 2, op. 35 in horn 1 and oboe. Simultaneously, at b. 42, the clarinets play what is traditionally the snare drum trill and beat from a gallows march however, in "Revelge" is seen in the string introduction. The oboe repeats the Revelge rhythm at bb. 46-47 while the viola and cello reassert theme A.

A new theme (C) appears at b. 48 in the double bass and contrabassoon/bassoon with the horn Revelge rhythm accompanying and finishing with a full stop on the timpani. The Cello and Double Bass repeat theme C accompanied by horns and violins to begin with, then joined by violins and finished again with a finality provided by the timpani. At b. 62, however, theme A returns with the pastoral triplet birdcalls seeming to reaffirm life by portraying nature and returning to the major mode. The full orchestra, octave doubling and homophonic nature of the section indicates the romantic topic. The canonic entry of theme A between bass clarinet, horns, contrabassoon, violins and cello/double basses does nothing to contradict the homophonic feel due to the crotchet movement of the theme but it does enhance the life-affirming temporal movement of the section in opposition to the inert character of what has come before. This movement doesn't last, however, as funeral rhythms re-emerge: at b. 69, the cello/double bass repeats the "Funeral march"; at b. 76 the trumpet repeats it alongside the major horn call and at b.78 flute, oboe, bass clarinet and finally timpani play the Revelge rhythm.

A complete change in topic and narrative occur at b. 83 as a "leisurely" *contradanse* is introduced and continues unspoiled or altered until b. 118 where the sensibility style illustrates a fragmentation of the middle-class dance into a reiteration of the introduction horn calls. The pastoral topic now includes the use of cowbells answering and then accompanying the horns. The bells mark out the physical space of the pastoral, in a way similar to the answering horn at the beginning of the movement that used the mute to sound further away. The horn calls reflect off the distant cowbells signifying a spatial difference between the pastoral and the dance topics, the fullness of the orchestra and homogeneity of the thematic material creating a closeness encapsulating the listener within the confines of the dance hall. In addition, they also signify artificiality on two different levels in a deconstructive manner. The "realness" of the cowbells bring an iconistic element to the signification; using cowbells to connote the Alpine mountains, while simultaneously emphasising the artificial nature of the horn call that imposes mankind in the idyllic scene and confirms the idealism inherent in the pastoral topic. Julian Johnson comments on the significance of this deconstructive view:

> Bells may denote the human world of religion, but Mahler's use of cowbells, like the call of horns, evokes a pastoral space in which the boundary between the realms of man and nature is blurred. That these realms are often evoked

together denotes a music that is concerned precisely with the relationship of one to the other.²³

What answers the horns call is the "Funeral March" in the cellos, English horn and clarinets before theme C interposes in the double bass. Theme A returns but with inverted instrumentation: the wind and horns play the melody while the triplet birdcalls are heard in the cello and bass. The sparse texture echoes the preceding pastoral mountain scene, however, the signification is now of the *ombra* topic. At b. 161 a four-bar static wind introduction leads to a tango heard in the oboe, with a rhythmic accompaniment in horn and pizzicato upbeat in cello and bass. The use of this dance is significant when regarded in an investigation into the waltz and its identification as an ironic archetype of Viennese civility as this dance has also altered in its signification, as Jane Desmond explains:

> The history of the tango traces the development of movement styles from the dockside neighbourhoods of Buenos Aires to the salons of Paris before returning, newly 'respectable', from across the Atlantic to the drawing rooms of the upper classes for a 'fundamentally taboo cultural form is a recurrent phenomenon'.²⁴

The "taboo" referenced here are the sexual connotations of the dance, the "passionate sensuality" associated with it along with other descriptors such as "hot" and "fiery". Desmond attributes the adoption of this low-class dance to the 'socially sanctioned way of experiencing sexuality'.

> On one level, by dancing 'Latin' or 'black' dance styles, the dominant class/ or racial group can experience a frisson of 'illicit' sexuality in a safe, socially protected and proscribed way, one that is clearly delimited in time and space. Once the dance is over, the act of sexualising oneself through a performance of a 'hot' Latin style, of temporarily becoming or playing at being a 'hot Latin' oneself, ceases. That dance then becomes a socially sanctioned way of expressing or experiencing sexuality, especially sexuality associated with subtle, sensuous rotations of the pelvis.²⁵

The parallel with the development of the waltz and its signification is marked; further, when understood in its syntagmatic placement within the narrative, alternating between an uncanny representation of the pastoral and the temporally static triplet and funeral march rhythm section surrounding theme A in the tubas and trombones signifying the hypnoid state, that collapses once again at b. 187. This suggests that the cause of the hypnoid state is multivalent, commenting on the baser ills of the breakdown of the Habsburg society: class prejudice and sex.

At b. 212, the transition begins with theme C in the cello and Double Bass with interjections of bird calls in flute and tremelo in harp. This leads to a fanfare passed between the trumpet, oboe, clarinet and flute until it forms the upbeat to a theme A full orchestra romance topic. At b. 232 the Funeral March returns in the horn and strings only returning the chamber music style briefly before theme A repeats with Eastern melodic adjustments.

At b. 262 the *contredanse* returns with the countermelody in flute, clarinet and oboe, however, this time the trumpet plays the Revelge rhythm lending the dance a militaristic feel while simultaneously injecting the dance, normally an affirmation of life, with an allusion to death that was previously missing from this theme. Theme A creeps back in as the full orchestra is gradually reintroduced but the wind reassert the *contredanse* with added percussion: the timpani, triangle and glockenspiel. The glockenspiel is, in Mahler's work particularly, associated with childhood or nostalgia. As the rest of the orchestra becomes more static with repetitive figures and, at b. 280, cowbells can be heard, the horn, oboe and flute melodies suggest it is the pastoral topic and the physical space denoted earlier that is being recalled and that is part of the trauma causing the hypnoid state surrounding the pastoral melodies.

This is retroactively confirmed at b. 293 when the answering horn call leads into a dysphoric development of theme A concentrated in the darker instruments of the orchestra accompanying the violins theme. The darkness continues with theme C heard in the bassoons, including the contra, and the English Horn sounding the Revelge. The pastoral triplets return, with drones in the cellos and basses and soon become static once more before the final collapse into long, low chords. The violin, then cello drop the same four octaves as the previous collapses and the piece ends on 2 bars of low chords, brightened only by cymbals and a final ray of hope in the cellos as they end on a harmonic dominant.

In the second *Nachtmusik*, movement four, the narrative tells of an alternation between a driving sensibility topic and static pastoral and *ombra* topics, the first two of which are introduced in the first eight bars. The themes for the rest of the piece are all introduced one after another beginning with a pastoral theme in the horn, then a birdcall like theme in the oboe and horn. The cello and violin then replay the sensibility theme from the introduction, which, at b. 28, develops into a serenade. The serenade was originally a piece composed for a suitor to play outside his loves window at night, but became a musical greeting to a beloved or a superior, still played outdoors in the evening and therefore mostly composed for instruments which can be played standing. The pastoral surrounds of the strings theme, the sensibility topic (marked *Mit Aufschwung* 'uplifting, impassioned') and the romance topic which is alluded to by the full orchestration and the quixotic violin solo, all point to a nocturnal love song (the movement itself confirms this, titled *Andante amoroso*). In addition, Hubert Unverricht suggests that 'any movement with an accompaniment on plucked strings (suggesting the lute, guitar or mandolin) carried serenade connotations'.[26] The sensibility introduction and the pastoral/*ombra* alternations bear strong resemblances to other serenades, such as Mozart's opp. K361 and K375 as well as Brahm's op. 11 and Richard Strauss's op. 7.

At b. 56 a slow dance ('Graziosissimo') begins sweetly, but soon a rising chromatic sequence leads to the *ombra* topic at b. 72 with bassoons and cello/bass figures. This charming dance returns, but alternates between the *ombra* and pastoral until at b. 148 heavy dark footsteps impose upon the narrative. The pastoral overcomes them, but the clarinet accompaniment switches between major and minor mode until the footsteps return at b. 176 referencing the previous movement's main features and linking the dark narrative to the *ombra* topic here. The pastoral and serenade combine, as a solo cello plays a passionate theme over the clarinets pastoral burble and a plucked accompaniment in the harp and double bass. At b. 199 the sensibility topic returns to be transformed into the serenade at b. 211. This topic is driven by the need for resolution, whether of an appoggiatura or through voice leading so when the "light figure", or what Anna Stoll Knecht terms the dream chords, stall the momentum at b. 253 it causes a suspension in the temporal movement, much as the hypnoid state in the previous two movements. However, rather than the suspension indicating the uncanny, in this instance it connotes something closer to a dawning, whether of the sunrise after the night the symphony has been enclosed in since the first movement or of a realisation and healing taking place after the darkness of the unconscious and uncanny narrative of the Scherzo.

Mahler often uses rising harp arpeggios to signify light, appearing mostly in *Kindertotenlieder*, a song cycle filled with polar images of light and dark (figure 6.3). The first example of this is in 'Nun will die Sonn' so hell aufgeh'n', which begins in darkness (illustrated by the *Nachtmusik* discussed above). Finally, the sun begins to rise at bar 47, as the contrary motion melodies in oboe and voice become diatonic and are joined by the 'light' figure,

Figure 6.3 *Mahler,* **Symphony 7,** *movement 4, bb. 253–254: 'light figure'.* (Berlin: Bote & Bock, 1960).

ascending arpeggios, in the harp. The father offers the listener advice: 'Du mußt nicht die Nacht in dir verschränken / mußt sie ins ew'ge Licht versenken!' (You must not enfold the night within you / you must immerse it in eternal light!). This does not seem to be the advice he would be able to follow or believe, however, given that the sun is not yet allowed to rise: no topic is wholly signified here, partly because all the constraints previously on the orchestra remain, so only half the orchestra is being utilised; and partly due to the pictorial nature of what is occurring. The figure's second appearance in the cycle is in the second song 'Nun seh' ich wohl'. The child's father contemplates the death of the child as an act of fate. He subjects a single moment (the moment of a look in his child's eyes) to intense scrutiny and signification. More than just eyes, they hold in them the fate of the child, as if in one look the father could have seen the consolation he so badly needs. He also feels he should have known, and by knowing perhaps acted to turn the child away from, this destiny. The dark atmosphere is set immediately through the sparse texture, using only muted low strings, clarinet in A (to give a murkier sound), horn and bassoon. The two chords, which are the focal points of the four-bar introduction, are dissonant, the first a G minor chord with a sharpened fourth, the second including the supertonic. The sigh motif is utilised, combined with an appoggiatura, signifying the topic of sensibility. The dark mood is lightened subtly by the ascending arpeggios in the harp, the light figure that in the first song symbolises the "eternal flame", and which here illuminates the darkness as the dark flame is reflected in the child's eyes.

In 'Der Schildwache Nachtlied' the ascending arpeggio initially appears to represent the ascension into the light from the *Nachtmusik* that preceded it, but its symbolisation of God and faith is retrospectively affirmed as the narrator expresses his belief that to have God's blessing is 'all possessing, who so believes!'. This becomes more poignant when his time, like the child's, is cut short as he dies at the end of the song. When the figure appears in Symphony No. 7 movement I, just as the main character, identified as Florio, breaks free of Venus's seductive spell, it is the light figure that symbolises this fateful act.[27] The hero is saved by his faith in God, just as in *Kindertotenlieder* the light figure presents faith and the eternal flame, or as the fate of the child to rest in heaven. Hence, the light figure symbolises not just "light" but also ascension achieved through faith, whether to heaven after death, or to a better state of life through realisation and belief.

Realisation here reintroduces the string sensibility topic and the pastoral topic from the introduction. As the orchestra cycles through the themes, the *ombra* allusions present from the start have disappeared and the movement finishes on a calm resolution, unlike the previous *Nachtmusik*.

The physical distance laid out at the start of the first *Nachtmusik* juxtaposes the major/minor alternations, the janissary music and the pastoral topic denoting an anxiety towards the natural world, or maybe an understanding that that world is unreal, idealised tainted by the artificialness of a civilised perspective. That the music descends into a hypnoid state immediately after confirms that it is part of the trauma from which the narrative is distancing itself. The narrative, however, soon returns to consciousness and the subject of death, or more specifically, the anticipation of death. The 'Revelge' rhythm and snare figure in the clarinets refer to the introduction of the *Wunderhorn* song which begins as the soldiers march off to battle, but it also brings to mind the introduction to 'Der Tambourg'sell', also from *Wunderhorn* that begins with a gallows snare drum rhythm as it leads a drummer to his death. It lends an air of inevitability to the idea of death found here. The pastoral topic reaffirms life, with the triplet birdcalls and major mode returning movement to a narrative that had been motionless and is followed by a romantic rendering of theme A which is quickly dominated by the urban Funeral March.

While a complete change of tack occurs with the leisurely *contradanse* it is still an urban topic, although this time it is middle-class, a firm favourite of the bourgeoisie in the dance halls. Even once the pastoral topic recurs, it is an artificial space portrayed. It is this narrative that is present then: with the presence of the sexual tango, the civilised but middle-class *contradanse*, the artificial pastoral setting – whose portrayal of physical distance creates a yearning not satisfied within this movement – and a funeral march anticipating death, one can understand the subject's desire for change. It is perhaps unclear whether the narrative desires to return to *Alt Wien*, or to the simpler times before the Industrial Revolution, the poverty and the collapse of the Viennese Empire, however, the inclusion of the glockenspiel which leads the movement into a dysphoric darkness gives the impression that a yearned for time has passed, the resulting darkness brightened only by the dominant cello harmonic.

As the narrative moves to the Scherzo the anxiety becomes more pronounced. The arrant rendering of the Uncanny narrative through the signification of the automaton, the madness and rage inherent in the representation of Grimalt's "inner subjective states" and the treatment of the waltz topic adheres to the *Nachtmusik*'s plot trajectory, but also sets the precedent for Webern's Symphony 21, in which the waltz is the pivot for the unconscious mind (see chapter 8). In Webern's Symphony, the waltz acts as a mirror image, as the access point to his unconscious, whereas here it forms the basis, the deepest reason for his dark psychological state. The lament acts as a second level to the rage and madness that consumes the first bars of this movement, the rage caused by the loss of the authentic, the lament an acknowledgement of the inevitability of that loss. The dark, uncanny waltz at the centre of the movement presents the artificial nature of the Viennese society, one that obscured the true stagnation of the Empire's policies, but it also symbolizes the collapse of that society as the waltz, the lament and the tempesta topic collapse with the *Kreischend* figure. The significations of the waltz the pastoral and the *ombra* topic together lead to the uncanny narrative: the beauty of nature coloured by the fear of the unseen and unknown; a collapsing of consciousness due to the fear of dance and death.

The third of the nocturnal movements, *Nachtmusik* IV, emplots the rise out of the unconscious hypnoid state, to a dawning realisation, illustrated by the serenade and the light figure which symbolises an ascension from the depths of the unconscious to a better consciousness where the anxiety has fled. Beginning with the sensibility and the pastoral topics a nocturnal love song is narrated utilising the serenade. A slow dance occurs, such as in the previous two movements, and, just like then, it is interrupted by uncanny footsteps. However, in this case, the charm of the dance wins, as the three main topics (pastoral, serenade and sensibility) combine. The drive these topics contain – the continued movement of a dance and the need for resolution of the sensibility topic – is suspended briefly by the light figure signifying a breakthrough caused by the continued forward motion of the analysis that leads to a calm resolution of the movement.

The Beginning and the End: I and V

While the central movements embody the uncanny narrative, the first movement provides us with the cause of the anxiety. A French overture combines with the arioso topic, a style of opera singing between recitative and aria, to humanise the instrumental solos and evoke its literary stylistic counterpart, poetry, as a form of expression that lies between speech and song. The accompanying topic, French overture, symbolises the supernatural sub-plot through its similarity to the *ombra* topic. This topic is signified here by the slow tempo, the heavily dotted rhythms conveying the high style ceremonial music that accompanied the entrance of King Louis XIV and his entourage to court. It was later adopted as the opening section for theatrical performances, suites and symphonies when a serious, elevated tone was called for. McClelland states, however, that the French overture was also used to invoke *ombra* allusions, but significantly adds that the topic can create a more sinister atmosphere. In an analysis of Handel's opera *Admeto* (1727), McClelland writes:

> The dotted rhythms and trills normally associated with the French overture here convey a more sinister meaning, especially in combination with the key of D minor and the sudden contrasts in dynamics. This scene is unlike the other Handel examples so far considered, in that the horrors presented on the stage and in the music are intended to portray the idea of mental torment. The demons,

although physically present on the stage in a ballet, are supposedly in the mind of the king. This device was to be explored by Hasse and especially Jomelli within a few years.[28]

Therefore, the rhythms present in the introduction to Mahler's Seventh Symphony could be acknowledged as instigating a creeping terror and symbolising heartbeats or footsteps (either the approach of impending menace or the procession of a funeral) and the tremolando in the strings and clarinets, which, when combined with *fp* markings at bar 6 create fear and agitation.

It should not be forgotten, however, that the French overture is still indicative of a procession, and moreover, has martial connotations – the dotted rhythm associated with the march 'are only elaborations of the upbeat impetus preparing for the [soldiers] next tread'.[29] But rather than connoting the common soldiers, as in the *Wunderhorn* songs ('Der Schildwache Nachtlied', 'Revelge', 'Der Tamboug'sell') the topic instead points to the higher ranks, the aristocracy and perhaps even the Imperial Family. The hunt topic that begins the exposition lends weight to this hypothesis, particularly as it contains allusions to the cavalry march. This topic is associated with the ideal of hunting, rather than the brutal reality; hence, it is correlated with nobility, courage, joy and being one with nature. Fitzpatrick suggests that 'the hunt stood for all that was desirable in worldly virtue, representing a new embodiment of the older *ritterlich-höfisch* [chivalrous-courtly]... ideals which were at the centre of aristocratic thought'.[30] The valiant associations of this topic connote two levels of signification here. They describe the characteristic aristocratic bearing as well as symbolising nature, immediately placing the listener outside. The horn evokes the woodland, and thus also mystery, romance and the unknown.[31] The second theme of the exposition is a drunken gavotte; the violins announce the melody while the horns slide through chromatic counterpoints. After a brief return to the galloping horse topic from the hunt, the musical language transforms into the romance topic at b.118. The *Empfindsamkeit* swells and pauses describe undulations of passion providing the listener with the love story that plays such an important part in the uncanny narratives of the centre movements.

The development begins at b. 193 with the Arioso theme, but now accompanied by the *ombra* topic rather than the French overture. It very quickly transforms into the sensibility topic using the thematic material from the romance topic of the exposition. The sensibility and romance topoi use similar signifiers – full orchestral timbre, large leaps and string melodies – but their signifiers differ due to the sensibility's use of appoggiaturas and *pianto* to represent an anxiety that is not present in the Romance topic. When theme B returns, originally within the hunt topic, it can now be heard in the trumpet rather than the tenor horn and is surrounded by discordant tremolo stings, which in the Allegro tempo indicate *tempesta* rather than *ombra*. With the addition of the timpani's march rhythm at b.220 the hunt topic has now become a military march as the quick repeated figures in the oboe, clarinet, strings and triangle have disappeared to be replaced by linear lines with movements of crotchets or larger notes. The military topic continues with developments of all the themes until there is a sudden low style topic heralded by fanfares in the trumpets marked 'wieder etwas bewegter, aber gemessen wie vorhin' (Again a bit more agitated, but measured as before). The serenade that follows has a nationalistic feel to begin with as the viola mimics a guitar or mandolin but the use of the darker English Horn to accompany the solo violin creates a night-time pastoral, conveying not only the serenades night associations, but also casts a shadow over the intended love song. This foreshadows the serenade in the second *Nachtmusik*.

Just as the movement reaches its most ominous the light topic makes its first appearance, heralding its use in the *Nachtmusik* as a moment of dawning or realisation. The romance topic surrounds it, but after 20 bars, the French overture recurs with fragments of theme B heard in the trombones pushing the signification towards the *ombra* topic. This push seems warranted as the recapitulation features the themes in the tuba and trombones, with the addition of timpani and bass drum creating a sinister atmosphere. The timpani and fanfares in the trumpet interrupt the recap of the gavotte and finally the military topic dominates with martial percussion including the tambourine, cymbals, snare drum and glockenspiel. The march slows to a procession combined with the march from b. 19, but at 523 the coda encapsulates the cavalry march.

The vast majority of this movement, then, can be said to be high class. The minority, rather than being low class as has been seen before, is associated more with the middle-class: the bourgeoisie. The sensibility topic, the romance and the gavotte are all signifiers of the salon, a particular favourite of the bourgeois and even the high-class topics are the idealised perspective of the aristocracy: the French overture, the hunt and the cavalry march. Its general lack of pastoral signifiers throughout, instead of describing the chambers and parade grounds, are at odds with the pastoral signification largely present in the other movements suggesting that the anxiety created here and played out in the next three movements is encapsulated in the disparagement of the contemporary society in which it is surrounded. This once again could suggest that the scorn Grimalt claims cannot be found in Mahler's work does exist, however it is perhaps not scorn but an acknowledgement of the society's ills, parodied as much in the saccharine Lehár-esque love song as in the "picture perfect" aristocratic marches. The bright marches, in particular the fast-paced cavalry march, jar against the funeral march that introduces the second movement, a stark warning of what the glory of battle actually entails and what the losses of these battles mean to the country they are fought for. The Empire's loss of territory in the thirty years before this composition had been responsible for a large decline in morale, battled, as described in the previous chapters, by the plethora of dances and operettas designed to distract and cocoon the population. That an uncanny waltz forms the centre of this Symphony's plot becomes more understandable and significant when seen in the context of this opening movement's satirical commentary.

The fifth movement follows the commencement of the healing process and everything about the movement signifies joy and triumph over the uncanny narrative of the first three movements. The narrative alternates between triumphant military marches, brilliant passages and pastoral dances, sometimes generic pastoral, but there are also *style hongrois* markers, such as the spondee (e.g. bb. 143, 240, 486) and *Ländlers* (bb. 420, 517) heard. The most significant moment in the movement, however, is the appearance of the hunt theme from the first movement that appears at b. 455. It is the first dark moment of the movement, but lasts only 30 bars before, at 486 the *style hongrois* style takes over building up in timbre and dynamics before the hunt theme is once again heard, in major this time and in the trumpets, rather than tenor horn, with a marking of "*strahlend*" (radiant) for the trumpets and "solemnly" for the rest of the orchestra. After a brief *Ländler* a triumphant march begins at b. 531 soon accompanied by the brilliant topic. At 581 the major hunt theme returns once more accompanied by gongs, bass drums and cowbells thereby presenting all the Symphony's specific narrative signifiers of the uncanny from the first four movements together as something to be triumphed over. Unlike in Schoenberg's op. 16, where the character lost their battle with their anxiety, here there is victory.

NOTES

1. Henry Louis De La Grange, *Mahler Studies*, ed. Stephen Hefling (Cambridge: Cambridge University Press, 1997), 138–139.
2. Speech marked quotes from Theodor Adorno, *Mahler: A Musical Physiognomy*. Trans. Edmund Jephcott (Chicago: 1992), 36, quoted in De La Grange, *Mahler Studies*, 139.
3. De La Grange, *Mahler Studies*, 138–139.
4. Donald Mitchell, *Gustav Mahler: The Early Years* (Berkeley: California University Press, 1995), 210–211.
5. Joan Grimalt, *Mapping Musical Signification* (Switzerland: Springer, 2020), 274.
6. Joan Grimalt, "Gustav Mahler's *Wunderhorn* Orchestral Songs: A Topical Analysis and a Semiotic Square" (PhD, Universitat Autònoma de Barcelona, 2011), 249–250.

7. Grimalt, "Gustav Mahler's *Wunderhorn* Orchestral Songs", 189–190.
8. The Eighth is not included as it is in two parts and therefore outside the remit of this manuscript.
9. See Joan Grimalt, *Mapping Musical Signification*; Anna Stoll Knecht, *Mahler's Seventh Symphony* (Oxford: Oxford University press, 2019).
10. Micznik, "Mahler and the Power of Genre", 148.
11. Monelle, *The Musical Topic*, 227–228.
12. Grimalt, *Mapping Musical Signification*, 274.
13. Julian Johnson, *Mahler's Voices. Expression and Irony in the Songs and Symphonies* (Oxford: Oxford University Press, 2009), 137.
14. See all Christmas movies, ever.
15. Nassar Al-Taee, *Representations of the Orient in Western Music: Violence and Sensuality* (Farnham: Ashgate, 2010), 137.
16. Keith Chapin, "Classicism/Neoclassicism" in *Aesthetics of Music: Musicological Perspectives,* ed. Stephen Downes (New York: Routledge, 2016), 144.
17. Natalie Bauer-Lechner, *Recollections of Gustav Mahler,* trans. Dika Newlin, ed. Peter Franklin (Cambridge: Cambridge University Press, 1980), 33.
18. McClelland, "*Ombra* and *Tempesta*", in *The Oxford Handbook of Topic Theory*, 286.
19. Grimalt, *Mapping Musical Signification*, 353.
20. Grimalt, *Mapping Musical Signification*, 353.
21. Stoll Knecht, *Mahler's Seventh Symphony*, 211.
22. William Mengelberg, from a complete program for the work based on Mahler's remarks during the rehearsals for the Seventh in Amsterdam, quoted in Stoll Knecht, *Mahler's Seventh Symphony*, 209.
23. Johnson, *Mahler's Voices*, 54.
24. Jane Desmond, *Meaning in Motion: New Cultural Studies of Dance* (Durham: Duke University Press, 1997), 33.
25. Desmond, *Meaning in Motion*, 41.
26. Hubert Unverricht, revised by Cliff Eisen, "Serenade" *Grove Music Online*, accessed on 4/09/2021. https://doi-org.nls.idm.oclc.org/10.1093/gmo/9781561592630.article.25454.
27. Danielle Hood, "Doubles and Duplicity: Topics in Vienna around the Long *Fin-de-Siècle*, 1874–1928" (PhD, University of Leeds, 2015). In an analysis of Symphony No. 7, movement I the musical narrative is compared to Eichendorff's novella *Das Marmorbild*, in which Florio is the protagonist.
28. Clive McClelland, *Ombra*, 144.
29. Allanbrook, *Rhythmic Gesture in Mozart*, 23.
30. H. Fitzpatrick, *The Horn and Horn-Playing, and the Austro-Bohemian Tradition from 1680-1830* (London: Oxford University Press, 1970), 20; quoted in: Monelle, *The Musical Topic*, 67.
31. Monelle, *The Sense of Music* (Woodstock: Princeton University Press, 2000), 40.

Chapter 6 Part 2

Mahler's Scherzos and the Uncanny Waltz

SYMPHONIC SCHERZOS

As Mitchell states, 'when one comes to the Scherzo of Mahler's Symphony V, [. . .] the *Ländler* has engulfed the entire Scherzo. The scale of Mahler's adoption of the *Ländler* is, then, a principal innovation in his development of the scherzo.[1] By following the development of the Scherzos from the Third Symphony to the Ninth, it reads as a mirror to the changes inherent in Viennese society that have been discussed thus far. Although Mahler wrote his Ninth Symphony after he had moved to America, the influence the decline of the Empire had on his work can still be seen in his combined use of the uncanny narrative and waltz topic. The use of the minuet and the gradual withdrawal from that aristocratic dance to the *Ländler* and the waltz, the resulting class conflict caused by the two triple time dances and, finally, the development of the uncanny narrative caused by the changing associations of the dances parallel the decay of Vienna between 1900 and 1918. The overall analyses of the Scherzo's from Symphonies Three to Nine show a darkening of the plot with each new Symphony.

Third Symphony, Movement II

The Third Symphony describes a superficial alternation between the minuet, the heavenly pastoral, the Romance topic and *style hongrois* themes. As such, it epitomises the high-/low-class dichotomy, predominantly in the opposition of the aristocratic minuet and the *hongrois* themes, but not between the dance and the pastoral, as would be expected. The second movement begins with a minuet played by a quartet consisting of the low strings with the melody (theme A) taken by the oboe. This high-class topic is soon spotted with pastoral allusions: the horn drone at b. 10 and the flute birdcalls from b. 15. At b. 20, the pastoral topic takes over as theme B (developed from the second half of theme A (A1)) emerges in the violin and then in the oboe and flutes. The grace notes in the violin melody and the semi-quaver to quaver descending leaps in the woodwind give the effect of birdcalls, while the harp's continuation of the accompaniment from theme A suggests this is the heavenly pastoral, and therefore not a sudden opposition of the minuet but a move instead only from the urban to the rural, from the civilised to the sublime. Mahler has kept the noble aspect of the music while simultaneously shifting the listener from the spectacle of the court to the wonder of nature.

At b. 28 the pastoral topic merges with the Romance topic, signified by the octave doubling in the strings, full chords in the harp and lush long chords in the horns and flutes, the moderate tempo, the presence of Alberti pizzicato bass and the rhythmically regular melody in the shape of an arch. The clarinets interject bird-like triplets keeping the pastoral allusion alive, but the trumpets emerge with a new dissonant chromatic theme (C) which is an inverted form of the second violin and viola falling scales that accompanied theme B. The Romance topic draws the narrative back towards the indoors, into the theatre or the salon as it is commonly associated with the love songs of the operettas (such as 'Dein ist mein ganzes Herz' from *Das Land des Lächelns* and in 'Deinen süßen Rosenmund' from Lehár's *Paganini*). This progression back to the city is then confirmed by the recap of the minuet at b. 35, including the reduction to a string quartet from bb. 44–50.

At b. 50, the trio begins and consists of two *style hongrois* themes, theme D in 3/8 at b. 50, then theme E at b. 70–91. Theme D bears little resemblance to anything that has come before. However, unlike the pastoral theme of the first part (bb. 20–36), the exotic connotation does bring the music down to the lower class as it is a topic that Bellman posits a 'lack of musical sophistication' through a 'mechanical approach to music-making' lending an air of contempt to the music and highlighting its use as a source of comic value.[2]

Part A returns at bb. 91–143, followed by the Trio from b. 143–210. Rather than just repeating once, as the first two parts of the western section were, they are revisited immediately in a greatly reduced, but far more tempestuous form. The multi-rhythmic essence of theme D begins in earnest at b. 192, with quaver triplets overlying semiquaver sextuplets after a loud trumpet, clarinet and oboe chord on the downbeat. The dotted theme E soon usurps the triple meter theme D (although played in the 2/4 time signature of theme E from the start of the section); the march-like comic stereotype usurping the more realistic rustic *style hongrois* dance conveyed by the fundamental triplet rhythms. The metamorphoses of the dance into the janissary march is confirmed by the dotted trumpet fanfare introducing the transition at b. 210 bearing out the low-class nature of theme E as a gypsy *halgató* emerges for seven bars, complete with trilling chords, a harp accompaniment, and a grace note embellished theme in the solo violin resembling the gypsy scale.

When the minuet returns it soon develops into a recapitulation of the other themes, utilised simultaneously and by solo instruments (although the only solo that is marked is the violin, playing theme E, it is standard to use only one or two woodwind players per part, in which case the flute (theme B), the clarinet (C) and the oboe (A) would sound as soloists). There is a descent of sorts as the rhythmic and timbral density thins during a *ritardando* leading to an unexpected new theme: a pastoral singing style theme (F) which descends gradually into a string quintet that finishes the movement with harp rising arpeggios reminiscent of the "light" figure discussed in the previous chapter as it appears in the Seventh Symphony. The romantic *Empfindsamkeit* quality of the pastoral topic here, along with the "light" figure once again denotes the heavenly pastoral contrasting powerfully with the tempestuous, and yet still comical, nature of the *style hongrois* topic. The amalgamation of the Eastern topic and the *tempesta* topic leads to an interesting layering of signification very similar to that of Mozart's topical painting of Osmin: the comical connotations along with a threatening undertone. This conveys an expression of the low-class national "Other's" rage at being marginalised, perhaps, or a scornful commentary on the unfairness of the Compromise of 1867 which resulted in the creation of the Dual Monarchy. As a Bohemian Mahler would have been aware of the perception of his nation being secondary to those of Viennese origin, indeed, Mitchell explains that

> as innovatory as, at one time, the practice of incorporating popular tunes and rhythms into the symphony may have been, at the stage when Mahler entered the lists as a composer the practice was sanctioned by custom and tradition, and facilitated, even in Mahler's case, who was not moved to express himself in terms of musical patriotism, by the wave of nineteenth-century nationalism which swept Europe, especially those regions which cherished independence but had not yet won it. (Mahler's provinces, Bohemia and Moravia, were among them. While I would not suggest that Mahler's artistic passport was anything but Austrian, I am convinced that what one might call his musical sense of locality was sensitive to his early environment, a sensitivity which in his first period, at least, could colour his music with – to state it crudely but starkly – village rather than Viennese culture, an aspect of style which brings Mahler into the orbit of nationalism.[3]

Then again, no words express the feeling of Otherness felt by the marginalised cultures as Mahler's own words: 'I am thrice homeless, as a native of

Bohemia in Austria, as an Austrian among Germans and as a Jew throughout all the world. Everywhere an intruder, never welcomed'.[4]

Fourth Symphony, Movement II

The nationalist dichotomy between city and country continues in the first movement of the Fourth Symphony where the topical narrative describes a conflict between urban and rural topical classes: those of the military and pastoral styles. Despite beginning with a rural pastoral topic introduction, the first and second themes signify the singing style and a march, introducing the urban styles that, other than the hunt topic appearing briefly at bb. 7 and 22 – which it could be argued is also an urban topic as it represents the noble hunt as perceived by urban aristocrats –, dominates the entirety of the exposition. The development describes a dialectic in which a march and a polka/hunt/singing style combination struggle to continue domination over nationalist, pastoral and *tempesta* topics, resulting in a pyrrhic victory as the funereal fanfares introduce Classical themes. The hypocrisy of that victory is emphasised by the insincere innocence of the sleigh bells, and the equally artificial society polka. The final brilliant topic, signalling the Classical finale, places these views firmly in the past. This, the narrative implies, is where decadent *Alt Wien* should lie, enabling a return to nature and innocence.

In the second movement Scherzo, that hypocrisy becomes less an anti-nostalgic sneer and more a death toll symbolised by Death's dance – the *scordatura* solo violin's dance line – that initially appears only during higher class topics, such as the string quartet waltz that takes over at bb. 7 and 27 separated by the *Ländler* at b. 22 with a new theme in folk-song reminiscent thirds (C). The temporal change between these sections confirm the waltz/*Ländler* contrast with the waltz noticeably faster than the *Ländler* in its first manifestation at b. 7. In addition, while the metronomic tempo doesn't change when the folksong theme emerges, the longer note values and sparcity of the orchestration – reducing further from the quintet that preceded it, and also acting with more homogeneity – slows the temporal perception of the section. Lastly, the beat emphasis changes, being on the second beat for the *Ländler* introduction and on the first as it changes to a waltz.

Death's dance, at b. 31, towards the end of the waltz theme leads into a pastoral section in C major evoking the opening of the first movement of Beethoven's Sixth Symphony. When the Death Dance reappears at b. 46 it is initially in the flute and oboe before the first violin takes up the tune with the *scordatura* violin doubling only the opening figure. This is the first time any instrument other than the solo violin plays Death's dance but it immediately dispels the pastoral topic for a fast swirling waltz until b. 63 when the rustic simplicity of the introduction interrupts. It seems then Death is beginning to collect souls, although, as it is the waltz he plays, it rather gives the impression that it is their culture Death takes, pulling the artificial Viennese society towards its end in order for the natural pastoral to take over.

The Trio begins at a much slower speed to the waltz it replaces, the pastoral topic now definitively dominating as a clarinet and horn fanfare introduce a folk dance, theme E, in 3rds with ornamentation such as trills and neighbour note sighs over horn-fifth drones and arpeggio figures in the harp which is then passed through the wind section. The dissonances of the previous scherzo are nowhere to be found here as the key shifts to F major and a new theme (F) begins at 81 bowed over the fingerboard of the violins producing a softer, warmer tone. This transforms in the strings into the romance topic as the second violins double the firsts at b. 94 overlaid by the hunt topic. The horn drone restarts and the first horn plays the second half of the folk dance theme E. This rhythmic figure is taken by the lower strings in a descending progression from b. 102 accompanied by chromatic movements in the horn drones. This indicates the *ombra* topic and helps to modulate back to the C minor key of the pastoral *Ländler* introduction to a repeat of the scherzo, beginning at b. 110. The introduction of the hunt topic—an artificial urban topic—into the natural pastoral section which *then* descends into darkness and fear implies a return to the scornful commentary on urban/artificial vs natural/rural of the first movement.

This time, however, the horn takes centre stage with a forte combination of the horn call and the repeated notes of theme A opposing the forte Death's dance (while the other strings play *piano*) and a partial trumpet fanfare that originates from the opening of the first trio. The trumpet usurps the oboe folk dance in 3rds (C) robbing it of its bucolic air and forcing the topic back towards an urban military fanfare. The woodwind attempts to retrieve it, and succeed, but only after a three-bar interjection by Death's dance. The C major pastoral theme D returns but this time the harp and flute birdcall, originally an F, is played by the *scordatura* violin which plays an Eb against the F in the flute and first violins creating, due also to the *sehr kurz und Gerissen* (very short and terse) marking, a sharp shock in the middle of this tranquil scene. The section finishes with an allusion to the *ombra* topic as the horns play theme A at the lower end of their range and a dissonant chord in the trumpets ushers in a discordant minor hunt before Death's waltz returns at b. 160, along with reinterpretations of theme A in the horn and woodwind. Gone is the sparse simple and rustic dance replaced by a chaotic fragmentation of the original. What follows is an angular, almost military reinvention of the folk dance from b. 22.

The repetition of the trio follows the first trio's pattern, although this time it moves to D major at b. 254 rather than F major. Raymond Knapp posits that the rising pattern of major key episodes – from C to F to D major – plots 'a generalised outward spiral, propelled (or led) by the dance, and advancing in gradual steps from vision, through pastoral removal, and eventually to transcendence'.[5] However, the pastoral topic is being undermined by topics that could be seen as urban, which are at the very least equated with humanity rather than nature. The solo instruments that perform the theme F and B2 create a chamber music atmosphere that individualises the narrative and which is confirmed when, at b. 266, the romance topic combines with the sensibility topic; the flutes, oboes, horns and violas presenting a series of appoggiaturas against the chromatic movement of the held chords.

While the romance topic is based on the emotional state of an individual it also signifies a nostalgia for *Alt Wien*, connoting the sentimental songs sung about Vienna, for example Oscar Strauss's 'Walzertraum' and 'G'stellte Mädeln' from *Ein Walzertraum*. The sensibility topic, however, is closely associated with human emotions as Matthew Head confirms: '[c]onsciousness, subjectivity and reflexivity are key terms in conceptualising sensibility, which referred not simply to a capacity to be moved but also to an awareness of that capacity and its moral obligations'.[6] As such, it is the humanisation of the pastoral that is in effect here, a realisation that society's perception and idealisation of sublime nature is being iconicised. It is the beginning of a consciousness within Mahler's Scherzo's, an awakening of a subjective voice that creates a further level of signification juxtaposing the acknowledged levels of urban versus rural or death versus childhood innocence/life which have already been explored by other scholars.[7] This concept of hearing the music through the subjective ears of the audience, particularly in this case a Viennese audience, explains the narrative of the last scherzo section, which Knapp – in his heavenly transcendence analysis – glosses over as an uneasy conclusion in C major with *Freund Hein* in retreat after the D Major breakthrough. On the contrary, in light of the narrative extended here – that is, an awakening of consciousness and differentiation between the "real" and the "perceived" – the alteration in instrumentation (utilising a bass drum, timpani, a triangle and a gong), the placement of more military rhythmic figures (the duplication of the repeated figure in theme A combined with the *ombra* figure in the bass instruments), and the accidentals which pepper the score in the last 37 bars express the Turkish style, a comic topic described in the Scherzo of the Third Symphony above. It is a parody topic, used to inject humour into operas by caricaturing a "low-class" culture as a stereotype. Once again, it is an ironic icon designed to represent not recreate, unlike the pastoral signification of the first scherzo and trio. From the superficial symbolisation of the civilised West versus the benighted East narrative of the Third Symphony, the Fourth has begun to echo the awakening of the society around it to the artificiality of their hedonism, a narrative that is continued in the Fifth Symphony.

Fifth Symphony, Movement III

Similar to the Third Symphony the Fifth Symphony's Scherzo begins with a *Ländler* introduced by a horn fanfare in D major.[8] The horn obbligato begins the *Ländler* (theme A) with the clarinets and bassoons joining it at b. 5, a very bright start to the movement, particularly in light of the end of the Fourth Symphony's D major key being associated by some scholars as transcendence to heaven. I don't believe, however, that that is what is being signified here, as the heavenly transcendence of the previous symphony was signified by the interior teleological hermeneutics rather than any exterior context. However, with the addition of cymbals, triangle and glockenspiel and pizzicato crotchets in the strings the Fifth Symphony Scherzo attains a vibrant quality that continues as the *Ländler* transforms into a "bold" waltz at b. 10 (theme B). The horn continues playing the *Ländler* while the first violins take up a waltz, distinguishable from the previous dance with its large leaps and three-quaver upbeat. At b. 40 a change in atmosphere occurs as a *fortissimo* quaver figure (theme C) in the cellos scurries under a clashing fanfare-style figure in the clarinets (C1), who are directed to lift their bells into the air. This creates a harshness of tone while simultaneously projecting the sound over the orchestra. The harshness is accentuated by the *ff* marking, the staccato accented articulation and the discordant stretto entries. When the *Ländler* and waltz themes re-enter at b. 47 they are altered to connote a darker atmosphere: the waltz theme falls chromatically with *fp* markings creating foreboding accents while the *Ländler*, also chromatically altered, accents an E against the F# in the oboe and is placed in the lowest instruments to affect a dark timbre. These low instruments are noticeably absent at b. 57 when the horn reintroduces the major *Ländler* theme A in the upper winds and strings, the second violins and viola providing the accompaniment with the triangle re-established as a brightening tool. The full orchestra returns at b. 70 with a development of the two main themes. The brightness does not last, however, as over the next twenty bars the topic darkens from aristocratic dance to *ombra*. At b. 90 the clashing fanfare from b. 40 reappears in the trumpets followed by the tuba, trombone and contrabassoon playing a form of the obbligato horn solo based on semitone rather than full tone intervals. The violins replay their chromatic waltz figure accompanying the horns diminished fanfare preceding a recap of the major wind *Ländler* that, in turn, leads onto a flamboyant example of the brilliant topic. This is signified by the sweeping contra-motion scales in the high strings and slower homophonic scales in the winds and low strings. The horn and trumpet repeat the introductory fanfare once each until at b. 131 the orchestra comes to a sudden stop and the horns play the fanfare once more to introduce the Trio and a modulation to Bb major. The sudden shifts between dark and light in the scherzo coincide with the waltz and *Ländler* alternations: the dark/*ombra* waltz in opposition to the sunlit *Ländler*. Mitchell avers that 'the contrast – conflict – between the two styles, one the primitive, peasant forerunner, the other, its brilliant, worldly successor, of the city, and sophisticated to a degree, presented the kind of dialectical complex which attracted Mahler's synthesizing musical intelligence; and from the attempted synthesis emerges part at least of the Scherzo's hectic tension'.[9] "Part", certainly, but what Mitchell terms the "brilliant" and "sophisticated" in this narrative appears more as the feared and unknown as the *ombra* signifies the supernatural. Not, in this circumstance, the supernatural of ghosts and spirits but the unknown as a simulated insincere reality in which the perception of "love, laughter, women and wine" Vienna is opposed to the authenticity of nature and the "primitive".

Nevertheless, after the introductory fanfare the waltz becomes serene, but inimitably urban as the string quintet indicates the chamber style. The string quintet waltz (theme D) opens the trio echoing the opening of the scherzo with intermittent interjections from the bassoon, oboe and flute. This serene dance continues for almost 40 bars until it is interrupted by the introduction of trumpet fanfares leading immediately into a tempestuous recapitulation of the scherzo ideas. A fugato on the repeated quaver figure pushes the movement on, the sudden and extreme dynamic changes, *"wild"* score markings and *abrupt fff* unison entries in the lowest strings at b. 213 signify the *tempesta* topic which continues into the trio introducing new thematic material at b. 222: an *ff* declamation (theme E) falling to a repeated *pianto*. The *pianto* signifies weeping, but is also a signified of the sensibility topic, which, combined with the swells and rising pitch (the initial figure rising from a C2 to an A2) and an augmentation in timbral density, increases the tension creating a suspense that dissipates at b. 241 due to a change in instrumentation and articulation. As if the stormy weather calms but hasn't abated, the wind section takes over the constant quaver figure, smoothly (with a *"Ruhig"* direction) performing them *pp* legato rather than the strings attacking dynamics and articulation. The horn develops the *pianto* figure into an expressive, though anxious, *Ländler* theme (F) but the *tempesta* topic is not forgotten and interjects in the form of the trumpet's pronunciation of the *ff* declamation.

The *tempesta* topic returns at bar 251 when the first violins reclaim the quaver figure, the woodwinds take the *Ländler* and the horns and trombones loudly assert the opening three notes of the scherzo, instilling it with an impending sense of foreboding until at b. 269 the *tempesta* transforms into the *ombra* topic. This is signified by a recitative by the horn obbligato repeating the *Ländler* melody twice, between low chords, then begins an imitative call and response between the horn obbligato and cello with the *pianto* theme, until the first horn with the declamation theme plays over a very quiet drone in the viola and cello.

A complete change in orchestration at b. 308 (figure 6.4) follows the recitative as solo pizzicato strings pick out the accompaniment, termed by Adorno as 'a prototype of the shadowlike', and the *Ländler* theme (E) with intermittent interjections of the declamatory figure in the viola.[10] The bassoon and oboe also interpose over the *Ländler*, the bassoon playing the *pianto* theme F from the recitative, and the oboe reintroducing the waltz from the beginning of the first trio at b. 136 (D).

The violin precedes it with an echo of the rhythmic form of the waltz, but the pitches of the *Ländler*. The horn recitative arrests the tempestuous urgency of the second trio constructing an atmosphere comparable to a time shard in its abrupt containment of the recitative horn and cello figures that circle without immediately developing. The recitative device is often used to push dramatic action, but here it works contrary to this purpose – holding it back – although it's other signification, to illustrate 'moments of intense dramatic crisis [. . .] [and] mental confusion (particularly madness)' tallies with my proposal that this moment indicates the beginning of the *ombra*'s transformation into the uncanny in Mahler's Symphonies.[11] When the "shadowlike" *Ländler* begins, it acts similarly to the second state ostinato of the

Figure 6.4 *Mahler,* Symphony 5, *Scherzo, bb. 308–319 showing interjections by bassoon: theme F, and declamatory theme in Viola.* (Leipzig: C F Peters, 1964).

uncanny narrative providing the unconscious base over which the conscious traumatic events or triggers, that is the waltz and the *pianto*, interject. The oboe line is marked "*schüchtern*" (bashful/shy) and pre-empts the modulation to Ab major and a pastoral rendition of the theme E *Ländler*, complete with horn drone on the dominant of the chord with an anacrusis.

The pastoral topic is gradually transformed into the *ombra* as the *pianto* theme gains prominence over the *Ländler*; *ombra* allusions beginning at b. 360 with a timpani roll as the lower instruments take over the timbral atmosphere with drones in the cello and bass against the trumpet, tuba and contrabassoon playing the *Ländler*. The themes are passed between the instruments, the density increasing gradually from the opening duet between violin and trumpet, to trios, quartets and so on. The *ombra* allusions continue, such as the high range of the flute, loud trombone fanfare (from the horn obbligato introduction), double bass pizzicato playing the waltz theme D doubling the bassoon and a tuba drone playing at the very low end of its range. Once more, Mahler completes the section with a horn solo and returns to a traditional rendition of the waltz theme.

The nostalgia of the *Alt Wien* dance, however, does not last but is interrupted at b. 447 by the aggressive theme C quavers in the cello and bass. The waltz tries to regain its dominance every two bars, but is ultimately subsumed at b. 462 by the *tempesta* topic, which significantly plays the original *Ländler* and waltz themes (A in the trombones, tuba and bass and B in the horns and woodwind). A *Holzklapper* (slapstick or whip) is used to accentuate sharply the trumpet playing the rhythm originally introduced by the glockenspiel then a cymbal and triangle roll lead the orchestra into the recapitulation.

Initially, the recapitulation follows the same topical lines as the original scherzo however at b. 527 *tempesta* inflections begin to creep in. The theme B waltz once again incorporates a chromatic falling line and sharply contrasting dynamic changes and the lower strings alter their accompaniment from a quickly moving lively scale to a slower leaping, but far more static and dark line. An *fff* marked discordant (C, D#, F# and G#) brass chord pauses the temporal movement at b. 560, but its sudden drop to *p* in the next bar releases the pause to regain the *tempesta* topic. The topic flickers between the brilliant topic (bright, exuberant, victorious) and the *tempesta* topic (dark, stormy, foreboding) – depending on the instrumentation and chromatic alterations of the theme – until the momentum is once again paused by a chorale-like section in the winds at bb. 614–632. The *tempesta* begins again with the waltz theme D, although as before, all themes make an appearance in anticipation of a final obbligato horn recitative playing the *Ländler* theme E at b. 700. Between the horn and later trombone solos the low strings play the quaver note theme C juxtaposing the stasis of the recitative style with the driven *tempesta* that theme C characterises. Just as at b. 308, the *Ländler* theme holds the temporal narrative back as if by staying in the past, in a stylised but stagnant simplicity, the narrative cannot move forward.

Eventually, at b. 745 the *Ländler* begins again in a traditional style. The horn obbligato and the trombone, however, continue their duet from the recitative, suggesting this is an artificial advancement, an attempt to gloss over the stagnation, and, true to the narrative, the idealised dance halts and is replaced by a beat in the bass drum at b. 764. The *tempesta* topic returns, scrolling through each of the topics until a final rendition of the opening fanfare, played now on all the horns finishes the movement.

In this Scherzo we see the beginning of the uncanny narrative appearing, the revolution of the *ombra* topic – an external fear of something originating in the physical world – to the uncanny narrative – a psychological or metaphysical fear of the unknown which causes a physical reaction, whether terror, anxiety, depression or hysterics. The narrative tells of a fantastical world, where light and dark diverge on a parallel with the realities of the Viennese cultural upheaval. As Mitchell says, 'If the mundane often succeeds the tragic, Mahler seems to say, there is no guarantee that the easeful security of the commonplace is anything more than a deceitful fantasy'.[12]

Sixth Symphony, Movement II

This movement begins with an *ombra* march, introduced by beats on the timpani that are accented on the third beat of each bar. The celli and basses join them, with the accent on the first beat, which along with the horns and strings dotted rhythms, drive the momentum forward. This momentum is halted at bar 32 by a high A on the piccolo and Eb clarinet. Movement resumes after two bars with beats in the low wind, low strings and bass drum, but the shrill note continues, albeit fading away over the next five bars. Once it has faded, there is a steady swirling fall in the low wind, brass and strings (B material) before a minuet begins at b. 42, with pastoral allusions in the oboe and flute trills. This is disrupted, however, by 4/8 bars, after which the light orchestration of the minuet gets denser and more martial with the inclusion of brass and percussion. This again stalls for three bars as the figures are repeated before the A theme, the *ombra* march returns, including the dark fall and finally the piccolo/clarinet shrill A over an orchestral chord and a dotted collapse over four bars. A repeated note ostinato sounds for 6 bars, but lightens over the last two *riterdando* bars as the flute and oboe lead into a *Ländler*, which converts into a Minuet when the strings take over at b. 103.

The first one hundred bars, then, plot a temporal thrust and delay, the forward momentum continuously disrupted, which, when combined with the *ombra* opening similar to the introductions to Schoenberg's Opp. 5, 16 and 17 (apart from the dynamic difference) indicate the uncanny narrative as the overall scheme of this movement. Even once the minuet commences the temporal delay plot continues. The minuet is marked "*Alväterisch*" (Old-fashioned) but is continuously disrupted by three to four bars of urgent fast staccato semi-quavers (bb. 111–114, 124–128) and a harsh *ff* clarinet interpretation of the tune at b. 134. The dance gradually gets faster, such that by b. 166 it fragments and leads back to the introduction material: the timpani beats.

Rather than a repeat of the introductory material, however, the *style hongrois* emerges, as the repeated notes now include chromatic acciaccaturas and chromatic lines in the horns and bass winds until at b. 190 it develops into a slow *csárdás*. The second violins, viola and celli play a dotted rhythm *col legno* along with the stopped horns, xylophone and bassoons. B. 199 speeds up the Hungarian dance but at b. 222 the B material drags the tempo down and with a marking of "*etwas zurückhaltend*" (somewhat reluctantly) the temporal movement comes to a halt, motion only conveyed through the semitone movements of the bass instruments and the occasional *piano diminuendo* staccato semi-quavers in the horn and bass clarinet. Floros notes that the "range of expression" here is "frightening" as the tam-tam, 'sound symbol of horror and death' is used "purposefully" here to accentuate the fatal aspect of the basic rhythm.[13] It is noteworthy that the *csárdás* was the only dance *not* temporally affected, until the B material from the Austrian (as opposed to Hungarian) march dispersed it and pulled the narrative back into the hypnoid state.

A slow regal dance begins at b. 238, but at 252 it begins to accelerate before climaxing at b. 261 and collapsing once again before the minuet returns at b. 273, again disrupted by 4/8 bars and sudden fast sections of *tempesta* lasting for only a few bars. The dance now seems to alternate between a steady minuet and a waltz, for example at b. 320 where the strings use light broken scales and upward leaps as well as soaring grace notes, whereas in the previous five bars the minuet's main feature is the three steady accented quavers, denying the waltz through the lack of the lilting *atempause*. This alternation continues until at b. 346 the *ombra* slow chromatic falls return, re-introducing the trio's Hungarian dance. The slow beginning of a csárdás emerges from the repeated note introduction, but rather than speeding up gradually the tempo changes suddenly at b. 372 to a *tempesta* section that, at 394 is once more arrested by the B material. This leads back to the *ombra* topic, which, at b. 401, collapses into a cycle involving the minuet and *csárdás* material then fragments, falling lower in pitch until in the last four bars the contrabassoon and the bass drum and timpani finish the movement.

As can be seen, the uncanny narrative is without doubt present in this Scherzo. From the introduction of the narrative in the Fifth Symphony, the narrative has asserted itself in this movement through Mahler's utilisation of the *ombra* introduction, the temporally disruptive plot. Apposed to this, Mahler outlines a Hungarian/Austrian opposition where the Hungarian dance breaks free of the dislocation imposed on the Austrian dances which Mahler never allows to truly express themselves, but are unremittingly blocked from making any progress: they become stagnant. Now that Mahler has begun to use the uncanny narrative, it persists through into the Seventh Symphony, which, as discussed in the first part of this chapter, embodies the uncanny through its illustration of the automaton and employment of the ostinato to symbolise the "hypnoid state". The Eighth has been omitted from this study as it is in two parts, rather than a traditional four or five movement form and as such does not contain a Scherzo movement. Therefore, the analysis moves on to Mahler's Ninth Symphony. Despite having moved to America when this was composed it still has a remarkable affinity to the Symphonies that precede it and shows, in a way similar to Webern's Symphony in the next chapter, how time (in Webern's case) or distance (in Mahler's) did not dull the effect the cultural milieu had on these composers.

Ninth Symphony, Movement II

The Scherzo of the Ninth Symphony begins with a pastoral *Ländler* marked '*Im Tempo eines gemächlichen Ländlers. Etwas täppisch und sehr derb*' (In the tempo of a leisurely *Ländler*. Somewhat clumsy and course). When at b. 9 Scottische allusions emerge with drones in fifths and "fiddles" playing a '*Schwerfällig*' (heavy, sluggish, ponderous or clumsy) melody the pastoral allusions grow with bird calls in the horn part. The *Ländler* returns as the main theme at b. 25 and remains the central topic until at b. 90 a string quintet takes charge with a striking waltz (I). This is not a traditional Straussian dream of love, laughter and wine, but a dysphoric dance filled with flattened sixths and sevenths, *sfp* and *ff* markings and lower brass interjections. At b. 147 the waltz I melody is heard in the bass clarinets, trombones, tuba and double basses while the rest of the orchestra, including the timpani, accompany them with the oom-pah-pah rhythm.

Waltz II is introduced with a swirling downward figure, but lasts only twelve bars before the *Ländler* returns, although at the Tempo II pace of the faster waltz I. The *Ländler*, waltz I and II swirl around each other gradually getting more sinister until finishing on an *ombra* passage signified by extremely low drones in the horns, bass clarinet and timpani. However, as the *ritardando* slows the tempo back to the *Ländler* tempo and theme, the bassoons and violas brighten the mood with pastoral utterings. The melody at b. 218, from the b. 9 *Ländler*, is marked expressive and sounds more as a singing style duet between the oboe and second violin than as the dance it is marked. Mitchell, in fact, names this a Minuet, which, if the emphasis on the first beat and the slow walking tempo is taken into account seems more likely. At b. 230, however, the original *Ländler* returns along with Tempo I, but is subsumed by the second waltz at b.243 – although still at the *Ländler* tempo – which in turn slows further as the first waltz is heard, each slower but less dysphoric than their original versions.

At b. 261 waltz I and II merge at the faster Tempo II but by b. 305 the dysphoria recurs with *sfp* chords in the horns, trumpets and upper woodwind and the cymbals joining the triangle to emphasise the waltz rhythm. Significantly, this, as in many of the Scherzos before this, is the centre of the movement although as this piece has only four movements it is not the centre of the entire piece. The key has moved to the relative B minor, and as more percussion interjects (timpani and bass drum in addition to what has already been heard) as well as *ffp* minims in the trombones at b. 318, *ombra* allusions are added to waltz II. The tempo arrests at b. 323 with a repeated note in the flute punctuating a slow chromatic line in the bassoons and trombones. A repeated quaver lift pulls the narrative out of the time shard and back into the aristocratic world with a recapitulation of the pastoral minuet in F major. The introductory *Ländler* recurs at b. 369 and gives way to the first waltz at b. 404 that quickly devolves into the *tempesta* topic with fast quaver leaps and long punching chords in the horns. The transition melody from waltz I to II (originally from b. 147–155) is now enacted in the violins providing a distinctly *tempesta* atmosphere, despite the tempo as the full orchestra play the waltz oom-pah-pah. The chromatic slides from waltz II in the horns confirm the waltz topic at b. 433 completing the transition cemented by the piccolo and high wind theme from bar 445. This grotesque waltz gradually accelerates over the next 80 bars before the Tempo I *Ländler* begins the recapitulation at b. 523 with a pastoral version of the dance as the horn plays the introductory fanfare rather than the viola and bassoon. At approximately b. 551, the second waltz begins to creep back in with the violins and the temporal narrative accelerates to quavers rather than crotchets. Even this does not last, however, fragmenting as the chromatic slides lead to a time shard created by repeated quaver fifths in the cellos and basses that provide a foundation for triplet fragments in the wind. The foundation drops away but is replaced by a drone in the horns and the timpani beating the listener into the next section: an *ombra* interpretation of the second waltz performed by bassoon, contrabassoon, horn and cello. However, at b. 595 the *Ländler* reappears and the timbre brightens as the pitch begins to lift and the orchestration thins. The *Ländler* finishes this movement as it began it, on a light sweet note of pastoral colour.

This Scherzo, therefore, epitomises the argument made throughout this book that the way in which the composers use the waltz and the *Ländler* symbolises the conflict in the cultural and political atmosphere of Viennese society. The *Ländler* represents the low-class denizens of Vienna. Nonetheless, the inherent unrefined vulgarity of the peasantry is not represented within the narrative. Instead, it symbolises the heavenly pastoral: the simplistic, sincere, authentic, *natural* side of the rural ethos that is instinctively the opposite of the aristocratic Viennese waltz. The movement begins and ends on the sweet pastoral *Ländler*, but in between the dysphoric, *ombra*, grotesque waltz satirises the Viennese bourgeoisie's hedonistic way of life. The uncanny time-shards characterise the awareness the composer has of the anxiety felt by the Viennese noble class as the Empire began to decline, just as can be seen in the contemporary literature of Joseph Roth, Herman Bahr, Karl Krauss and Hugo von Hofmannsthal. The movement summarises the narrative arc that has led through the Scherzo's from Three to Nine but also expounded on the advancement of the transformation from external fear of the unknown to a psychological anxiety that is symbolised by the uncanny narrative. In the Third Symphony, the Scherzo described the difference between high and low classes using the high-class minuet and the expression of "Otherness" felt by the marginalisation of the smaller nations. On the surface, it is the artificiality of society that is opposed to the "realness" of nature in the Fourth, however, the topical layering instead describes an acknowledgment by the composer that the heavenly transcendence of the pastoral is a perceived idealisation, no better than the artifice of the urban sophistication. The Fifth Scherzo describes a narrative in which a "dark" waltz and "bright" *Ländler* conflict, but the *Ländler* acts to rein in the progressive darkness, to halt its progress somewhat. Nostalgia affects the temporal line of the musical narration, conceding perhaps that holding on to the perception of *Alt Wien* was the cause of the anxiety described by the uncanny narrative that makes its first appearance here.

The uncanny is a definitive part of the narrative of the Sixth Symphony, fully associating itself with the political and psychological problems that go along with the fragmentation and concessions of the Austrian empire, as well as the consequent restrictions that follow as the Empire attempts to control what it has left. The commentary here on the conflict caused by the 1867 Hungarian concession is depicted by an uncanny narrative of temporal disturbance and constriction of the Austrian waltz while freedom is given to the Hungarian csárdás. The narratives of these Scherzi, from the Third onward have guided us to the quintessential example of the uncanny narrative in Mahler's Symphonies: that of the Seventh. The waltz acts in this Scherzo as a trigger of the second state, and the collapses that pierce the movement characterise the uncanny fall into the unconscious. The *Ländler*'s attempt to lift the musical narrative, couple with the romance topic signifying the quixotic charm associated with *Alt Wien*, also collapses into the waltz and the winding down of the automaton that symbolises Hoffmann's uncanny.

NOTES

1. Mitchell, *Gustav Mahler: The Early Years*, 208.
2. Bellman. "Toward a Lexicon for the *Style Hongrois*", 218.
3. Mitchell, *Gustav Mahler: The Early Years*, 207.
4. Michael Kennedy, *Master Musicians: Mahler* (Oxford: Oxford University Press, 2000), 2.
5. Raymond Knapp, *Symphonic Metamorphoses: Subjectivity and Alienation in Mahler's Re-Cycled Songs* (Middletown: Wesleyan University Press, 2003), 249.
6. Matthew Head, "Fantasia and Sensibility", *Oxford Handbook of Topic Theory*, 264.
7. See Knapp, Mitchell, Floros etc.
8. All keys analysed in concert pitch.
9. Mitchell, *Gustav Mahler: The Early Years*, 210–211.
10. Theodor W. Adorno, *Mahler: eine musikalische Physiognomik* (Frankfurt am Main, 1960); Eng. Trans. *Mahler: A Musical Physiognomy* (Chicago, 1991), 139 quoted in Constantin Floros, *Mahler: The Symphonies (Aldershot: Amadeus, 1994)*, 150.
11. Dale E. Monson *et al.*, "Recitative".
12. Donald Mitchell, *Gustav Mahler the Wunderhorn Years* (Woodbridge: The Boydell Press, 2005), 76.
13. Floros, *Gustav Mahler: The Symphonies*, 165.

Chapter 7

The Waltz as Pivot Point in Webern's Symphony Op. 21

Despite the Habsburg Empire officially ending in 1918, the repercussions of its years of decline were still felt by those who had lived through it. The symbols of the *Alt Wien* era and their contemporary associations were still known, understood and utilised by composers who had historical allegiances and connections to the city and its former artists. Such a composer is Webern: pupil of Schoenberg's and devotee of Mahler; his works – while drastically different in musical language and style from his predecessors – still mirrored the cultural struggles they had all lived through. Webern's musical language has been interpreted as abstract, un-Romantic, and lacking the "Viennese traditions" of Mahler and Schoenberg. The musical narrative of his Symphony Op. 21 (1928), however, will disprove these interpretations and show that the Viennese traditions – the anxieties, prejudices and idealisations – are still very much alive in his work.

When Webern discussed his Symphony Op. 21 in a series of lectures in 1932, now collected under the title *The Path to New Music*, he declared that 'greater unity is impossible'.[1] Despite the network of connections the composer created, the piece is peppered with contradictions and conflicts, with reversals on all levels of the work.[2] In the last lecture Webern summarises the second movement of his symphony as an attempt to 'create as many connections as possible', thereby justifying its basis on a twelve-note row the second half of which is the retrograde of the first.[3] As such, the number of row forms reduces to twenty-four, rather than the usual forty-eight. Webern's subsequent treatment of these rows using canons and palindromes creates a system of relations leading him to the above declaration. Webern's is the first of many analyses of this piece which centre almost solely on the row structure of the work, in particular the utilisation of canons and the symmetry of palindromes which allowed him to construct a larger scale work than his previous compositions.

H. Wiley Hitchcock's article, for example – written in answer to R. P. Nelson's claims that Webern's comments on his symphony were 'imprecise and conjectural' – aims only to prove the precision of Webern's own analysis through a formal breakdown of the row series and transpositions of the second movement.[4] Mark Starr concentrates more on the palindromic aspects of the second movement, although he does introduce an investigation on the palindromic treatment of not just the rows, but also the dynamics and timbre.[5] As an example, Starr illustrates the way in which all the various musical elements, which he categorises as pitch, rhythm, instrumentation, dynamics and articulation, do not always follow the canonic treatment of the rows; hence, in the second voice in variation 2 (rows P6 and P10) the pitch and rhythm are in canon, while the remaining three are not. None of these analyses, however, make any comment on the overall form of the symphony, concentrating as they do on the second movement, nor is there a discussion about the context of the piece in the symphonic genre itself.[6] This discussion was left to later scholars, such as Christopher Ballantine and Peter Brown.[7] In his overview of the work, Brown cites Webern's justification for the absence of the third movement as following the traditions set out by Beethoven, but calls it 'ironic in light of the many aspects of Opus 21 that are outside of normal cyclic and, even more specifically, symphonic practice'.[8] However, other than the length of the work and the small size of the orchestra ('only nine quiet instruments and ten minutes') Brown does not clarify which aspects are 'outside symphonic practice', concentrating in the most part, just as the scholars mentioned above, on the row form and palindromic structure.

It is the question of the symphonic tradition that Ballantine endeavours to answer, as he suggests that, while

> the two-movement work is at a technical level pure monism, built as it is on the implications of a single tone row […] it unmistakably engages with the traditional symphonic ethic of musical dualism insofar as it is profoundly and uniquely involved with a polarity of *Symmetry* and *Asymmetry*.[9]

What follows is, once again, an analysis of the structure in terms of the treatment of the row in which there is 'a struggle against imbalance and asymmetry', where 'each section has some greater or lesser "fault", which calls for a renewed attempt and so propels the music on into the next variation'.[10]

This seeming preoccupation with the form of Webern's Symphony is summarised concisely by Ballantine:

[t]here is no reason in principle why the dialectic should not make itself felt as, say, structure; why, that is, the music's own *form* of coming into being should not be subject to countervailing demands or principles, and why therefore the conflict should not realize itself as *tensions internal to the music's own structural process.*[11]

What this fixation appears to suggest, then, is that the traditional dialectic felt between 'disjunct keys and themes' in traditional symphonies, and the extra-musical meaning created by this dialectic, is not present in Webern's work. The reason for this concentration by scholars on the technical aspects of Webern's works seem to be a "tradition" of understanding Webern's music as what critic Olin Downes described in a review in the *New York Times* as 'the ultimate significance of nothing'.[12] Even Brown, who, having written his overview of the Symphony in 2003, therefore had available to him interpretive techniques which were not available to the newspaper critic in 1929, claims that this work has 'none of the overt Romanticism that informs Schoenberg's Opus 9. Webern seems to have erased from his symphony the ghost of Gustav Mahler and the Viennese symphonic tradition'.[13]

It is this claim that the present study endeavours to overturn: that there is no "Viennese" quality to the Symphony, that it cannot be interpreted as a musically meaningful work, only as a technical exercise in unity and conciseness. Further, not only is it Viennese, it can be understood topically as emplotting the same cultural uncanny narrative as Mahler's Scherzos and Schoenberg's opuses. 'The music', Busch suggests – although it is important to note she is not referring specifically to the Symphony, rather her thoughts are a general commentary on understanding Webern's compositions – 'evidently seems to frighten people; at all events it does not make things easy for them. It has not become familiar, or at least not self-evident, even to experienced interpreters'.[14] Busch further comments that while traditional musical concepts were important to Webern, appearing consistently throughout his writings on his works (for example *The Path to New Music*) musicologists have shied away from regarding the music as in any way traditional. This is possibly one of the most overlooked sources available for the argument that, rather than Webern's music being revolutionary, in fact it is steeped in tradition. It has been noted by Peter Stadlen, a pianist who studied Webern's Op. 27 with the composer, that in *The Path to New Music* Webern describes the journey towards twelve-tone composition as a progression in line with tradition. It was not a sudden rebellion against convention, just the next step along the path.[15] It is the essence of the collapse in meaning in Freud's uncanny: *'that class of the frightening which leads back to what is known of old and long familiar'*.[16] The unfamiliar musical language, which Busch claims frightens people, lies over Classical foundations: the sonata, and theme and variations.

This analysis seeks to rectify the misapprehension described by Busch by investigating the theme of reversal within the Symphony presented on three different levels. These levels are, first, the structure of the movements; second, the topical narrative; and third, an exploration of how the work follows, simultaneously, the external referential paths set out by Mahler and Strauss II, and the psychological turn inwards explored by Schoenberg. The formal analysis establishes the foundation of the argument, discussing the ways in which the Symphony slips between traditional and new paths in its construction. I will then demonstrate how the topics interact with the structure and each other to form a narrative in which traditional significations are upturned to form oxymoronic topics such as the urban pastoral in the second movement. The individual explorations of these domains then combine with a social and cultural exploration positing that the binary oppositions between society and nature espoused by Mahler and Strauss and described in the previous chapters are still present in combination with the expression of the inner psyche from Schoenberg's "New Music", as the unfamiliar musical language represses, or hides, the familiar traditional forms and social issues.

FIRST MOVEMENT

The first movement of the Symphony is in sonata form, which Bailey suggests follows the binary outline of the Classical form as both sections, the exposition and the development/recapitulation, are repeated.[17] However, the formal expectations are subverted, as the tonal identity does not follow the traditional course – that is, the exposition ends away from the tonic and the recapitulation returns to it. In Webern's rendition, the row series of the exposition, bars 1–26, repeats exactly in the recapitulation, bar 42 to the end. Hence, although this piece cannot be discussed in terms of traditional tonality, the comparative structural system, that is the row order, does not return to the "tonic" when the second theme is recapitulated; instead, it retains the transposition pattern of the exposition. That Webern may have intended this analogy with tonality is addressed by Busch:

> The title originated with Schoenberg, yet with a variant: 'Composition *with* 12 Notes'. In his 1932 lectures, Webern continued to speak of composition *in* 12 notes. This enabled him to create in his listeners' minds the connexion with a conception of music into which the new methods of composing could also be seamlessly incorporated. [. . .] One might say even one with some degree of concreteness, insofar as this spatial conception enables the 'concrete' musical experience of music that 'is in C major' to be communicated by analogy.[18]

Further, Arnold Whittall confirms that 'all three [Schoenberg, Berg, and Webern] used terminology suggesting that they needed to project the new developments against a tonal background: they tended to refer to the Prime as "T" (tonic) and the transposition of the basic series at the triton – not at the perfect fifth – as "D" (dominant)'.[19]

Bailey also identifies two other departures from the Classical form: the use of the canon, which tends to be associated with the development rather than the exposition, and the difference between the melodic material of the exposition and the recapitulation.[20] The two are usually melodically similar; however, while the row structure here is an exact replica, the musical material is different. The exposition's themes are also presented unconventionally in that, as Bailey puts it, 'Webern has rotated the exposition ninety degrees, so that events one customarily encounters in succession in this section occur simultaneously instead'.[21] The two themes share the exposition, as Canon I and Canon II, the first utilising more lyrical material, while the second uses shorter notes and angular phrases with pizzicato and staccato markings.

Bailey recognises that the conclusion that this piece is in sonata form is not universally recognised; other scholars have presented it as ternary, or described it as "structural variation".[22] However, while the musical material is superficially different, when looked at closely it is only a rhythmic diminution and textural augmentation of the original material (figure 7.1). As such, although this demonstration of the similarities confirms Bailey's assertion that the movement is structured in sonata form, it disagrees with her conclusion as to how much Webern altered it.[23]

The row form of the recapitulation is only one of the ways in which the Symphony's first movement differs from traditional sonata form; the movement's development is also significant. In *Fundamentals of Musical Composition*, Schoenberg discusses the nature of the development, which he terms the elaboration or *Durchführung*:[24]

> The elaboration is essentially modulatory, and for very good reasons. [. . .] In the exposition, though some parts modulate and others express a (related) contrasting tonality, apart from transitions, everything stands solidly within the region of definite tonality. In other words, the harmony is essentially stable. This requires a different kind of contrast in the elaboration.[25]

Schoenberg lists examples of contrasts between the exposition and the elaboration, most of which are based on tonal modulations but also include rhythmic features, thematic material, structure and length. What is clear is that the traditional development section, as Schoenberg would have taught it to Webern, tends towards instability and lacks ruling features other than that it contrasts with the stable exposition.

Theme 1: bb. 1–6.

Theme 2: bb. 3–7.

Theme 1 and 2: bb. 44–47.

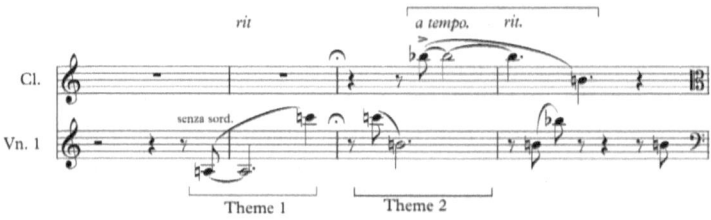

Figure 7.1 *Motivic Similarities in Bars 1–26 and 43–end.* Webern, Symphony Op. 21/I for chamber ensemble (c) by kind permission of Universal Edition AG, Wien / PH368).

This is possibly the most significant way in which Webern has reinterpreted sonata form in the Symphony. The development (bars 26–42) is an extremely strict symmetrical structure, not the unstable 'working out' which Schoenberg describes in his essay. Consisting of a pair of mirrored canons, one of prime rows and one of inverted rows, all four voices are identical with respect to rhythm and segmentation. These are set within a palindrome, which pivots between the last quaver of bar 34 and the first quaver of 35. Therefore, the development acts independently from the rest of the Symphony. Other than one of the rows corresponding with the last row of Canon II (P11), so that there is a continuation in some form from the exposition to the development, the palindrome structures the section into a self-contained module ending with a general pause on the bar line preceding bar 46. This is a reversal of the function of the traditional development and forms the basis of the topical analysis. In that later section, it will be suggested that the implication of perpetuity in a section removed from the rest of the movement is analogous with the ostinati so far seen in Schoenberg and Mahler's music signifying Freud's repressed hypnoid, or second, state.

The exposition begins with the *Nachtmusik* topic, signified by the low range of the instruments and the scarcity with which they are used. The higher violin and clarinet are employed only briefly in each canon, and again use only low pitches. The melodic movement is slow and steady, like footsteps, which, combined with the pizzicato technique, could suggest the *ombra* topic; however, with the absence of *sul ponticello* technique and with the utilisation of a horn call as the melodic base of the first canon signification veers more towards the pastoral. This could suggest a location, similar to the way in which Schoenberg used the *ombra* topic in his Opp. 16 and 17 to signify dark forests, which without the *ombra* signifiers may now have become the mountains so important to Webern. In Freud's *Interpretation of Dreams*, the psychoanalyst suggests that 'many of the landscapes seen in dreams, especially those that contain bridges or wooded mountains, may be readily recognized as descriptions of [female] genitals', and therefore signify the castration complex.[26] In his analysis of the second movement of the Symphony, Johnson emphasises the signification of nature throughout the theme and variations, which he then associates with the gravesites of Webern's parents, adducing that Webern was visiting the sites in Schwabegg when the pieces were written. The overwhelming effect of the *Nachtmusik* style introduction is a sense of space and stillness, which, combined with the enclosed row progression, creates an environment at once infinite and static, but which is opposed by the use of two movement-inducing canons. This environment might be held to emulate Webern's mountain climbing experiences: Moldenhauer notes that Webern's ambition when climbing 'was not for conquest; he wished only to immerse himself in the wonders of nature and in the stillness of the heights'.[27]

The *Nachtmusik* style also has darker connotations of mourning, as seen in Mahler's 'Nun will die Sonn' so hell aufgeh'n' from *Kindertotenlieder* and 'Der Schildwache Nachtlied' from *Des Knaben Wunderhorn*. Hence, this style acts multivalently; the mountains and graves are signified simultaneously, as are the notions of time eternal and the finality of death. There is also, according to Shreffler, a third level evoking Webern's religious beliefs: 'a pantheistic piety that blended elements of Lutheranism and nature worship with his native Catholicism, never closely associated with an institutional church'.[28] Moreover, Shreffler notes, Webern drew religious inspiration from musical and literary sources more than theological ones, for example the folk poetry of Rosegger, which, while relegated to anthologies of children's literature after the Second World War, was at the time respected in literary circles.[29] A recurring theme within Rosegger's stories is that of God represented in nature. In *Mein Himmelreich*, Rosegger exclaims:

> I would still have found such a tightly knit, unified world of belief upon the awakening of my reason. And if I had not encountered something like this, no church, no pulpit, no altar, no pious mother and no father to point me to God, I believe that I would still have believed from the depths of my being. I imagine that for example the flower, the storm, the stars in the heavens, the mountains, the sea, the entire world-essence life![30]

This would certainly resonate with Webern's idea of nature, as set out by Julian Johnson, and would further polarise the dichotomy between the idyllic mountainside and the Vienna metropolis. Schreffler, here citing Dean Garrett Stroud, explains that

> God's presence in nature, according to Rosegger, is revealed most immediately and purely on the mountain peaks [...] The mountain excursions that figure so prominently in his stories represent the voyage into the soul, in which 'the mountain represents the goal of the journey, and [...] serves as the place where union with the Divine is most likely to take place'.[31]

The diminution of the rhythmic values from bar 13 onwards, however, begins to move against the static nature of the *Nachtmusik* style as it increases the temporal movement, while at the same time the tempo markings – *calando* (bars 17 and 19) and *ritardando* (bar 23) – attempt to reduce the temporal movement. This appears to create a restrictive atmosphere, similar to that produced by the instrumentation constraints in his Op. 16 *Fünf Canons*.

Once again, then, there is a reversal at play within the topical narrative. The temporal movement of the second half of the exposition only *appears* to create restrictions that have actually been present throughout the entire 26 bars. This constriction takes the form of the learned style, signified by the canonic structure and is placed in opposition to the pastoral topic. The learned style, and particularly the strict style subtopic, connotes both the church and the adherence to laws. Therefore, the perpetuity implicated by the *Nachtmusik* style and the repetition of the exposition is reversed by the structured canons of the themes, effectively overturning the signification of the strict style. Hence, Webern integrated the signified "church", the goal-led restrictive style, with the signified "nature", containing signifiers which connote space, stillness, expansion and perpetuity; therefore, to all intents and purposes, reversing both significations to include the other. Tom Service echoes George Benjamin's thoughts that there is a 'sense of stasis in this first movement of the Symphony, the uncanny feeling that time is not moving like an unstoppable arrow, but rather softly expanding and exploding in all directions, like the growth of a crystal – or [...] a snowflake'.[32] The atmosphere of "expansion" ironically causes the *Nachtmusik* canons to act similarly to the ostinati in Schoenberg's works to signify the hypnoid state and, subsequently, the notion of the double consciousness, or unconscious. Freud states that if something is 'withdraw[n] from knowledge, it becomes unconscious': it is repressed. In the above quotation, Busch suggests that the traditional musical concepts (such as form) are not "self-evident", but hidden by the unfamiliar musical language, withdrawn from the surface and therefore repressed.

The *a tempo* in the second time bar, b. 25, signals the beginning of the development and the apparent temporary relaxation of the restraints. The canonic entries are closer together, the dotted semibreve entries, based on theme one, begin only a bar apart, the high violin line causing dissonances alien from the calm stillness of the exposition. Where the exposition entries were always on a crotchet beat, the entries here are often on the second or sixth quaver of the bar, adding syncopation to the sensation of movement initiated by the shorter canonic intervals and dissonances – a movement swiftly arrested by a silent pause at bar 34. The closer entries turn the long notes into drones, which underscore birdcall figures and grace notes in the harp, clarinet and strings. This suggests that the pastoral is still dominant, but with brighter allusions than the previous *Nachtmusik*. The pivot point at bb. 34–35 is another example of an uncanny "time-shard". A steady pulse stream in a musically static environment—in this case, in between two pauses – it is, Cherlin writes, 'the ghostly presence of the way time "used to go"', referring to the teleological characteristic of Classical music, and therefore referencing the music not only from the previous bars, but also from an earlier tradition. The *ombra* signifiers also present here, the low cello and harp notes, the grace notes, and the triple *pianissimo* dynamic marking, confirms the time shard as a signifier of the uncanny narrative.

The row form is also worthy of note here as each row follows the same rhythmic pattern, creating a strictly imitated melodic line. This appears contrary to the idea of this section as a development of bars 1–24 as it is far stricter than the previous section, where developments are usually unfettered and unstable, as seen in previous case studies where the *tempesta* topic has been utilised, for example, in the first movements of Mahler's Fourth and Seventh Symphonies. However, in each of these the unstable topic has juxtaposed a stable, goal-oriented topic like the military topic, which in Mahler's

Fourth Symphony, Movement I dominated the *tempesta* signifiers. This, combined with the tonal progression – leading traditionally, albeit on a winding path, to the tonic of the first theme –, formed an extended transitory period leading to the recapitulation. As discussed above, however, this development section is an enclosed unit in which two stable topics, the strict style and the pastoral, are juxtaposed.

Although the second eight bars of the development are the retrograde of the first eight bars, the topic alters slightly. The pastoral topic now incorporates the allusions to the *ombra* topic absent from the first half of the movement, caused initially by the *ombra* signifiers of bars 34–35 colouring the subsequent material, but also because of the placement of the grace notes. In order for the grace notes to appear before the main note, the pitches of the two notes affected are swapped. This means that, rather than a long low note ending on a higher pitch, an elevation which lightens the mood of the musical material, there now appears a short high note that drops quickly to a lower long note (clarinet, bb.32 and 37; violin II, bb. 32–33, 36–37), an action which invokes an anticipatory mood of anxiety or dread. This change is emphasised by the addition of staccato accents to the quavers, giving them a harsher quality. The gradual metamorphosis into the *ombra* topic continues in the four-bar transition, bars 42–46, which introduces harmonics, forte-*piano* dynamics and an A minor stretto chord unexpectedly resolving onto a high C# triple *pianissimo* quaver in the harp. At bar 46 the *ombra* topic is fully manifested, signified by harmonics, *sforzando* and forte-*piano* and forte dynamics, high range orchestration, and dissonant chords. The alpine horn call is now brash, with no mute and a forte dynamic marking, and the bird song is peppered with grace notes and harmonics, and *is* muted, therefore subtly altering the signification from a bright, spacious pastoral to a harsh, subdued unstable hunt. The retrograde of the movement therefore reverses the signification of the topics. What seems to be small alterations in articulation and technique produce substantial changes in signification. The pivot acts as a turning point between the conscious and the unconscious, signified by the double coding of the various inflections of the pastoral topic.

SECOND MOVEMENT

The second movement is a theme and variations form, the theme of which is the first time the prime row is played by one instrument, in this case clarinet. The structure of the movement corresponds to Schoenberg's description of a theme and variations movement in *Fundamentals* in that the theme is 'simple' and 'consists of closely related motive-forms'.[33] These small

Figure 7.2 *Motivic Segmentation.* Webern, Symphony Op. 21/ii for chamber ensemble (c) by kind permission of Universal Edition AG, Wien / PH368), bb. 1–11; 14–20.

motives (labelled a–d, illustrated in figure 7.2), can be seen in various states of development throughout the seven variations. However, the Symphony differs from the traditional variations form in one significant sense. In his lecture of 1932, Webern stated that the theme and variations is as close to total unification as is possible, containing not just thematic, but also serial and formal unity:

> The second movement of my Symphony (Op. 21, written in 1928). It's peculiar in that the second half is the cancrizan of the first. This is a particularly intimate unity. So here there are only 24 forms, since there are a corresponding number of identical pairs. In the accompaniment to the theme the cancrizan appears at the beginning. The first variation is in the melody a transposition of the row starting on C. The accompaniment is a double canon. Greater unity is impossible. Even the Netherlander didn't manage it. In the fourth variation there are constant mirrorings. This variation is itself the midpoint of the whole

movement, after which everything goes backwards. So the entire movement is itself a double canon by retrograde motion!³⁴

The unity, or to use Schoenberg's word, "comprehensibility" of the Symphony is akin, in Webern's opinion, to Goethe's *Urpflanze* – the primeval plant in which 'the root is in fact no different from the stalk, the stalk no different from the leaf, and the leaf no different from the flower: variations on the same idea'.³⁵ In the same way as the development of the first movement's sonata form deviates from the Classical convention, so too the inherent unity of Webern's variations departs from the essentially paratactic tradition outlined by Sisman and Schoenberg. Sisman equates variation form to the oratory style parataxis. She contrasts the 'fragmented, "chopped up"' paratactic style with the "rounded" hypotactic, or periodic style.³⁶ Hernstein Smith categorises these opposing styles through the internal connections among the variation segments. She writes that

> when repetition is the fundamental principle of thematic generation, the resulting structure will tend to be *paratactic*; that is, the coherence of the poem will not be dependent on the sequential arrangement of its major thematic units. In a non-paratactic structure [. . .] the dislocation or omission of any element will tend to make the sequence as a whole incomprehensible or will radically change its effect. In paratactic structure, however, [. . .] thematic units can be omitted, added, or exchanged without destroying the coherence or effect of the poem's thematic structure.³⁷

Thus, the Symphony's second movement is not paratactic; if one section is removed the palindrome is compromised and the movement becomes structurally incomprehensible. The cohesive substance of the conventional variations form is only thematic, unlike the tonal and thematic comprehensibility of structures such as the sonata form. Rosen argues that in the nineteenth century, Classical forms, including the variation form, took on features of the sonata such as the integrity of both the harmonic and thematic structure.³⁸ Consequently, rather than the paratactic, 'abstract model of variation form' of the Classical period, Webern references the Romantic form of works such as Beethoven's *Appassionata* sonata, Op. 57.³⁹

This radical digression from tradition parallels Samuel Taylor Coleridge and Hegel's development of idealism and organicism in the nineteenth century.⁴⁰ In her article "The Living Work", Ruth Solie reviews the advancement of biological philosophy over mechanistic thought, noting that this 'particular manifestation of idealism places much emphasis on the transcendence of the multifarious, diverse substances of the apparent world in a higher and unified reality'.⁴¹ Solie describes a reorientation of philosophical consideration, from the prevalence of the 'part-to-whole construction of the world' hypothesis in pre-Romantic times, to one in which 'the whole is primary and its constituent parts derived therefrom'.⁴² The Symphony's unified departure from paratacticism, then, encompasses Coleridge's concept of the organism:

> The difference between an inorganic and organic body lies in this: In the first [. . .] the whole is nothing more than a collection of the individual parts or phenomena. . . while in the second, the whole is everything, and the parts are nothing [. . .] Depend on it, whatever is grand, whatever is truly organic and living, the whole is prior to the parts.⁴³

Therefore, despite the superficial difference of the sections, each variation connects to another, revolving around the pivot point at bar 50 (figure 7.3). Variation five is the retrograde of variation three; six is the retrograde of two; and seven of one. Variation four is the only one which is not obviously symmetrical, using a subtler type of palindrome, but it does contain the pivot point. Instead, there is an intimate pitch relationship between P0 and I3 in which the reversal takes place on two levels. The pairs of notes in the rows remain intact and operate as units. Bailey explains how this is significant, stating that

Figure 7.3 Webern, Symphony Op. 21/ii for chamber ensemble (c) by kind permission of Universal Edition AG, Wien / PH368). Variation IV, b. 50.

in the outer tetrachords, the units appear in reverse order in the answering row, while the internal order of their elements is unaltered. Conversely, the order of the units within the central tetrachord is the same in both rows, but the internal order of their members is reversed. At no point in the row do both levels reverse simultaneously. Thus none of the tetrachords is answered by its exact retrograde; this is prevented by the maintenance of the original ordering at one level or the other.[44]

The whole is therefore an integral network of connections rather than the linear thematic variations of old, which makes it, in Coleridge's, Goethe's and Webern's eyes, truly organic.

The chordal nature of the accompaniment and the slow, steady crotchet movement of the clarinet's prime row statement suggest a recitative style, although one with a calm lyricism. The first variation takes the form of a mirrored canon played by the string quartet. The syncopation, alternating pizzicato and arco articulation, and grace notes combine with what Johnson termed the 'light, tripping figures' which, he claims, signify early spring.[45] Certainly, it is the pastoral topic signified here, but Webern once again constrains it within an extremely strict structure associated firmly with the learned topic and therefore urbanity. The simultaneity of these two topics could then be considered an "urban pastoral", an oxymoron describing the employment of a "man-made" topic such as the learned style in a structural role within which pastoral musical signifiers have been utilised as musical material. The dialectic caused by the "urban pastoral" is similar to Mahler's use of these topics in his Fourth and Seventh Symphony's Scherzos that represented his commentary on the perceived idealisation of the rural peasantry. The divergent nature of these topics is exploited in the second variation as a brash hunt topic takes over, significantly the topic Mahler used to fully represent the urban pastoral concept. All the instrumental voices here are palindromic, rotating around the beginning of bar 29, except the driving horn quavers, increasing the impression of moving forward after the previous two calmer topical fields. The hunt topic presented highlights the collision between the rural and urban topical associations, as it is not the chivalrous, noble atmosphere normally signified by the hunt that is suggested here, but a vulgar parody, ironically closer to an authentic hunt than the romanticised version traditionally symbolised.

At b. 34 an abrasive fanfare introduces the third variation and the *tempesta* topic, with the forte fanfares introducing the beginning and end of each row, all of which elide by two notes: 11/1, 12/2. Alternating between I3/RI3 and P6/R6, the palindrome pivots around b. 39 and a moment of stillness reminiscent of the uncanny topic at bb. 34–35 in the first movement which was the pivotal bar for the development's palindrome. The *tempesta* topic gives way at b. 45 to the fourth variation's waltz topic. This is the only variation which is not palindromic, but it does contain the palindromic centre of the piece at b. 50 (19). Unlike the first movement, where the musical material and the row are in retrograde, the musical material from this point on is not the same as the first half. Some aspects of the previous variations remain intact – the horn standing apart from the palindrome in variations II and VI, and some of the motives are repeated in their original form – but the overall melodic material is unrecognisable to the listener. This suggests that the waltz has drastically altered the world of the narrator.

The waltz topic of variation IV contrasts the previous *tempesta* topic with its slow lyricism, which Johnson asserts 'relate[s rhythmically] directly to the Schwabegg pieces such as the slow movement of Op. 24'.[46] In the example Johnson cites, from bb. 19–22 of the Concerto, one can see the rhythmic similarities with the fourth variation of the Symphony, but, owing to the differences in articulation, dynamics and instrumentation the effect in the Concerto is quite forceful, almost aggressive, and therefore in stark contrast to the waltz seen here. Johnson proposes that the gravesites, and the surrounding landscape, were 'the physical embodiment of a *Heimat* rooted in his family past'.[47] It is interesting then that the waltz topic is used in this context, as its traditional association is with the cultured upper classes of the city and therefore carries urban rather than pastoral connotations. While slower and more lyrical than the usual Strauss waltz, possibly suggesting a wistful nostalgia, it still carries the double coding of the Viennese waltz seen in the previous chapters. Signifying the upper-class Viennese identity, the waltz also invokes the *Ländler*, associated with the low-class primitive Austrian peasant who is simultaneously idolised as happy and simple. This double signification of the waltz therefore epitomises the relationship between the elevated society and the brute peasantry, the yearning for the freedom of nature and the obligations inherent in being part of civilisation.

In addition to the evocation of the double by the waltz topic, at the centre of the fourth variation there is a bar of repeated notes, another uncanny "timeshard", used once again at the pivot point. Bailey demonstrates that although this bar appears to relax the strictness Webern has shown in the rest of the work, in actuality all of the notes except the central B♭ in the clarinet are in their proper place within the row.

That this bar is contained within the only inaccurate palindromic variation is significant. As suggested by the second variation horn figures, the unconstrained line drives through the non-linear accompaniment, signifying a movement of some sort. Johnson posits that 'the centre of the palindrome, the mystery of the fourth variation, transforms the nature imagery of the first half into the increasingly "abstract" journey of the second'.[48] In the second variation, the movement is suggestive of the galloping hunting horse; here it implies a different type of journey, in which the musical narrative refocuses from the external world to the internal psyche.

The tense ostinato of the fifth variation retrospectively confirms this uncanny narrative and consists of accented staccato semiquavers overlaid with a cowbell-like triplet figure in the harp. In a 1932 letter to Adorno, Webern expressed his happiness that Adorno had interpreted these figures as such: 'And when speaking of the harp passage in the fifth variation of my Symphony you interpret it as "cowbells", this image makes me extremely happy, because I gather from that you have rightly heard'.[49] Once more, Webern references Mahler's Seventh Symphony, this time the first *Nachtmusik*, although in not quite as obvious a way. In Mahler, the cowbells denoted the physical open space of the mountains and the emotional/metaphysical space between the dance and the pastoral topics in addition to imposing mankind on the idyllic scene.[50] The syntagmatic position of the waltz and the pastoral topic in this movement implies a similar interpretation here. The pastoral references in the ostinato, and the suspenseful atmosphere generated by the staccato and accent articulation of the repeated semiquavers, suggest that this is a signifier of the repression seen in the first movement, in which the signifieds "church" and "nature" collapsed into each other. It creates an impression of a tense atmosphere but includes signifiers traditionally associated with idyllic cowherds living simplistic lives. The tense mood of the fifth variation continues as the large leaps and sudden alterations in dynamics and rhythms echo the brash hunt topic, including the non-palindromic horn, of the second variation. The clarinets each play a row (I10 and P2) and then the retrograde of that row so that they are palindromes, but the horn has two rows which run simultaneously and are not palindromic. This is the retrograde of the second variation row series, in which the horn quavers alternate between I0 and P11.

In this instance, however, the horn is not playing driving quavers, but rather the rhythm is unpredictable and unstable. The rests act as simultaneously anticipatory and restraining, in that the variation does not progress as a goal-oriented driving force, but nevertheless leads to variation VII, an inflected repeat of the first variation's pastoral topic. Finally, the coda repeats the rows from the theme, P0/R0, but neither the topic nor the motivic material is similar. Instead, a solo violin melody plays a lyrical line, more suggestive of a folksong than of a recitative. The absence of the canon in the coda is significant; the freedom from restriction combines with the simple folksong of the peasants, symbolising the return to the surface of the structure repressed throughout the movement. Bailey also claims significance for the simplistic coda in this way, positing that it is one of the only parts of the movement where it is likely the listener will hear the "ingeniously constructed" palindrome without the benefit of a score:

To the listener is presented the most deceptively simple string of variations, each with its own distinctive instrumentation, rhythms, articulation, and so forth—features which do not recur in symmetrical fashion. The listener could never be expected to know that he is hearing a palindrome which encompasses the movement as a whole. [. . .]. He will hear the numerous small palindromes in [the] Variations [. . .] but will probably not hear any complete section as a palindrome until the Coda.[51]

Bailey describes the organic nature of this movement as she suggests that the parts are incomprehensible until they have all been heard: 'the whole is everything, the parts are nothing'.[52] The construction of the topical syntax means that individual topics are meaningless outside their context, whether that is within the narrative of one piece, or their position within the cultural context as a whole. However, until the whole narrative is realised, it is not entirely possible to understand the unifying qualities of the piece under the surface complexities. Bailey claims this impenetrable surface is "carefully contrived" by Webern, as in some variations, such as Variation I, 'it is unlikely that the listener will hear two mirror and retrograde canons in this variation because of his inability to comprehend the wealth of complex relationships which are exposed in a very short period of time'.[53] In Variation V, on the other hand, the simplicity of the variation 'entirely hides the real structure'.[54] The "real structure", or meaning, is therefore repressed beneath surface signifiers which act similar to a series of images in a dream, becoming clear only once analysed as a whole. Freud describes dreams in the same way, as a "rebus", a series of 'hieroglyphics, whose symbols must be translated, one by one, into the language of dream-thoughts'.[55] Once translated, these seemingly unconnected symbols are understood as a whole, just as, without an understanding of each variation's structure and topical narrative, the topical meaning in Webern's Symphony cannot be revealed.

Most analyses or descriptions of Webern's Symphony, and indeed most of his works, concentrate on the technical compositional method, in this case the twelve-tone technique and his use of symmetry. Even Webern's own comments on the work focus on the unifying element of the tone row and the thematic and formal connections which embody Goethe's conceptual organicism. The superficiality of these analyses – the fact that they direct their attentions only to the surface functionality, without investigating the expressionistic quality of the works – is summed up by Brown, when he states that 'Webern seems to have erased [...] the Viennese symphonic tradition'.[56] However, although Webern's comments regarding the Symphony itself focus on its formal unity, the basis of the surrounding lectures is to situate the "new" method within the compositional tradition of the Netherlanders and Classical composers.

Busch's observation, that the music "frightened" listeners through its unfamiliarity, brings to light the aspect in which Webern's music follows Viennese traditions, not only as set out by Webern's mentor, Schoenberg, but also by Mahler and Strauss. The analysis of the three domains of form, topical narrative and Freudian methodologies have demonstrated that, although the Symphony is based in tradition, there are reversals at play, moments where there are twists on the conventions almost to the point of parody, particularly in the topical domain. In the first movement, the sonata form is altered without the "tonality", the thematicism nor the use of canon following the Classical conventions. The exposition and first half of the development exhibits the multivalent properties of the integration of the strict and *Nachtmusik* styles, the infinite and the static signifying the amalgamation of the signifieds "church" and "nature" and the notion of the double. The narrative therefore encompasses commentaries from both *Alt Wien* and "New Music". The ironic social narratives inherent in Strauss's *Die Fledermaus* and Mahler's Scherzos and *Des Knaben Wunderhorn* are present in the repression of intrusive reality on the civilised utopian ideal, while the psychoanalytical uncanny narrative symbolises the repression of the very traditions Mahler and Strauss mocked, shown by the final tranquillity as the traditional structure is revealed in the coda. The second movement confirms the melding of these two narratives with the utilisation of the waltz/*Ländler* double at the pivot point of the variations. The topical meaning of the waltz, both as an Austrian dance and an upper-class topic is double-coded with the *Ländler* signification. As the waltz developed from the *Ländler*, the lower-class dance is necessarily present simultaneously: the waltz is a *Ländler* that has entered civilisation. A waltz, in Freudian terms and in Webern's hands, is always already a repressed *Ländler*.

NOTES

1. Anton Webern, *The Path to New Music*, ed. Willi Reich (London: Theodore Presser, 1963), 56.

2. Kathryn Bailey discusses the way in which Webern transforms rather than diverges from tradition in his use of row forms in her article: Kathryn Bailey, "Webern's Op. 21: Creativity in Tradition", *The Journal of Musicology*, 2, no. 2 (Spring 1983), 184–195.

3. Ibid. Donna Lynn's article chronicles the compositional process of the row through Webern's sketches and demonstrates how, originally the row was four three-note gestures, in which the second (G♯–A–B♭) is the mirror image, by retrograde inversion, of the first (G–F♯–F); Donna Lynn, 12-Tone Symmetry: Webern's Thematic Sketches for the Sinfonie, Op. 21", *The Musical Times* 131, no. 1,774 (Dec., 1990): 644–646. See also George Perle, "Webern's Twelve-Tone Sketches", *The*

Musical Quarterly, 57, no. 1 (Jan., 1971): 1–25. Other literature on the composition of the rows, and the possible segmentation of the music includes Catherine Nolan "New Issues in the Analysis of Webern's 12-Tone Music", *Canadian University Music Review*, 9, no. 1 (1988): 83–103.

4. H. Wiley Hitchcock, "A Footnote on Webern's Variations", *Perspectives of New Music* 8, no. 2 (Spring/Summer, 1970), 123; R.P. Nelson, "Webern's Path to Serial Variation", 80.

5. Mark Starr, "Webern's Palindrome", *Perspectives of New Music*, 8, no. 2 (Spring/Summer 1970): 127–142.

6. One insightful analysis based solely on the first movement of the Symphony is Lejaren Hiller and Ramon Fuller, "Structure and Information in Webern's Symphonie, Op. 21", *Journal of Music Theory* 1, no. 1 (Spring 1967): 60–115. This is a comparative study between a structural analysis (of the row series) and an information theory analysis.

7. Christopher Ballantine, *Twentieth Century Symphony* (London: Denis Dobson, 1983), 194–201; A. Peter Brown, *The Symphonic Repertoire: The Second Golden Age of the Viennese Symphony* (Bloomington: Indiana University Press, 2003), 875–884.

8. Brown, *The Symphonic Repertoire*, 875.

9. Ballantine, *Twentieth Century Symphony*, 194. How prevalent symmetry actually was in the music of the composers of the Second Viennese School is discussed in David J. Hunter and Paul T. von Hippel, "How Rare is Symmetry in Musical 12-Tone Rows?", *The American Mathematical Monthly* 110, no. 2 (Feb., 2003): 124–132. The authors demonstrate that although symmetrical rows were rare in Viennese twelve-tone music, they are far rarer in the universe of all row classes.

10. Ballantine, *Twentieth Century Symphony*, 194–198.

11. Ballantine, *Twentieth Century Symphony*, 186.

12. Olin Downes, *New York Times*, December 19, 1929.

13. Brown, *The Symphonic Repertoire*, 883.

14. Regina Busch, "On the Horizontal and Vertical Presentation of Musical Ideas and on Musical Space (I)", *Tempo* New Series no. 154 (Sept, 1985), 2.

15. Peter Stadlen, "The Webern Legend", *The Musical Times* 101, no. 1,413 (Nov. 1960): 695.

16. Freud, "The Uncanny", *The Standard Edition*, vol. XVII, 218–219.

17. Bailey, *The Twelve-note Music of Anton Webern*, 163.

18. Busch, "On the Horizontal and Vertical Presentation of Musical Ideas and on Musical Space (I)", 6.

19. Arnold Whittall, *The Cambridge Introduction to Serialism* (Cambridge: Cambridge University Press, 2008), 87.

20. Bailey, "Webern's Op. 21: Creativity in Tradition", 187.

21. Bailey, *The Twelve-note Music of Anton Webern*, 166.

22. Bailey, *The Twelve-note Music of Anton Webern*, 164.

23. Bailey, *The Twelve-note Music of Anton Webern*, 164.

24. Schoenberg's choice of the term "elaboration" rather than development stems from his conviction that '[development] suggests germination and growth which rarely occur. The thematic elaboration and modulatory "working out" (*Durchführung*)

produce some variation, and place the musical elements in different contexts, but seldom lead to the "development" of anything new' (Schoenberg, 1967, 206).

25. Arnold Schoenberg, *Fundamentals of Musical Composition,* ed. Gerald Strang and Leonard Stein (London: Faber and Faber, 1967), 206.

26. Freud, "The Interpretation of Dreams", *The Standard Edition,* vol. IV, 356.

27. Hans Moldenhauer and Rosaleen Moldenhauer, *Anton Webern: A Chronicle of his Life and Work* (London: Gollanz, 1978), 285.

28. Anne C. Schreffler, "'Mein Weg geht jetzt vöruber'", The Origins of Webern's Twelve-Tone Composition", *The Journal of the American Musicological Society* 47, no. 2 (Summer, 1994), 320.

29. Schreffler, "'Mein Weg geht jetzt vöruber'", 325.

30. 'Eine solche enggeschloffene, einheitliche Welt des Glaubens hatte ich noch vorgefunden bei dem Aufwachen meiner Vernunft. Und hätte ich nichts desgleichen vorgefunden, keine Kirche, keine Kanzel, keinen Altar, keine fromme Mutter und keinen zu Gott weisenden Vater, so meine ich doch, daß ich meiner ganzen Natur nach glauben hätte müssen [...] ich vermute, daß z.B. die Blume, der Sturm, der Sternenhimmel, die Gebirgswelt, das Meer, die ganze Wesenheit der Welt allmählich so eindringlich zu mir gesprochen hätten: Ein Gott, ein ewiges Leben!' (Peter Rosegger, *Mein Himmelreich: Ein Glaubensbekenntnis* (Leipzig: Staackmann, 1924), 9).

31. Dean Garrett Stroud, *The Sacred Journey: The Religious Function of Nature Motifs, in Selected Works by Peter Rosegger* (Stuttgart: Akademischer, 1986), 18.

32. Tom Service, "The Symphony Guide: Webern's Opus 21", The 50 Greatest Symphony Series, The Guardian, entry posted December 17, 2013. http://www.theguardian.com/music/tomserviceblog/2013/dec/17/symphony-guide-webern-op-21 (accessed August 8, 2014); Service here expands on George Benjamin's description of the Symphony in his chapter "Canonic Codes", *Sing, Ariel: Essays and Thoughts for Alexander Goehr's Seventieth Birthday,* ed. Alison Latham (Aldershot: Ashgate, 2003), 25.

33. Schoenberg, *Fundamentals of Musical Composition,* 167.

34. Webern, *The Path to New Music,* 56.

35. Anton Webern, *The Path to New Music,* 53.

36. Elaine Sisman, *Haydn and the Classical Variation* (London: Harvard University Press, 1993), 8.

37. Barbara Hernstein Smith, *Poetic Closure: A Study of How Poems End* (Chicago: University of Chicago Press, 1968), 98–100.

38. Charles Rosen, *The Classical Style: Haydn, Mozart, Beethoven* (New York: Norton, 1972), 438.

39. Sisman, *Haydn and the Classical Variation,* 10.

40. German Idealism began with Kant's *Critique of Pure Reason* (1781), and was taken up by philosophers such as G.W.F Hegel, Johann Fichte, Friedrich Schelling and Arthur Schopenhauer.

41. Ruth Solie, "The Living Work: Organicism and Musical Analysis", *19th-Century Music* 4, no. 2 (1980): 150.

42. Solie, "The Living Work: Organicism and Musical Analysis", 150.

43. Coleridge, *Philosophical Lectures*, 196; quoted in M.H. Abrams *The Mirror and the Lamp*, Oxford: Oxford University Press, 1953, 171.

44. Bailey, "Webern's Op. 21: Creativity in Tradition", 184.

45. Bailey, "Webern's Op. 21: Creativity in Tradition", 201.

46. Bailey, "Webern's Op. 21: Creativity in Tradition", 202. This piece, along with the Quartet Op. 22, and the String Quartet Op. 28 were written after Webern's visit to his parents' grave sites in Schwabegg and Annabichl in July 1928. In each of these works Webern sketched a programmatic outline in his sketchbook with references to the mountains and to these two places. The Symphony is not directly linked in the sketchbook to a particular place, however, there is a plan outlined, dated November–December 1927:

   I. Rondo: lively – sun
   II. Variations: moderately
   III. Free form: very calmly – moon

The variations movement was completed in March 1928, four months before his visit, and in June he completed movement III, which was published as the first movement.

47. Bailey, "Webern's Op. 21: Creativity in Tradition", 187.

48. Johnson, *Webern and the Transformation of Nature*, 202.

49. Heinz-Klaus Metzger and Rainer Riehn, eds., *Musik-Konzepte Sonderband: Anton Webern I* (Munich: edition text + kritik, 1983), 20; quoted in Johnson, *Webern and the Transformation of Nature*, 7.

50. See Chapter 6 part 1.

51. Bailey, "Webern's Op. 21: Creativity in Tradition", 192.

52. Coleridge, *Table Talk*, quoted in Solie, "The Living Work", 150.

53. Kathryn Bailey, "Webern's Op. 21: Creativity in Tradition", 193.

54. Ibid., 193.

55. Freud, "The Interpretation of Dreams", *The Standard Edition*, vol. IV, 277.

56. Brown, *The Symphonic Repertoire*, 883.

Conclusion

The concept of the waltz as a repressed *Ländler* epitomises the uncanny nature of the final years of the Habsburg Empire. The association of the waltz by Strauss with, not only the high-class, but the immoral, hedonistic and decadent nature of high society in opposition to the "natural" rural *Ländler* of the simple lower classes can be understood in terms of Freud's *doppelgänger* and its notion of opposites collapsing into one another. Clare Rosenfield suggests the Double could parallel the protagonist/Antagonist narrative: 'a juxtaposition of two characters; the one representing the socially acceptable or conventional personality, the other externalising the free, uninhibited self'.[1] The waltz and *Ländler* derive from the same humble origins, from more spirited rural dances like the *Dreher*, however, the *Ländler* continues to connote the conventional triple dance while the waltz plays at being high class eventually representing the "free, uninhibited self". The waltz, therefore, came to symbolise Vienna in all ways. It was danced by society and servants alike; it encapsulated glitz and glamour, but therefore also symbolised the artificial nature of that glamour as it covered over the decadence of the Austrian Empire. It is this decadence that the composers of *fin-de-siècle* Vienna railed against as they created satirical commentaries concerning the class system and the juxtaposition of nature/mankind, rural/urban, "wine, women and song"/poverty and loss and Viennese/"Other".[2] The dualistic nature of the waltz and its surrounding topical narrative enabled the composers to create narrative arcs within their own compositions. Moreover, it enables an emplotment of the changes in the attitudes and opinions of Viennese composers and – through the implication that the composers, having been ensconced in the same population and cultural milieu as everyone else will understand and reflect the popularist view – the Viennese public over the eighty years discussed in this manuscript. That narrative arc demonstrates the change in the waltz's signification from signpost for deception and artifice in Strauss's *Die Fledermaus* in 1874 to its development as part of the uncanny narrative and eventually ends with the waltz signifying the repression of the anxieties inherent in being part of the Viennese society in Webern's Op. 21 in 1928. Symbolising individual anxiety about their place in society and the pressures society places on an individual, the uncanny narrative also represented the anxiety Vienna/Austria-Hungary as a whole felt about their place in the global society as they were ravaged by war, suffering losses in pride and territory while the government remained stagnant and paralysed. In Mahler's Scherzos the man versus nature argument is enforced with the use of the waltz and its juxtaposition to the other side of the triple-time dance coin, the rural *Ländler*, while the class divide is still emphasised with the employment of other topic's relationships to the waltz and *Ländler*, such as the minuet, marching band and pastoral. The 1907 operetta *Ein Walzertraum* by Oscar Straus also employs this narrative as the city soldier, despite being made a Prince, longs for the Viennese charms. The dull rurality of his newly acquired kingdom holds no allure and he leaves his wife on their wedding night to fall in love with a Viennese singer. The immoral nature of this act is illustrated by waltzes and *Ländlers*, the ethical rural princess underscored with a pastoral gavotte. Finally, the waltz acts as the primal trauma in Webern's Symphony Op. 21 as it acts as the pivot point between the conscious and unconscious, reflecting the subjects repressed superego back at him. This deployment of the waltz as a pivot between unconscious immorality and conscious morality is reflected in Lehár's operetta *Die lustige Witwe* as the deliberate misdirections and immoral behaviour by the characters get cleared up and the real feelings of the main couple are exposed and revealed to be ethical.

Strauss II focussed on the class system, denouncing the decadent nature of the upper class as, even when he should be going to jail, the protagonist Eisenstein instead goes to a ball with his friend Dr. Falke. His wife also attends, masked and he attempts to seduce her while he believes she is a Hungarian Countess. The next day he discovers a man he believes to be her lover in jail in his place and accuses her of adultery, until she produces evidence she was the Countess. He then apologises and blames it on the champagne, which she accepts and immediately forgives him. This immoral behaviour is highlighted by Strauss with a version of the waltz at each deception point, and while he does not paint the lower classes in an angelic light (Alfred attempts to seduce Rosalinde and Adele goes to the ball in a stolen dress) their stories are overshadowed by the extravagance of the aristocratic ball and the actions of the Eisenstein and Falke. It is therefore the artifice of Vienna, the *Wiener Schmäh*, which is being parodied here.[3] Meanwhile, in Oscar Straus's *Ein Walzertraum*, the class distinction is seen from the other side as a Viennese Lieutenant marries a rural Princess, but yearns for the insular revelry of Vienna. The singer of a Viennese band then teaches the Princess how to affect the Viennese charms in order to win the Lieutenant back. This also highlights the nationalist Otherness perceived by the audiences of the time that the happy ever after moment came only once the naïve rural Princess – initially introduced by the heavenly pastoral – "becomes" Viennese. The nationalist theme is continued in *Die lustige Witwe* with the rivalry set between the East and West – Pontevedria (a fictional mix between Poland, Czechoslovakia, Russia and Hungary) and Paris – with the West depicted as untrustworthy and self-indulgent and the East as ethical and moral but naïve. The waltz represents neither side instead acting as a pivot point or as the point of repression between them. The waltz accompanies the recognition of the feelings between Hanna and Danilo and is therefore the only true representation of love in the operetta, sounding in opposition to the falsity of marrying for any reason other than love.

As such, rather than it being used as a signifier for deceptiveness, as in *Die Fledermaus* and *Ein Walzertraum*, it is used by Lehár in a way similar to Schoenberg: to signify ethical behaviour in line with his view of the struggle to impose authenticity and morality on the Viennese people while simultaneously introducing the Freudian concept of doubles and repression that becomes intrinsic to the argument from then on. The operettas, therefore, despite being "light" music have set out most of the same dualistic musical narratives depicted in the "art" music of Mahler, Schoenberg and Webern, apart from the narrative Mahler is best known for: nature versus mankind. His Seventh Symphony displays a narrative arc that travels in the first three movements from a bourgeois serenade undermined by anxiety, through a story of the baser ills of the Habsburg society: class prejudice and sex. A stormy lamentation of the loss of the ignorance and bliss of *Alt Wien* instigates a descent into the unconscious and the uncanny narrative in the Scherzo with parodic grotesque waltzes and "screeching" collapses after waltz instances. The arc begins to ascend in the fourth movement, *Nachtmusik II* as the serenade combines with pastoral topics due to the dawning temporal suspension and light figure that begins the healing process to be completed in the triumphant fifth movement.

The Seventh Symphony Scherzo encapsulates the uncanny narrative as well as the use of the waltz as the representation of repression and doubles that is seen in Schoenberg's Op. 16. Furthermore, it uses this narrative four years earlier than Schoenberg, although there are uncanny elements in *Verklarte Nacht* (1899) and *Pelleas und Mellisande* (1903) the full narrative expressed in Opp. 16 and 17 does not appear until 1909. The second part of chapter six plots the development of this narrative from Mahler's Third to his Ninth Symphonies (1893–1910) by analysing the Scherzo of each work. The progression from a rather superficial dialectic between classes and idealised nationalism and rural and urban in the Third Symphony lead to a death toll to the upper class's artifice (symbolised by the waltz while the *Ländler* represents the natural *Volk*) in the Fourth. The Fourth Scherzo also introduces a consciousness into the narrative, a "subject", as the sensibility is combined with the pastoral topic to create an awareness of the idealisation of nature and the peasantry and the insincere gaiety and superiority of the urban civilisation, a differentiation between the real and the perceived. The Fifth Symphony marks the beginning of the *ombra*'s metamorphosis into the uncanny with a shadowlike *Ländler* and the use of ostinati to represent the second state with a narrative telling of a world where light and dark parallel the cultural upheaval of Vienna, the "easeful security of the commonplace" exposed as "deceitful fantasy".[4]

The temporal thrust and delay that disrupts the beginning of the Sixth Symphony Scherzo cements the *ombra* topic's transformation into the uncanny narrative and initially describes the yearning for the golden age of Vienna. An "*Alväterisch*" minuet is continually disrupted by an *ombra* march and a pastoral *Ländler*. Here, Mahler also outlines a Hungarian/Austrian dialectic where, although the Hungarian dances aren't disrupted like the Minuet they are impeded and become stagnant. With the Viennese/Other dialectic described in the Sixth Symphony and the collapse of the *Alt Wien* façade in the Seventh Symphony, the Ninth Symphony Scherzo uses the waltz and the *Ländler* to symbolise the conflict in the cultural and political atmosphere. The *Ländler*, far from representing the crudeness of the peasantry, symbolises the heavenly pastoral – the simple, sincere, *natural* side of the rural ethos – and places it in opposition to the dysphoric, grotesque aristocratic waltz.

The subject that has been inherent in these symphonies since the fifth symphony is characterised by the time-shards that state the anxiety felt by the decline of the noble class and the Empire. The Ninth symphony, despite, or perhaps because of, the physical and temporal distance to the plot (as Mahler was in America at time of composition), summarises both the narrative of the decline of the Empire, the decadence of the last century and the transformation from external fear of the supernatural and the known to a psychological anxiety of the unknown that is symbolised by the uncanny narrative.

Webern also used the same narratives ten years after the Empire dissolved, whether as a reflection of the times he had lived through or as a commentary on what was still a tense time in which the same anxieties were prevalent after the Great War. However, Webern's new musical style meant that the Classical conventions Mahler used were twisted or reversed almost to the point of parody in the topical domain. The narrative plots create commentaries on *Alt Wien* and "New Music" and the repression of the civilised utopian ideal by an intrusive reality. The second movement cements the waltz/*Ländler* double as an embedded part of the Viennese uncanny narrative as once again, just as in Mahler's Scherzos, the waltz appears at the centre of the movement and combines with a time shard to symbolise the entry of the psyche into the unconscious. That the double signification of the waltz and the *Ländler*, that one would not be possible without the other while signifying different but vital elements of the Viennese culture – rural and urban, aristocrat/bourgeois/peasant, conscious/unconscious –, proves that the surrounding political, cultural and social issues of the time made their way into even the most technical and "abstract" of music and was felt long after the Empire's decimation.

NOTES

1. Claire Rosenfield, "The Shadow Within: The Conscious and Unconscious Use of the Double", in *Daedalus*, 328.

2. Johann Strauss, *Wein, Weib und Gesang*, Op. 333 (1869). The title is taken from an old hedonistic adage "Who loves not wine, women and song, remains a fool his whole life long".

3. In Austrian German slang *Schmäh* means "gimmick," "trick," "swindle" or "falsehood" as well as "compulsory friendliness", "saying" or "joke". https://www.duden.de/suchen/dudenonline/Schm%C3%A4h (accessed January 16 2022).

4. Donald Mitchell, *Gustav Mahler the Wunderhorn Years* (Woodbridge: The Boydell Press, 2005), 76.

Bibliography

Abbate, Carolyn, *In Search of Opera* (Princeton, NJ: Princeton University Press, 2001).

———, *Unsung Voices: Opera and the Musical Narrative in the Nineteenth Century* (Princeton: Princeton University Press, 1991).

———, "What the Sorcerer Said", *19th-Century Music* 12, no. 3 (Spring, 1989), 221–230.

Abrams, M.H. *The Mirror and the Lamp*, Oxford: Oxford University Press, 1953.

Adorno, Theodor, *Mahler: A Musical Physiogmany*. Trans. Edmund Jephcott (Chicago: 1992).

Agawu, Kofi, "The Musical Language of *Kindertotenlieder* No. 2", *The Journal of Musicology* 2, no. 1 (Winter 1983), 81–93.

———, *Music As Discourse: Semiotic Adventures in Romantic Music* (New York: Oxford University Press, 2008).

———, *Playing with Signs*: *A Semiotic Interpretation of Classical Music* (Princeton: Princeton University Press, 1991).

Allanbrook, Wye J., *Rhythmic Gesture in Mozart: Le Nozze Di Figaro and Don Giovanni* (London: University of Chicago Press, 1983).

———, *The Secular Commedia: Comic Mimesis in Eighteenth-Century Instrumental Music* (Berkeley, CA: University of California Press, 2014).

Almén, Byron, *A Theory Of Musical Narrative* (Bloomington, IN: Indiana University Press, 2008).

Al-Taee, Nassar, *Representations of the Orient in Western Music: Violence and Sensuality* (Farnham: Ashgate, 2010).

Auner, Joseph, *A Schoenberg Reader: Documents of a Life* (New Haven, CT: Yale University Press, 2003).

Bailey, Kathryn, *The Life of Webern* (Cambridge: Cambridge University Press, 1998).

———, *The Twelve-tone Music of Anton Webern* (Cambridge: Cambridge University Press, 1991).

——, "Webern's Op. 21: Creativity in Tradition", *The Journal of Musicology* 2, no. 2 (Spring 1983), 184–195.

Baines, Anthony, revised by Robert A Green and Meredith Ellis Little, "Musette", *Grove Music Online*. https://doi-org.nls.idm.oclc.org/10.1093/gmo/9781561592630.article.19398 (accessed April 3, 2021).

Ballantine, Christopher, *Twentieth Century Symphony* (London: Denis Dobson, 1983).

Barea, Ilsa, *Vienna: Legend and Reality* (London: Secker and Warburg, 1966).

Barthes, Roland, *Image–Music–Text*, trans. Stephen Heath (New York: The Noonday Press, 1977).

Bartók, Béla, *Essays*, ed. Benjamin Suchoff (London: Faber and Faber, 1976).

——, "Gypsy Music or Hungarian Music?", *The Musical Quarterly* 33, no. 2 (1947), 240–325.

Bauer-Lechtner, Natalie, *Recollections of Gustav Mahler*, trans. Dika Newlin, ed. Peter Franklin (Cambridge: Cambridge University Press, 1980).

Beller, Steven, *A Concise History of Austria* (Cambridge: Cambridge University Press, 2006).

——, *Rethinking Vienna 1900*. Vol. 3 of *Austrian and Habsburg Studies* (Oxford: Berghahn, 2001).

——, *Vienna and the Jews, 1867–1938: A Cultural History* (Cambridge: Cambridge University Press, 1989).

Bellman, Jonathan, *The Exotic in Western Music* (Boston: Northeastern University Press, 1998).

——, *The Style Hongrois in the Music of Western Europe* (Boston: Northeastern University Press, 1993).

——, "Toward a Lexicon for the *Style Hongrois*", *The Journal of Musicology* 9, no. 2 (Spring 1991), 214–237.

Berlin, Jeffrey B., Jorun B. Burns and Richard Lawson, eds., *Turn of the Century Vienna: Essays in Legacy of Donald G. Daviau* (Vienna: Edition Atelier, 1993).

Bettelheim, Bruno, *Freud's Vienna and Other Essays* (New York: Alfred A. Knopf, 1990).

Born, Georgina, and David Hesmondhalgh, *Western Music and Its Others* (Berkeley: University of California Press, 2000).

Botstein, Leon, "Modernism", in *The New Grove Dictionary of Music and Musicians*, 2nd ed., vol. 16, ed. Stanley Sadie and John Tyrell (London: Macmillan, 2001).

Boulez, Pierre, "Schoenberg is Dead", in *Stocktakings from an Apprenticeship*, collected Paule Thévenin, trans. Stephen Walsh (Oxford: Oxford University Press, 1991).

Brand, Juliane and Christopher Hailey, ed., *Constructive Dissonance: Arnold Schoenberg and the Transformations of Twentieth-Century Culture* (Berkeley: University of California Press, 1997).

Braunstein, Néstor, A., "Desire and Jouissance in the Teachings of Lacan", in *The Cambridge Companion to Lacan*, ed. Jean-Michel Rabaté (Cambridge: Cambridge University Press, 2003).

Broch, Hermann, *Hugo von Hofmannsthal and His Time: The European Imagination 1860–1920* trans. and ed. by Michael P. Steinberg (Chicago: University of Chicago Press, 1984).

Brown, A. Peter, *The Symphonic Repertoire: The Second Golden Age of the Viennese Symphony* (Bloomington, IN: Indiana University Press, 2003).
Burkhart, Charles, "Schoenberg's *Farben*: An Analysis of Op. 16, No. 3", *Perspectives of New Music* 8, no. 2 (Autumn, 1973–Summer, 1974),141–172.
Busch, Regina, "On the Horizontal and Vertical Presentation of Musical Ideas and on Musical Space (I)", *Tempo* New Series 154 (September, 1985), 2–10.
Butler, Christopher, *Early Modernism: Literature, Music, and Painting in Europe 1900–1916* (Oxford: Oxford University Press, 1994).
Caplin, William, "On the Relation of Musical Topoi to Formal Function", *Eighteenth Century Music* 2, no. 1 (2005), 113–124.
Carner, Mosco, "Ländler", *The New Grove Dictionary of Music and Musicians*, ed. Stanley Sadie, 2nd ed. (London: Macmillan, 2001).
Carpenter, Alexander, "A Bridge to a New Life: Waltzes in Schoenberg's Chamber Music", in *Schoenberg's Chamber Music, Schoenberg's World*, ed. James K. Wright and Alan M. Gilmour (New York: Pendragon, 2009).
———, "Schoenberg's Vienna, Freud's Vienna: Re-examining the Connections between the Monodrama Erwartung and the Early History of Psychoanalysis", *Musical Quarterly* 93, no. 1 (2010),144–181.
Černušák, Gracian *et al.*, "Polka", in *Grove Music Online. Oxford Music Online*. http://0-www.oxfordmusiconline.com.wam.leeds.ac.uk/subscriber/article/grove/music/22020 (accessed November 25, 2015).
Chatman, Seymour, *Story and Discourse: Narrative Structure in Fiction and Film* (New York: Ithaca, 1978).
———, "What Novels Can Do That Films Can't (and Vice-Versa)", *Critical Inquiry* 7, no. 1 (Autumn, 1980), 121–140.
Cherlin, Michael, "Schoenberg and Das Unheimliche: Spectres of Tonality", *The Journal of Musicology* 11, no. 3 (Summer, 1993), 357–373.
———, *Schoenberg's Musical Imagination* (Cambridge: Cambridge University Press, 2007).
Cobley, Paul, *Narrative* (New York: Routledge, 2001).
Cohn, Richard, "Uncanny Resemblances: Tonal Signification in the Freudian Age", *Journal of the American Musicological Society*. 57, no. 2 (2004), 285–323.
Compan, Charles, *Dictionnaire de Danse* (Paris: Cailleau, 1787).
Cone, Edward T., "Schubert's Promissory Note: An Exercise in Musical Hermeneutics", *19th-Century Music* 5 (1982), 233–241.
———, "Three Ways to Read a Detective Story—Or a Brahms Intermezzo", *Georgia Review* 31 (1977), 554–574.
Crittenden, Camille, *Johann Strauss and Vienna: Operetta and the Politics of Popular Culture* (Cambridge: Cambridge University Press, 2000).
Dahlhaus, Carl, *Nineteenth-Century Music*, trans. J. Bradford Robinson (Berkeley: University of California Press, 1989).
Desmond, Jane, *Meaning in Motion: New Cultural Studies of Dance* (Durham: Duke University Press, 1997).
Dickensheets, Janice, "Nineteenth-Century Topical Analysis: A Lexicon of Romantic Topics", *Pendragon Review* 2, no. 2 (2003), 5–19.

Downes, Olin, *New York Times*, December 19, 1929.
Downes, Stephen, ed.,, "Classicism/Neoclassicism", in *Aesthetics of Music: Musicological Perspectives* (Routledge, 2016).
———, "Mazurka", in *Grove Music Online, Oxford Music Online*. http://0-www.oxfordmusiconline.com.wam.leeds.ac.uk/subscriber/article/grove/music/18193 (accessed July 27, 2015).
Fantel, Hans, *Johann Strauss: Father and Son and their Era* (Newton Abbott: David and Charles, 1971).
Floros, Constantin, *Gustav Mahler: The Symphonies* (Aldershot: Amadeus, 1994).
Freud, Sigmund, *The Standard Edition of the Complete Psychological Works of Sigmund Freud*, ed. and trans. James Strachey (London: Hogarth, 1964).
Frigyesi, Judit, "Bela Bartok and the Concept of Nation and Volk in Modern Hungary", *The Musical Quarterly* 78, no. 2 (Summer, 1994), 255–287.
Gammond, Peter and Andrew Lamb, "Waltz", in *The Oxford Companion to Music*, ed. Alison Latham, *Oxford Music Online*. http://0-www.oxfordmusiconline.com.wam.leeds.ac.uk/subscriber/article/opr/t114/e7260 (accessed July 21, 2015).
Garrett Stroud, Dean, *The Sacred Journey: The Religious Function of Nature Motifs, in Selected Works by Peter Rosegger* (Stuttgart: Akademischer, 1986).
Gartenberg, Egon, *Johann Strauss: The End of an Era* (Pennsylvania State: Pennsylvania State University Press, 1974).
Genette, Gerard, *Narrative Discourse: An Essay in Method*, trans. Jane E. Lewin (New York: Ithaca, 1980).
Geretsegger, Heinz, and Max Peintner, *Otto Wagner 1841-1918: The Expanding City, the Beginning of Modern Architecture*, Associate Author: Walter Pichler. Introd. by Richard Neutra; Translated (From the German) by Gerald Onn (London: Rizzoli, 1979).
Gill, Graeme, *Bourgeoisie, State and Democracy—Russia, Britain, France, Germany, and the USA* (Oxford: Oxford University Press, 2008).
Grimalt, Joan, "Gustav Mahler's *Wunderhorn* Orchestral Songs: A Topical Analysis and a Semiotic Square" (PhD, Universitat Autònoma de Barcelona, 2011).
———, *Mapping Musical Signification* (Switzerland: Springer, 2020).
Gronburg, Tag, *Vienna: City of Modernity, 1890–1914* (Bern: Peter Lang, 2007).
Grun, Bernard, *Gold and Silver: The Life and Times of Franz Lehár* (London: W.H. Allen, 1970).
Haimo, Ethan, *Schoenberg's Transformation of Musical Language* (Cambridge: Cambridge University Press, 2006).
Harris-Warrick, Rebecca, "Dance", *Grove Music Online*. https://doi-org.nls.idm.oclc.org/10.1093/gmo/9781561592630.article.45795, accessed April 3, 2021).
Hatten, Robert S., *Interpreting Musical Gestures, Topics, and Tropes: Mozart, Beethoven, Schubert* (Bloomington, IN: Indiana University Press, 2004).
———, *Musical Meaning in Beethoven: Markedness, Correlation, and Interpretation* (Bloomington, IN: Indiana University Press, 1994).
———, "On Narrativity in Music: Expressive Genres and Levels of Discourse in Beethoven", *Indiana Theory Review* 12 (1991), 75–98.

Hayes, Jeremy. "Orfeo ed Euridice". *Grove Music Online (8th ed.)*. Oxford University Press. doi:10.1093/gmo/9781561592630.article.O008226 (accessed January 3, 2022).

Head, Matthew, *Orientalism, Masquerade, and Mozart's Turkish Music* (London: Royal Musical Association, 2000).

Heartz, Daniel, "The Beginnings of the Operatic Romance: Rousseau, Sedaine, and Monsigny", *Eighteenth-Century Studies* 15, no. 2 (Winter, 1981–1982), 149–178.

Heartz, Daniel and Alan Brown, *"Empfindsamkeit"*, in *Grove Music Online, Oxford Music Online*. http://0-www.oxfordmusiconline.com.wam.leeds.ac.uk/subscriber/article/grove/music/08774 (accessed July 27, 2015).

Hefling, Stephen, ed., *Mahler Studies* (Cambridge: Cambridge University Press, 1997).

Hernstein Smith, Barbara, *Poetic Closure: A Study of How Poems End* (Chicago: University of Chicago Press, 1968).

Hickman, Hannah, *Robert Musil & the Culture of Vienna* (Kent: Croom Helm, 1984).

Hiller, Lejaren and Ramon Fuller, "Structure and Information in Webern's Symphonie, Op. 21", *Journal of Music Theory* 1, no. 1 (Spring 1967), 60–115.

Hitchcock, H. Wiley, "A Footnote on Webern's Variations", *Perspectives of New Music* 8, no. 2 (Spring/Summer, 1970), 123–126.

Hood, Danielle. "Doubles and Duplicity: Topics in Vienna around the Long *Fin-de-Siècle*, 1874–1928" (PhD: University of Leeds, 2015).

———, "Schoenberg's *Pelleas und Melisande:* Hidden Agendas of the Sonata Form", *Musicology Review* 8/i, 2013.

Hunter, David J. and Paul T. von Hippel, "How Rare is Symmetry in Musical 12-Tone Rows?", *The American Mathematical Monthly* 110, no. 2 (Feb., 2003), 124–132.

Jacob, Heinrich, *Johann Strauss Father and Son: A Century of Light Music*, trans. Marguerite Wolff (London: Hutchinson, 1940; originally published as *Johann Strauss und das neunzehnte Jahrhundert. Die Geschichte einer musikalischen Weltherrschaft, 1819–1917* [Amsterdam: Querido-Verlag, 1937]).

Janik, Alan and Stephen Toulmin, *Wittgenstein's Vienna* (London: Weidenfeld and Nicolson, 1973).

Johnson, Julian, "Mahler and the Idea of Nature", in *Perspectives on Gustav Mahler*, ed. Jeremy Barham (Aldershot: Ashgate, 2003).

———, *Mahler's Voices: Expression and Irony in the Songs and Symphonies* (Oxford: Oxford University Press, 2009).

———, *Webern and the Transformation of Nature* (Cambridge: Cambridge University Press, 1999).

Jung, Hermann, *Die Pastorale: Studien zur Geschichte eines musikalischen Topos* (Bern: Francke, 1980).

Kálmán, Emmerich, *Gräfin Mariza* (Vienna: Josef Weinberger, 1924).

Kant, Immanuel, *The Critique of Judgement*, trans. James Creed Meredith (Oxford: Oxford University Press, 2007).

Kennedy, Michael, *The Master Musicians: Mahler* (Oxford: Oxford University Press, 2000).

———, "Mazurka", *The Oxford Dictionary of Music*, 2nd ed. http://0-www.oxfordmusiconline.com.wam.leeds.ac.uk/subscriber/article/opr/t237/e6658 (accessed July 27, 2015).

Kerman, Joseph, "Beethoven's Op. 131 and the Uncanny", *19th-Century Music* 25, no. 2–3 (2002), 155–164.

Klein, Michael, "Chopin's Fourth Ballade as Musical Narrative", *Music Theory Spectrum* 26, no. 1 (2004), 23–56.

———, *Intertextuality in Western Art Music* (Bloomington, IN: Indiana University Press, 2005).

Klein, Michael, and Nicholas Reyland, eds., *Music and Narrative since 1900* (Bloomington, IN: Indiana University Press, 2013).

Knapp, Raymond, "Suffering Children: Perspectives on Innocence and Vulnerability in Mahler's Fourth Symphony", *19th-Century Music* 22, no. 3 (Spring, 1999), 233–267.

———, *Symphonic Metamorphoses: Subjectivity and Alienation in Mahler's Re-Cycled Songs* (Middletown: Wesleyan University Press, 2003).

———, *The American Musical and the Performance of Personal Identity* (Princeton: Princeton University Press, 2006).

Koch, Heinrich C., *Musikalisches Lexicon* (Hildesheim: George Olms, 1964).

Korhonen, Joonas Jussi Sakari, "Urban social space and the development of the public dance hall culture in Vienna, 1780–1814", *Urban History*, 40, no. 4 (Nov. 2013), 606.

Kramer, Jonathan, *The Time of Music: New Meanings, New Temporalities, New Listening Strategies* (New York: Schirmer, 1988).

Kramer, Lawrence, "Musical Narratology", *Indiana Theory Review* 12 (1991), 141–162.

———, *Music as Cultural Practice 1800–1900* (Berkeley, CA: University of California Press, 1990).

Krenek, Ernst, *Music Here and Now*, trans. Barthold Fles (New York: Norton, 1939).

Kurth, Richard, "Music and Poetry, A Wilderness of Doubles: Heine—Nietzsche—Schubert—Derrida", *19th-Century Music* 21, no. 1 (1997), 3–37.

La Grange, Henry-Louis de, *Vienna: The Years of Challenge (1897–1904)*, vol. 2 of *Gustav Mahler* (Oxford: Oxford University Press, 1995).

———, *Vienna: Triumph and Disillusion (1904–1907)*, vol. 3 of *Gustav Mahler* (Oxford: Oxford University Press, 1999).

Lamb, Andrew, "Waltz (i)", in *Grove Music Online. Oxford Music Online*. http://0-www.oxfordmusiconline.com.wam.leeds.ac.uk/subscriber/article/grove/music/29881 (accessed July 21, 2015).

Latham, Alison, ed., *Sing, Ariel: Essays and Thoughts for Alexander Goehr's Seventieth Birthday* (Aldershot: Ashgate, 2003).

Lehár, Franz, *Das Land des Lächelns* (Vienna: Josef Weinberger, 1931).

Locke, Ralph, *Musical exoticism: Images and Reflections* (Cambridge: Cambridge University Press, 2009).

Lowe, Melanie, "Falling from Grace: Irony and Expressive Enrichment in Haydn's Symphonic Minuets", *The Journal of Musicology* 19, no. 1 (Winter 2002), 171–221.

Loya, Shay, *Listz's Transcultural Modernism and the Hungarian-Gypsy Tradition* (New York: University of Rochester Press, 2011).
Lynn, Donna, "12-Tone Symmetry: Webern's Thematic Sketches for the Sinfonie, Op. 21", *The Musical Times* 131, no. 1774 (December, 1990), 644–646.
Mahler, Gustav, *Fifth Symphony* (Leipzig, C F Peters, 1919).
———, *Seventh Symphony* (Berlin: Bote & Bock, 1909).
Martin, Peter, J., *Sounds and Society: Themes in the Sociology of Music* (Manchester: Manchester University Press, 1995).
Maus, Fred E., "Music as Drama", *Music Theory Spectrum* 10 (1988), 56–73.
———, "Music as Narrative", *Indiana Theory Review* 12 (1991), 1–34.
Mayes, Catherine, "Reconsidering an Early Exoticism: Viennese Adaptations of Hungarian-Gypsy Music around 1800", *Eighteenth Century Music* 6, no. 2 (September, 2009), 161–181.
McClelland, Clive, "Ombra Music in the Eighteenth Century: Context, Style and Signification" (PhD diss., The University of Leeds, 2001). In *White Rose Etheses Online*. http://etheses.whiterose.ac.uk/id/eprint/412 (accessed July 20, 2015).
———, *Ombra: Supernatural Music in the Eighteenth Century* (Plymouth: Lexington, 2012).
———, *Tempesta: Stormy Music in the Eighteenth Century* (London: Lexington, 2017).
McClymonds, Marita P. and Daniel Heartz, "Opera seria (It: 'serious opera')", *Grove Music Online*. https://doi-org.nls.idm.oclc.org/10.1093/gmo/9781561592630.article.20385 (accessed January 3, 2022).
McKee, Eric, *Decorum of the Minuet, Delirium of the Waltz: A Study of Dance Music Relations in 3/4 Time.* (Bloomington: Indiana University Press, 2012).
McQuillan, Martin, *The Narrative Reader* (New York: Routledge, 2000).
Meyer, Imke, "The Insider as Outsider: Representations of the Bourgeoisie in *Fin-de-Siècle* Vienna", *Pacific Coast Philology* 44, no. 1 (2009), 1–16.
Micznik, Vera, "Mahler and 'The Power of Genre'", *The Journal of Musicology* 12, no. 2 (Spring, 1994), 117–151.
———, "Music and Narrative Revisited: Degrees of Narrativity in Beethoven and Mahler", *Journal of the Royal Musical Association* 126, no.2 (2001), 193–249.
Miller, Hillis J., *Reading Narrative* (Norman, OK: University of Oklahoma Press, 1998).
Mirka, Danuta, ed., *Oxford Handbook of Topic Theory* (Oxford: Oxford University Press, 2014).
Mitchell, Donald, *Gustav Mahler: Songs and Symphonies of Life and Death* (London: Faber & Faber, 2002).
———, *Gustav Mahler: The Early Years* (Berkeley: California University Press, 1995).
———, *Gustav Mahler: The Wunderhorn Years* (London: Faber & Faber, 1975).
Moldenhauer, Hans and Moldenhauer, Rosaleen, *Anton Webern: A Chronicle of his Life and Work* (London: Gollanz, 1978).
Monelle, Raymond, "Genre and Structure in Nineteenth-Century Instrumental Music". http://www2.siba.fi/Yksikot/Sate/SMT/SMT952/Monelle.html, 2009, 1–12 (accessed July 27, 2015).

———, Review of *Playing with Signs: A Semiotic Interpretation of Classic Music* by Kofi Agawu *Music and Letters* 73, no. 2 (May 1992), 315–317.
———, "Structural Semantics and Instrumental Music", *Music Analysis* 10, no. 1/2 (March–July 1991), 73–88.
———, *The Musical Topic: Hunt, Military and Pastoral* (Bloomington, IN: Indiana University Press, 2006).
———, *The Sense of Music* (Princeton and Oxford: Princeton University Press, 2000).
Monson, Dale E. et al., "Recitative", *Grove Music Online, Oxford Music Online.* http://0-www.oxfordmusiconline.com.wam.leeds.ac.uk/subscriber/article/grove/music/23019. (accessed July 27, 2015).
Morris, William, *William Morris on Art and Socialism*, ed. Norman Kelvin (New York: Dover Publications, 1999).
Münz, Ludwig and Gustav Künstler, *Adolf Loos: Pioneer of Modern Architecture* (Santa Barbara: Praeger, 1966).
Musil, Robert, *The Man without Qualities*, vol. 1 (London: Secker & Warburg, 1953).
Nattiez, Jean-Jaques, and Kathryn Ellis, "Can One Speak of Narrativity in Music?", *Journal of the Royal Musical Association* 115, no. 2 (1990), 240–257.
———, *Music and Discourse: Towards a Semiology of Music*, trans. Carolyn Abbate (Princeton, NJ: Princeton University Press, 1990).
Nelson, Robert P., "Webern's Path to Serial Variation", *Perspectives of New Music* 7, no. 2 (Spring/Summer, 1969), 73–93.
Newbould, Brian, ed., *Schubert the Progressive: History, Performance Practice, Analysis* (Aldershot: Ashgate, 2003).
Newcomb, Anthony, "Schumann and Late Eighteenth-Century Strategies", *19th-Century Music* 11, no. 2 (Autumn, 1987), 164–174.
Nolan, Catherine "New Issues in the Analysis of Webern's 12-Tone Music", *Canadian University Music Review*, 9, no. 1 (1988), 83–103.
Notley, Margaret, "Brahms as Liberal: Genre, Style, and Politics in Late Nineteenth Century Vienna", *19th-Century Music* 17, no. 2 (Fall 1993), 107–123.
Panos, Nearchos et al, eds., *Proceedings of the International Conference on Music Semiotics in Memory of Raymond Monelle* (Edinburgh: IPMDS, 2012).
Pasler, Jann, *Writing through Music: Essays on Music, Culture, and Politics* (New York: Oxford University Press, 2007).
Perle, George, *Serial Composition and Atonality: An Introduction to the Music of Schoenberg, Berg, and Webern*, 6th ed. (Berkeley, CA: University of California Press, 1991).
———, "Webern's Twelve-Tone Sketches", *The Musical Quarterly* 57, no. 1 (January, 1971), 1–25.
Piotrowska, Anna, *Gypsy Music in European Culture* (Boston: Northeastern University Press, 2013).
Pople, Anthony, *Theory, Analysis, and Meaning in Music* (Cambridge: Cambridge University Press, 1994).
Radano, M. and Philip V. Bohlman, *Music and the Racial Imagination*, ed. Ronald (Chicago: University of Chicago Press, 2000).

Ratner, Leonard G., *Classic Music: Expression, Form, and Style* (London: Collier Macmillan, 1980).
Reeser, Eduard, *The History of the Waltz*. Trans. from the Dutch by W.A.G. Doyle-Davidson (Stockholm: The Continental Book Company A.B., 1949).
Reyland, Nicholas, "*Livre* or Symphony? Lutosławski's *Livre pour orchestre* and the Enigma of Musical Narrativity", *Music Analysis* 27, nos. 2–3 (2008), 253–294.
Robinson, Jenefer, ed., *Music and Meaning* (Ithaca: Cornell University Press, 1997).
Rosegger, Peter, *Mein Himmelreich: Ein Glaubensbekenntnis* (Leipzig: Staackmann, 1924).
Rosen, Charles. *The Classical Style: Haydn, Mozart, Beethoven* (New York: Norton, 1972).
Rosenfield, Claire, "The Shadow Within: The Conscious and Unconscious Use of the Double", *Daedalus* 92, no. 2 (1963), 326–344.
Roth, Michael S., "Performing History: Modernist Contextualism in Carl Schorske's *Fin-de-Siècle* Vienna", *The American Historical Review* 99, no. 3 (June 1994), 729–745.
Rousseau, Jean-Jacques, "Menuet", vol. 10 of *Encyclopédie*, ed. Denis Diderot and Jean d'Alembert (Paris: Briasson, 1751–1772).
Sage, Jack, *et al.*, "Romance", *Grove Music Online*. *Oxford Music Online*. Oxford University Press. http://0-www.oxfordmusiconline.com.wam.leeds.ac.uk/subscriber/article/grove/music/23725 (accessed January 2, 2016).
Samson, Jim, "Romanticism", in *Grove Music Online, Oxford Music Online*. http://0-www.oxfordmusiconline.com.wam.leeds.ac.uk/subscriber/article/grove/music/23751 (accessed July 27, 2015).
Samuels, Robert, *Mahler's Sixth Symphony: A Study in Musical Semiotics* (Cambridge: Cambridge University Press, 1995).
———, "Narrative Form and Mahler's Musical Thinking", *Nineteenth-Century Music Review* 8 (2011), 237–254.
Sansone, Matteo, "Verismo", in *Grove Music Online, Oxford Music Online*. http://0-www.oxfordmusiconline.com.wam.leeds.ac.uk/subscriber/article/grove/music/29210. (accessed July 27, 2015).
Sárosi, Bálint, *Gypsy Music* (Budapest: Corvina Press, 1978).
———, "Gypsy Musicians and Hungarian Peasant Music", *Yearbook of the International Folk Music Council* 2 (1970), 8–27.
Sassman, Hans, *Das Reich der Träumer; Eine Kulturgeschichte Oesterreichs vom Urzustand bis zure Republik* (Berlin: Verlag für Kulturpolitik, 1932).
Scheibe, Johann Adolph, *Critische Musikus* (Leipzig: Breitkopf, 1745).
Schnitzler, Henry, "'Gay Vienna'—Myth and Reality", *Journal of the History of Ideas*, 15, no. 1 (Jan. 1954), 94–118.
Schoenberg, Arnold, *Erwartung* (Vienna: Universal Edition, 1916).
———, *Fundamentals of Musical Composition*, ed. Gerald Strang and Leonard Stein (London: Faber and Faber, 1967).
———, *Fünf Orchesterstücke* (Leipzig: C F Peters, 1912).
———, "Generational Tension and Cultural Change: Reflections on the Case of Vienna", *Daedalus* 107, no. 4 (Fall, 1978), 111–122.

———, *Style and Idea*, ed. Leonard Stein, trans. Robert Black (Berkeley: University of California Press, 1975).
———, *Verklärte Nacht* (Berlin: Verlag Dreililien, 1905).
Schorske, Carl E., *Fin-de-Siècle Vienna: Politics and Culture* (New York: Vintage, 1981).
Schreffler, Anne C., "'Mein Weg geht jetzt vöruber'. The Origins of Webern's Twelve-Tone Composition", *The Journal of the American Musicological Society* 47, no. 2 (Summer, 1994), 275–339.
Schubert, Franz, *String Quintet in C Major D956* (Leipzig: Breitkopf & Härtel, 1888).
Schwarz, David, *Listening Subjects: Music, Psychoanalysis, Culture* (Durham: Duke University Press, 1997).
Scott, Derek, B."Orientalism and Musical Style", *The Musical Quarterly* 82, no. 2 (Summer 1998), 309–335.
———, *Sounds of the Metropolis: The 19th Century Popular Music Revolution in London, New York, Paris and Vienna* (Oxford: Oxford University Press, 2008).
Service, Tom, "The Symphony Guide: Webern's Opus 21" The 50 Greatest Symphony Series, The Guardian, entry posted December 17, 2013. http://www.theguardian.com/music/tomserviceblog/2013/dec/17/symphony-guide-webern-op-21 (accessed July 28, 2015).
Sheinberg, Esti, ed., *Music Semiotics: a Network of Significations—In Honour and Memory of Raymond Monelle* (Aldershot: Ashgate, 2012).
Shepherd, John, and Kyle Devine Mueller, ed. *The Routledge Reader on the Sociology of Music* (New York: Routledge, 2015).
Simms, Bryan, *The Atonal Music of Arnold Schoenberg, 1908–1923* (Oxford: Oxford University Press, 2000).
Sisman, Elaine, *Haydn and the Classical Variation* (Cambridge, MA: Harvard University Press, 1993).
———, *Mozart: The Jupiter Symphony* (Cambridge: Cambridge University Press, 1993).
Smith, Joan Allen, *Schoenberg and his Circle* (London: Collier Macmillan, 1986).
Solie, Ruth, "The Living Work: Organicism and Musical Analysis", *19th-Century Music* 4, no. 2 (1980), 147–156.
Spector, Scott, "Beyond the Aesthetic Garden: Politics and Culture on the Margins of "Fin-de-Siècle Vienna", *Journal of the History of Ideas* 59, no. 4 (October 1998), 691–710.
Stadlen, Peter. "The Webern Legend", *The Musical Times* 101, no. 1,413 (November 1960), 695–697.
Starr, Mark, "Webern's Palindrome", *Perspectives of New Music* 8, no. 2 (Spring/Summer, 1970), 127–142.
Stępień, Wojciech, "Musical Categories of the Uncanny in Edvard Grieg's "Troll Music", *Studia Musicologica Norvegica* 38 (2012), 47–65.
Stoll Knecht, Anna, *Mahler's Seventh Symphony* (Oxford: Oxford University press, 2019).

Strauss, Johann II, *Die Fledermaus* (Leipzig: August Cranz, n.d., 1890).
Street, Alan, "Narrative and Schoenberg's *Five Orchestral Pieces,* Op. 16", in *Theory, Analysis and Meaning in Music*, ed. Anthony Pople (Cambridge: Cambridge University Press, 1994).
Sulzer, Johann Georg, *Allgemeine Theorie der schönen Künste*, 2nd ed., vol. 1 (Hildesheim: Georg Olms, 1994).
Sutton, Julia, "Dance", *Grove Music Online.* https://doi-org.nls.idm.oclc.org/10.1093/gmo/9781561592630.article.45795 (accessed April 3, 2021).
Swartz, Anne, "The Polish Folk Mazurka", *Studia Musicologica Academiae Scientiarum Hungaricae* 1, no. 4 (1975), 249–255.
Tarasti, Eero, *A Theory of Musical Semiotics* (Bloomington, IN: Indiana University Press, 1994).
Taylor, A.J.P., *The Habsburg Monarchy: 1809–1918* (London: Penguin, 1990).
Thompson, Wendy, and Jane Bellingham, "Gavotte", in *The Oxford Companion to Music*, ed. Alison Latham. *Oxford Music Online.* http://0-www.oxfordmusiconline.com.wam.leeds.ac.uk/subscriber/article/opr/t114/e2800 (accessed July 20, 2015).
Timms, Edward, *Karl Krauss: Apocalyptic Satirist* (London: Yale University Press, 1986).
Timms, Edward and Ritchie Robertson, eds., *Vienna 1900: From Altenberg to Wittgenstein* (Edinburgh: Edinburgh University Press, 1990).
Traubner, Richard, *Operetta: A Theatrical History*, rev. ed. (London: Routledge, 2003).
Unverricht, Hubert, revised by Cliff Eisen, "Serenade", *Grove Music Online* (accessed April 9, 2021). https://doi-org.nls.idm.oclc.org/10.1093/gmo/9781561592630.article.25454.
Välimäki, Susanna, *Subject Strategies in Music: A Psychoanalytic Approach to Musical Signification* (Helsinki: The International Semiotics Institute, 2005).
Wank, Martin, "Oedipus in the Fin de Siècle: A Reinvention of Legitimacy", *New Political Science* 19, no. 3 (1997), 59–73.
Warren, Jackson Eliot, "The *Style hongrois* in the music of Johann Strauss Jr" (PhD diss., University of Arizona, 2012).
Weber, Carl Maria von, *Der Freischütz* (Leipzig: C F Peters, 1986).
Webern, Anton, Symphony Op. 21 (Vienna: Universal Edition AG, PH368).
——, *The Path to New Music*, ed. Willi Reich (London: Theodore Presser, 1963).
Weiss, Piero and Julian Budden, "Opera Buffa", in *Grove Music Online, Oxford Music Online.* http://0-www.oxfordmusiconline.com.wam.leeds.ac.uk/subscriber/article/grove/music/43721 (accessed July 27, 2015).
Whittall, Arnold, *The Cambridge Introduction to Serialism* (Cambridge: Cambridge University Press, 2008).
Zychowicz, James, *Mahler's Fourth Symphony* (New York: Oxford University Press, 2000).

Index

Italicized pages refer to figures.

Abbate, Carolyn, 67, 86, 93
accompagnato recitative, 15
Admeto (Handel), 133–34
Adorno, Theodor, 147, 170
aestheticism, 2
Agawu, Kofi, 7
Alberti basses, 20, 37, 140
Alceste (Gluck), 88
Allanbrook, Wye J., 19, 21, 47
alla turca, 18, 19, 60
alla zoppa, 58
Almén, Byron, 67–69, 71
Al-Taee, Nasaar, 118–19
'*An der Schönnen Blauen Donau*,' 48
Andrian, Leopold von, 29
Anna O., case of, 3, 83, 93
anti-narrative, 70
anxiety of alienation, 108–10
architecture, 51
arias, 15–16
Atempause, 47
Austro-German racism, 38
Austro-Hungarian Empire, 38–39
authenticity, 36

Bach, J. S., 20, 99
Bailey, Kathryn, 158, 159, 167–71
Ballantine, Christopher, 156–57

'Ballroom Dances of the Late Eighteenth Century' (McKee), 21
Bartók, Béla, 40, 52, 55–58, 61
Beethoven, 156; *Appassionata* sonata, Op. 57, 167; Sixth Symphony, 142
Beller, Steven, 2, 29, 49
Bellman, Jonathan, 4, 19, 55, 56, 58, 59, 140
Berg, A., 47, 79
Bettelheim, Bruno, 83
The Blue Danube (Strauss), 2
bókazó, 58
Botstein, Leon, 85
bourgeois class: moral clarity, 29; new, emergence of, 116–17; rise of, 51; self-perception of being, 29; values of, 28–29
bourrée, 19, 21
'Brahms the Progressive' (Schoenberg), 86
Breuer, Josef, 84, 93–94
Brinkmann, Reinhold, 83–84
Broch, Hermann, 30, 51
Brown, Peter, 156
Burkhart, Charles, 105–6
Busch, Regina, 157–58, 163, 172
Busoni, Ferruccio, 84

195

Cage, John, 70
Carpenter, Alexander, 69, 85, 110
Carré (Stockhausen), 70
castration complex, 86, 91–93, 104–6, 110, 161
Catholic Church, 28
Cavalleria Rusticana (Mascagni), 76
Cernušák, Gracian, 53–54
chamber music, 11
Champagner-Polka Op. 211, 54
Chapin, Keith, 13
Chatman, Seymour, 69
Cherlin, Michael, 3, 69, 85, 86, 92–94, 110, 163
'Chopin's Fourth Ballade as Musical Narrative' (Klein), 68
Christian Social Party, 28
cimbalom, 56
civilisation, *Ländler* entering into, 108–10
"Civilisation and its Discontents" (Freud), 104
civil societies, 1
class conflicts, 2
Classical works, 35
Classicism, 34–35
Classic Music (Ratner), 7
Cobley, Paul, 68
Cohn, Richard, 69, 86
Coleridge, Samuel Taylor, 167–68
Compan, Charles, 21
Cone, Edward T., 67–68, 78
conscious logic, 85
contredanse, 21–22, 46, 77, 129
contredanse allemande, 21
contredanse anglaise, 21
contredanse française, 21
coup d'archet, 71
critical modernism, 2, 30–31
csárdás, 45, 55, 56, 59, 61, 150, 153
cultural hunt, 13

dance, 19–22; commercialisation, 49; low-class, 19; nationalist, 19; upper-class, 19. See also *Ländler*/waltz; *specific dance*

Danican Philidor, François-André, 37
Death's dance, 142–43
Dehmel, Richard, 88
Der Freischütz (Weber), 88, *88*
'Der Schildwache Nachtlied' (Mahler), 131, 161
Der Traum ein Leben (*A Dream is Life*) (Grillparzer), 50
'Des Antonius von Padua Fischpredigt' (Mahler), 106, 117–19
Des Knaben Wunderhorn (Mahler), 117, 161, 172
Desmond, Jane, 128
Deutsch, Max, 36
dichotomy between urban/rural, 61, 117–18, 139, 142, 162
Die Entführung aus dem Serail (Mozart's opera), 18, 37, 118
Die Fackel, 30, 50
Die Fledermaus (Strauss), 2–5, 37, 41, 53, 54, 62, 71–73, 75–76, 78, 86, 117, 118, 172, 178, 179
Die Lustige Witwe (Lehar), 40, 41, 53, 71, 75–79
doubles (*doppelganger*), 2, 3, 5, 62, 75–79, 94, 109, 110, 163, 169, 172, 177, 179–81
Downes, Olin, 157
Dreher, 45–46
Dual Monarchy, 2
Durchführung, 159
Dvořák, 54, 77

Ein Walzertraum (Straus), 71–75, 78–79, 144, 178–79
Empfindsamkeit, 17–18
equestrian marches, 14
Erwartung (Schoenberg), 3, 83–85, 90, 91, 93, 94, *95*, 106
exit arias, 15

Fantel, Hans, 1
Fasching, 49
father-imago split, 3

father/son conflict. *See* Oedipus complex
fiddle, 56
Fifth Symphony, Scherzo (Mahler), 145–49
folk dances, 45–47
folk music, 52
forest, 14
Fourth Symphony, Scherzo (Mahler), 142–44
Fragment of an Analysis of a Case of Hysteria (Freud), 91
Franco-Austrian War, 39
Freud, Sigmund, 2–3, 5, 83–84, 91–94, 163, 171; as central psychoanalytical personality, 31–34; "Civilisation and its Discontents," 104; *Fragment of an Analysis of a Case of Hysteria*, 91; *The Interpretation of Dreams*, 31–33, 83, 91, 161; "The Medusa's Head," 91, 93; Oedipus complex, 32–33. *See also* castration complex; doubles (*doppelganger*)
"Freud's Vienna" (Bettelheim), 83
Frigyesi, Judit, 40, 52
Fundamentals of Musical Composition (Schoenberg), 159
funeral march, 126–27
"Funeral March" (Chopin), 126–27
Fünf Orchesterstucke, Op. 16, 'Vorgefühle', 'Farben', 'Vergangenes', 'Peripetie' and 'Das obligate Rezitativ' (Schoenberg), 5, 96–110, 115, 119, 124, 136

Gartenburg, Egon, 48–51, 62
gavotte, 19, 20, 37
gavotte tendre, 37
generational rebellion, 29
generation's values, 29
Genette, Gérard, 69
genre, 9
German nationalist sentiment, 38–39
gigue, 15, 19
Gluck, C. G., 16

Goscombe, Stanley, 54
Grabócz, Márta, 71
grell (piercing), 126
Grétry, André, 37
Grillparzer, Franz, 50
Grimalt, Joan, 4, 16, 21–22, 115–17, 119, 120, 132, 135
Grun, Bernard, 76
Gung'l, Josef, 54
Gurrelieder (Schoenberg), 88–89, 93, 94
Gypsies, 55, 59
Gypsy music, 55–61; *alla turca*, 60; idealised concept of, 60; *style hongrois* and, 60–61
Gypsy Music in European Culture (Piotrowska), 60

Habsburg Monarchy, 1, 3
hallgató style, 55, 56
Handel, George Frideric, 133–34
Hanslick, Eduard, 48
Hasse, Johann A., 16
Hatten, Robert, 9, 13, 68, 69, 71, 81n33
Hauptstimme, 99, 102–3, 105, 107
Head, Matthew, 17–18, 105
Heartz, Daniel, 15
heimlich, 93
high style/class topics, 8–10, *12*, 13–18
Hitchcock, H. Wiley, 156
Hofmannsthal, Hugo von, 29, 33–34, 153
horn calls, 127–28
Hungarian-Gypsy music. *See* Gypsy music
Hunter, Mary, 19
hunt topic, 10, *12*, 13–14
hypnoid state/second state, 3, 5, 93–94, 101, 102, 104, 106–7, 119, 124, 126, 128–30, 132, 133, 150, 151, 163
hysteria, 93–94

id, 94
impressionism, 2
industrialisation, 15

In Search of Opera (Abbate), 86
The Interpretation of Dreams (Freud), 31–33, 83, 91, 161
Intertextuality in Western Art (Klein), 86

Janik, Allan, 27, 28, 30–31, 84
Jews, 28
Johann Strauss (Fantel), 1
Johnson, Julian, 117, 127–28, 161, 162, 168, 169
Jommelli, Niccolò, 16
Josef, Franz, 51
Joseph, Franz, 2
Joseph II, 49
Jung, Hermann, 15

Kahlert, Karl August, 35
Kant, Immanuel, 35, 109–10
Kindertotenlieder (Mahler), 88, 130, 131, 161
Klein, Michael, 5, 67–70, 86, 93, 99
Knapp, Raymond, 143–44
Knecht, Anna Stoll, 130
Koch, Heinrich C., 21, 99
Korhonen, Joonas Jussi Sakari, 48–49
Kramer, Jonathan, 70
Kramer, Lawrence, 5, 67, 69, 71
Kraus, Karl, 2, 30, 34, 36, 50, 153
kreischend, 122–26
kujawiak, 61
Kurz, Josef, 47

Labitzky, Joseph, 54
La Grange, Henry-Louis de, 115
Lamb, Andrew, 54
L'amitié à l'épreuve (Grétry), 37
Ländler/waltz, 1, 5, 45–52, 177–81; characteristic feature, 47; entry into civilisation, 108–10; Fantel on, 1; Fifth Symphony, Scherzo (Mahler), 145–49; *kreischend*, 122–26; melody in, 48; Ninth Symphony, Scherzo (Mahler), 151–53; origin, 45–47; overview, 4–5; as a *Schleifer*, 47; Seventh Symphony, Scherzo (Mahler), 115, 119–36; significations, 4; Symphony Op. 21 (Webern), 5–6, 155–72
Langhaus, 46
Lanner, Josef, 48, 54
learned style, 13, 17, 20, 34, 71, 99, 104, 105, 162, 168
Lehár, Franz, 30, 37
Le roi et le fermier (Monsigny), 37
Le sorcier (Danican Philidor), 37
liberalism, 27–31
librettos, 15
Lied style, 35, 107
"The Living Work" (Solie), 167
Livre pour orchestre (Lutosławski), 70
Loos, Adolf, 2, 51
Louis XIV, 133
Lowe, Melanie, 20
low style/class topics, 9, 10, 18–22
Loya, Shay, 61
Lueger, Karl, 28

Mahler, Alma, 109
Mahler, Gustav, 3–7, 10, 47, 69–71, 77, 79, 105, 106, 157. *See also* Scherzo (Mahler)
The Man without Qualities (Musil), 28
Mapping Musical Signification (Grimalt), 4
march, 14; funeral, 126–27
Mariza, Gräfin, 59
Mascagni, Pietro, 76
Mattheson, Johann, 8
Maus, Fred E., 67–68
Mayes, Catherine, 55, 60
mazurka (*mazur*), 61–62
McClary, Susan, 69–70
McClelland, Clive, 4, 7, 17–18, 87, 88, 90, 93, 120, 133–34
McClymonds, Marita P., 15
McKee, Eric, 7, 19–21
McQuillan, Martin, 69
"The Medusa's Head" (Freud), 91, 93
Mein Himmelreich (Rosegger), 162

Mengelberg, William, 123
The Merry Widow (Lehár), 3, 5
Metastasio, Pietro, 16
Metternich, 1; laws, 49–50, 62
Meyer, Imke, 28–30
Micznik, Vera, 10, 47, 110, 116
middle style, 8–9
military topic, 13–14; hunt topical class and, 14
minuet, 19–21; fundamental style, 20–21; triple time signature, 20
Mirka, Danuta, 4, 7, 8
Mitchell, Donald, 115, 139, 141–42, 146, 149, 151–52
Mit Humor, 118
modernism, 30; critical, 2, 30–31; satirical attacks on others, 30
Monelle, Raymond, 7, 9–11, 13–15, 18, 27, 75, 116–18
Monsigny, Pierre-Alexandre, 37
Mozart, 18
Mueller, John H., 34
musette, 15, 19, 22, 88
music: patriotic marches, 53; rationalisation of, 34; temporal narrative, 3
Music and Narrative (Almén and Hatten), 71
Music as Discourse (Agawu), 9
Musikalisches Lexicon (Koch), 99
Musil, Robert, 28

Nachtmusik, 115, 124, 126–33, 161–63
narrative, 67–79. *See also* uncanny narrative
Narrative in Music Since 1900 (Klein and Reyland), 67
narratology, 5
nationalism, 2, 38–41; as an exotic Other, 40–41, 52. *See also* style hongrois
Nattiez, Jean-Jaques, 67
Nebenstimme, 103, 105
Nelson, R. P., 156

Newcomb, Anthony, 68
New York Times, 157
Nietzsche, Friedrich, 2, 29
Ninth Symphony, Scherzo (Mahler), 120, 139, 151–53
noble simplicité, 20
non-narrative works, 70
nóta songs, 59

oberek, 61
Oedipus complex, 32–33
ombra, 4, 5, 7, 16–17, 34, 161, 163, 164, 180; Fifth Symphony, Scherzo (Mahler), 145–49; Fourth Symphony, Scherzo (Mahler), 143–44; Seventh Symphony, Scherzo (Mahler), 122–36; Sixth Symphony, Scherzo (Mahler), 149–51; transformation into uncanny, 87–93, 96–97, 99, 102, 109
Ombra (McClelland), 4
opera buffa, 16, 18–19
opéra comique, 37
opera seria, 15, 16
Orfeo ed Euridice, 16
Otherness, 2
Oxford Handbook of Topic Theory (Mirka), 4, 8

Pappenheim, Marie, 83, 84
paratacticism, 167
Paschen, 46
Pasler, Jann, 70
pastorale, 15, 19
pastoral topic, 13–15
The Path to New Music (Webern), 155, 157
Pelleas und Melisande (Schoenberg), 90, 91, 94, 179
phallic symbols, 91
pianissimo, 74, 88, 90, 163, 164
pianto, 18
Piotrowska, Anna, 60–61
Playing With Signs (Agawu), 7
polka, 4, 19, 41, 52–54, 62, 72–75, 78

Polka française, 54
"*Potemkimsche Stadt*" ("Potemkin City"), 51
private realms, 9–10
progressive modernism, 2
psychoanalysis, 83–85
psychological topics, 34

rationalism, 34; sociological concept of, 34
Ratner, Leonard, 7–9, 13, 17–21
recitativo obbligato, 15
Reeser, Eduard, 45–46
Revolutionary Dream, 32–33
Reyland, Nicholas, 67
'Rheinlegendchen,' 117
Ringstraße, 2, 34, 51, 62
Ritter, William, 120
romance, 36–38; operatic, 37
Romanticism, 35
Rosegger, Peter, 162
Rosen, Charles, 167
Rosenfield, Claire, 74
Roth, Michael S., 33
Rousseau, Jean-Jacques, 21
Rute, 118

Sage, Jack, 37
Samson, Jim, 35
sarabande, 19, 20
Sassman, Hans, 51
Scarlatti, Alessandro, 16
Scheibe, Johann Adolphe, 8–10
Scherzo (Mahler), 4, 5, 110, 115, 116, 119–36, 139–53; Fifth Symphony, 145–49; Fourth Symphony, 142–44; Ninth Symphony, 120, 139, 151–53; Seventh Symphony, 115, 119–36; Sixth Symphony, 149–51; Third Symphony, 139–42
Schmäh, 49
Schnell-Polka, 54
Schnitzler, Arthur, 29, 33

Schoenberg, Arnold, 2–6, 30, 36, 49, 69, 70, 78, 83–87, 155, 157–61, 163–64, 166, 172, 179; 'Brahms the Progressive,' 86; *Erwartung*, 3, 83–85, 90, 91, 93, 94, 95, 106; *Fundamentals of Musical Composition*, 159; *Fünf Orchesterstucke*, Op. 16, 'Vorgefühle,' 'Farben,' 'Vergangenes,' 'Peripetie,' and 'Das obligate Rezitativ' (Schoenberg), 5, 96–110, 115, 119, 124, 136; *Gurrelieder*, 88–89, 93, 94; "New Music," 158; "A Self-Analysis," 86; *Verklärte Nacht*, 88, 89, 91, 179
Schorske, Carl E., 27–34, 36, 38, 39, 51
Schreffler, Anne C., 161–62
Schubert, Franz, 48, 56, 86, 87
Schwartz, David, 86
Scott, Derek, 4
secco recitative, 15
second movement, 164–72
Second World War, 162
"A Self-Analysis" (Schoenberg), 86
Semper, Gottfried, 51
The Sense of Music (Monelle), 7
sensibility, 17–18
Seventh Symphony, Scherzo (Mahler), 5, 115, 119–36
shards. *See* time-shards
siciliano, 15, 19
Simms, Bryan, 84, 102, 108
Sisman, Elaine, 13, 99, 166
Sixth Symphony, Scherzo (Mahler), 149–51
Smith, Hernstein, 166–67
Smith, Peter, 86
Solie, Ruth, 167
Spector, Scott, 38
spondee, 58
Stadlen, Peter, 157
Starr, Mark, 156
Stockhausen, Karlheinz, 70

Stop (Stockhausen), 70
Strauss, Johann, II, 2, 3, 30, 48, 50, 52, 71, 72, 76, 79, 117, 118, 158, 178
Strauss, Oscar, 5, 71, 72, 76, 144, 178–79. *See also Ein Walzertraum* (Straus)
Strauss, Richard, 109
Stroud, Dean Garrett, 162
Studies of Hysteria (Freud), 93
Sturm und Drang, 17–18
style hongrois, 4, 5, 19, 52, 55–59, 136, 139–41, 150; Gypsy music and, 60–61; instrument, 56; rhythmic characteristics, 57–58; signification, 59–62
The Style Hongrois in the Music of Western Europe (Bellman), 55
styles, 7–8
Subject Strategies in Music (Välimäki), 86
sublime, 109–10
sul ponticello technique, 161
Sulzer, Johann Georg, 9
superego, 94
Sutton, Julia, 22
Symphony Op. 21 (Webern), 5–6, 155–72; Ballantine on, 156–57; first movement, 158–64; second movement, 164–72; twelve-tone technique, 171

táragató, 56
Tauber, Richard, 37
tempesta, 4, 7, 16–18, 34–35, 107, 120, 122, 124, 126, 133, 135, 141, 142, 146, 148–50, 152, 163–64, 168–69
Tempesta (McClelland), 4
Third Symphony, Scherzo (Mahler), 139–42
'Three Ways to Read a Detective Story—Or a Brahms Intermezzo' (Cone), 68–69

time-shards, 92–94, 110
Timms, Edward, 36, 39
tonal structure, 35
topics/topic theory, 3–4, 7–22; dance, 19–22; defined, 7; high style/class, 8–10, *12*, 13–18; low style/class, 9, 10, 18–22; private realms, 9–10; public realms, 9
topoi, 7, 11–12
Toulmin, Stephen, 27, 30, 84
The Tower (*Der Turm*) (Hofmannsthal), 33
Trakl, Georg, 30
Traubner, Richard, 39, 76
types, 7–8

Uncanny, concept of, 2–3
uncanny narrative, 4, 5, 83–110; development of, 83–110; *Fünf Orchesterstucke*, Op. 16, 'Vorgefühle' (Schoenberg), 5, 96–106, 115, 119, 124, 136; Scherzo (Mahler), 139–53. *See also* Schoenberg, Arnold
unconscious, 32; hysteria and, 94; repression of, 94; time shard, 94
Unverricht, Hubert, 130
Urpflanze (Goethe), 166

Välimäki, Susanna, 86
value vacuum, 30
verbunkos, 55, 59
verismo, 76
Verklärte Nacht (Schoenberg), 88, *89*, 91, 179
Viennese, 1
Violin Concerto (Berg), 47

Wagner, Otto, 36, 51
Wagner, Richard, 2, 29
waltz. *See Ländler*/waltz
Walzertraum (Strauss), 5
Webern, Anton: *The Path to New Music* (Webern), 155, 157

Weh dem, der lügt! (Woe to Him Who Lies!) (Grillparzer), 50
Weissweiler, Eva, 84
Werbung, 59
Whittall, Arnold, 158
Wiener Schmäh, 116
Wittgenstein, Ludwig, 30

Wolf's Glen scene in *Der Freischütz* (Weber), 88, *88*
Wozzeck (Berg), 47
Wunderhorn songs (Mahler), 117, 132, 134

Zemlinsky, Alexander von, 71

About the Author

Danielle Hood completed a PhD at the University of Leeds in 2015 under the title of *Doubles and Duplicity: Topics in Vienna Around the Long Fin-de-Siècle, 1874–1928* supervised by Martin Iddon and Michael Spencer. Her published works include 'Schoenberg's *Pelleas und Melisande:* Hidden Agendas of the Sonata Form' in the *Musicology Review* 8/i, (2013) and 'The Jewish Florio: Eichendorff narratives in the first movement of Mahler's Seventh Symphony' in the *Proceedings of the International Conference on Music Semiotics in Memory of Raymond Monelle* (2013). She also edited the footnotes and bibliography for *The Oxford Handbook of Topic Theory* (2014).

www.ingramcontent.com/pod-product-compliance
Lightning Source LLC
Chambersburg PA
CBHW020743020526
44115CB00030B/902